SOUTHERN COOKING FOR COMPANY

More than 200 Southern Hospitality Secrets
and Show-Off Recipes

NICKI PENDLETON WOOD

NELSON
BOOKS

An Imprint of Thomas Nelson

© 2015 by Nicki Pendleton Wood and Bryan Curtis

Photos © 2015 by Thomas Nelson

Published in Nashville, Tennessee, by Nelson Books, an imprint of Thomas Nelson. Nelson Books and Thomas Nelson are registered trademarks of HarperCollins Christian Publishing, Inc.

Photography by Stephanie Mullins

Food and Prop Styling by Teresa Blackburn

Thomas Nelson, Inc., titles may be purchased in bulk for educational, business, fund-raising, or sales promotional use. For information, please e-mail SpecialMarkets@ThomasNelson.com.

Library of Congress Control Number: 2015937026

ISBN-13: 978-1-4016-0541-4

Printed in the United States of America

15 16 17 18 19 QC 6 5 4 3 2 1

CONTENTS

INTRODUCTION

Some people were born to host. Years ago, as a bridesmaid in an East Tennessee wedding, I encountered the most gracious, detail-oriented, and natural hostess I could ever hope to meet.

As mother of the bride, she'd taken care of every small detail, from housing for her guests, hairstyling for the bridesmaids, and beautiful homemade meals for the bridal party. Her food was lovely looking and perfectly suited for the occasion. She had a warm manner, and her sweet, funny stories about each bridesmaid had everyone relaxed and giggling like old friends. Generous with her recipes, she fetched and shared original handwritten cards for tomatoes stuffed with creamed spinach and a sublime pimento cheese, the best I have ever eaten.

For most people, though, entertaining involves more effort. They have a spirit of generosity and the urge to invite people, but the details get in the way. How many to invite? What to serve and how to serve it? How to create that elusive but important energy that makes a party great?

As it turns out, there are hundreds of ways to host a successful gathering. In *Southern Cooking for Company*, we collected the recipes and advice of hosts and cooks from Texas to Maryland, Kentucky to Florida. They shared their best Southern and Southern-accented recipes and offered ample hosting tips and strategies that work for them.

Plenty of traditional Southern recipes are included here, as well as lots of recipes that are a new take on Southern food. The cooking of the South, from the coasts and uplands to the hills of east Texas, is in a spell of reinvention.

As more Americans from other parts of the country and immigrants move to the South, Southern dishes and ingredients are getting more attention, both from newcomers and nationally. Nothing's stopping these new Southerners from changing up traditional food ways, adding "buffalo" spices to creamed chicken or curry spices to okra.

At the same time, native Southerners cook and eat a lot of foods that aren't Southern. Cooks naturally meld the flavors and techniques of Chinese, Mexican, Italian, Japanese, Korean, and Thai cuisines with their own Southern cooking.

In restaurants and on food blogs, chefs and home cooks are innovating with traditional Southern fare like barbecue, fried chicken, and biscuits. Fifty years ago, who would have imagined that deviled eggs and pimento cheese would move from lunchbox to restaurant menu to food blog preoccupation?

Back to the party. There's always a reason to invite people for a bite of something Southern. It could be a holiday crowd for country ham and Lane Cake. Maybe it's an after-work gathering with margaritas and fajitas. Seasonal overabundance provides an excellent opportunity to invite friends—it's satisfying to share all that wild duck gumbo, Silver Queen corn, or country ham.

Look at your party style and adapt the advice offered here so it works for you. My usual style is to invite people impulsively, or when I have a lot of something, such as ribs, chili, or pie. I count on a dramatic entrée, a good party story, and interesting music as backdrop to good company, the most important element of a successful gathering.

When I concentrate on organizing a more detailed occasion, it's a pleasure to pamper guests with juleps in silver cups or seating with individual place cards. Someday maybe I'll be as gracious as the host who etches individual wine glasses or the one who hires musicians from Craigslist.

Of all the great ideas in *Southern Cooking for Company*, the best bit of advice is this: Don't wait to entertain. Have people over whenever you can, however you can.

Amen. Now pass those pimento cheese sandwiches.

Nicki Pendleton Wood
Nashville, Tennessee

APPETIZERS

While food, drink, and venue are all players in the story of a party, the host is the soul of any gathering. The gathering of friends or family is the act of gracious giving. Ever wonder why an office party feels more like an obligation than a cherished occasion? It's probably because there's no real host, no single individual conveying that you are a valued guest worthy of the effort.

Gracious hosting comes from a place of purposeful caring. The warmth you share with guests suffuses the party with a spirit of pampering and the generosity of an open hand. Show your guests your party spirit the second they walk in the door by setting out special drinks, snacks, and starters.

A splash of something festive and a bite of something delicious really roll out the red carpet for guests. After all, who doesn't have a little thrill of anticipation whenever good food and good times in the care of a genial host are on the menu?

Nashville, Tennessee, food stylist and cook Teresa Blackburn is a fearless inventor of cocktails, like this one she made for her potluck group. She calls it "Poire et Jacques, Y'all." You can prepare a pitcher of it and store it in the refrigerator for days, ready for a last-minute party. However you present this drink—over ice in vintage glasses or warm in kitschy mugs—it feels special in any season.

From pitcher to tablecloth, Blackburn lets her serving style be her unique welcome. In her work as a food stylist, she collects vintage and "shabby-chic" props. She loves the look of old glassware, linen napkins, and woven runners and placemats. Even old pieces of corrugated metal, burlap, and battered tin plates find a place in her tablescapes for guests.

PEAR, GINGER, AND JACK

6 cups pear cider

2 cups honey whiskey (such as Jack Daniel's Tennessee Honey)

1 cup pear liqueur

2 tablespoons ginger jam or preserves

1 to 2 whole pears, peeled

Combine the cider, whiskey, liqueur, and jam in a bowl or pitcher. Add 1 or 2 whole pears. Refrigerate until ready to serve. Serve over ice or warm in mugs. (Save the whole pears—they make a very nice dessert.)

▶ Makes about 2 quarts, or 8 servings

"I'm a single girl. I do a lot of social stuff with friends," says Dr. Carmen April of Nashville, Tennessee. Featuring a tall glass, a generous portion of sugar, and a maraschino cherry for decoration, April's strong, sweet drink hits the spot. It's a sweetly delectable julep that's a horse of a different color on Derby Day or any day that calls for a celebratory drink.

10 fresh mint leaves, plus more for garnish

4 teaspoons sugar

Splash of water

Crushed ice

3/4 cup bourbon

Maraschino cherries for garnish

CARMEN APRIL'S UNEXPECTED MINT JULEP

Divide the mint, sugar, and water between two tall glasses. Muddle with a wooden spoon. Fill the glasses with crushed ice. Pour in the bourbon. Stir to combine. Garnish with cherries and additional mint leaves.

▶ Makes 2 servings

If your guest list stretches beyond a handful of close friends, make a point of circulating through the party to check on guests. Make sure no one is left out and that everyone has someone to speak with.

Mindy Merrell and R. B. Quinn of Nashville, Tennessee, note that when getting ready for company, "We adhere to the Houdini school of cooking—creating the illusion of complexity to disguise the utter simplicity of our work." Shrub, a beverage dating back to Colonial America, is their go-to trick for summer cocktails and a conversation starter for guests. Just a couple of tablespoons of this intensely fruity, sweet, tart syrup is the secret potion for transforming a highball—like a gin and tonic, vodka and soda, whiskey sour, or Jack and ginger—into a magical libation. Blackberries make brilliant shrub, though Merrell and Quinn recommend experimenting with other fruits and berries, fresh ginger, serrano peppers, and fresh basil.

BLACKBERRY SHRUB

1 cup distilled vinegar
1 cup fresh blackberries
1 cup sugar

Combine the vinegar, blackberries, and sugar in a quart jar with a lid. Shake to blend the ingredients. Refrigerate at least 24 hours and up to 2 days. Strain the mixture into a bowl by pouring it through a fine sieve or a sieve layered with cheesecloth. Pour into a clean jar, cover, and refrigerate for up to 1 month. Spoon 1 tablespoon over your favorite cocktail.

▶ **Makes enough for 16 drinks**

Note: You can also freeze the shrub in ice cube trays to use as needed.

When Sonia Chopra of Atlanta, Georgia, serves hot or spicy foods, especially to guests who may not be acclimated to them, she offers cool, fruity drinks, like this lightly sweet sangria. It's a natural with her Green Tomato Pakoras (page 30).

PEACH MANGO SANGRIA

For the Simple Syrup, combine the sugar and water in a small saucepan. Heat over low heat, stirring, until the sugar dissolves. (Or combine sugar and water in a microwaveable cup. Stir well. Microwave 2 minutes. Stir again. Repeat until sugar is dissolved.) Let cool.

For the Sangria, combine the Simple Syrup, wine, and cognac in a pitcher. Stir in the mint, mango, and peaches. Refrigerate until serving time. Serve over ice (if desired) in wine glasses or tall glasses.

▶ Makes 6 servings

SIMPLE SYRUP

1/3 cup sugar

2 tablespoons water

SANGRIA

1 (750-ml) bottle white wine

1 cup orange-flavored cognac (such as Grand Marnier)

1/4 cup fresh mint leaves

1 ripe mango, pitted, peeled, and sliced

2 peaches, pitted and sliced

Pimm's Cup is an aperitif that steals the spotlight because of its unique flavor and easy drinkability, says Randle Browning of Waco, Texas. In this version, Ruby Red grapefruit brings a taste of Texas to the refreshing cocktail. An aperitif has very little alcohol, unlike a highball or even a glass of wine. It refreshes guests without all the buzz. It's a thoughtful drink for designated drivers or parents with kids in tow. It's also a nice alternative during hot weather, when strong drinks might "over-refresh" thirsty guests.

8 fresh mint leaves, julienned

1/4 cup thinly sliced cucumber

2 cups fresh red grapefruit juice, strained (such as Riostar or Ruby Sweet, varieties that are grown in south Texas)

1 cup Pimm's No. 1

2 tablespoons Simple Syrup (see the Simple Syrup in the Peach Mango Sangria on page 7)

1 1/2 cups ginger ale or mild ginger beer

4 lemon wedges

1 small cucumber, peeled and cut into 4 spears

4 thin slices lemon

TEXAS RUBY RED GRAPEFRUIT PIMM'S CUP

Combine the mint and sliced cucumber in a pitcher and muddle with a wooden spoon. Add the grapefruit juice, Pimm's No. 1, and Simple Syrup. Divide the mixture among four tall glasses, about 6 ounces per glass. Add ice. Pour about 3 ounces of ginger ale into each glass. Finish each drink with a squeezed lemon wedge and stir gently with a straw. Garnish the glasses with cucumber spears and lemon slices. Serve immediately.

▶ Makes 4 servings

Note: The herbal flavor of Pimm's lends itself to other fresh herbs. Try adding rosemary, basil, or lemongrass to mix things up.

Serving a signature drink makes a party one-of-a-kind and makes guests feel privileged, according to Warren Bobrow of Morristown, New Jersey. Rather than stocking a full bar, mix up a large batch of one festive drink. Then offer beer, wine, and sparkling water as other choices to make everyone happy. This cocktail is a riff on classic Southern bourbon punch, a bit puckery with grapefruit juice and lightly sweetened with pineapple juice. To play up the smoky taste of the bourbon, Bobrow grills thick slices of grapefruit until it's just charred before juicing.

RINGS AND THIMBLES

1/2 cup bourbon

1/4 cup grapefruit juice

1/4 cup pineapple juice

1 tablespoon fresh lemon juice

1 tablespoon fresh orange juice

Sparkling water

Dash or two Angostura bitters

Lime slices

Fill a cocktail shaker or mixing glass three-quarters full of ice. Pour in the bourbon, grapefruit juice, pineapple juice, lemon juice, and orange juice. Stir until chilled. Put some crushed ice in two tall glasses. Strain the drink over the ice, add a splash of sparkling water, and dot the drink with bitters. Serve with a lime slice.

▶ Makes 2 servings

Tasia Malakasis, proprietor of Belle Chevre Creamery in Elkmont, Alabama, usually welcomes guests to her home with one of two drinks: champagne or a julep. For brunch, though, a Bloody Mary bar lets her guests get their drinks just right. "Everyone is their own Bloody Mary expert," she says. She prefers hers spicy and in a glass with a salted rim, garnished with lots of pickled things.

Malakasis's young son learned the first lesson of hospitality at age 4, when his "aunt" Terri taught him to ask guests, "May I offer you a drink?" He repeated the question to everyone who arrived at the house for weeks, a gesture that delighted his "aunt" and chagrined his mother.

BLOODY MARY BAR

Combine the vegetable juice, vodka, lemon juice, salt, pepper, Worcestershire sauce, and hot pepper sauce in a large pitcher and mix well. Arrange the okra, celery, horseradish, olives, and lemon in pretty dishes or glasses and set the bottle of hot pepper sauce alongside. Provide tall glasses and ice. Let your guests customize their drinks as desired.

▶ Makes 6 servings

BLOODY MARY MIX

4 cups tomato-based vegetable juice blend

3/4 cup premium vodka

1 tablespoon fresh lemon juice

Generous shakes of salt and pepper

4 generous dashes Worcestershire sauce

4 generous dashes hot pepper sauce

GARNISHES

Pickled okra

Celery sticks

Fresh horseradish

Pimento-stuffed olives

Lemon or lime wedges

Hot pepper sauce

Milk punch is making a comeback among mixologists, and for good reason. A spirited blend in a generous bowl or jug just might be the universal symbol for party. A punch bowl surrounded by glasses is unusual at parties these days, but think of the impression it makes. Jean Button of Fayetteville, Arkansas, says her recipe, a mixture of spirits, milk, and ice cream, tastes like "a bourbon milkshake." Button says it works for lots of different occasions. "This is delicious with brunch, and my family has always had it for Thanksgiving, Christmas, and Mardi Gras," she says. Whether an heirloom cut glass round or a sleek modern square, a punch bowl stirs anticipation.

2 quarts vanilla ice cream, softened

1 (750-ml) bottle bourbon

2 quarts whole milk

Ground nutmeg, optional

BOURBON MILKSHAKE

Scoop the softened ice cream into a large bowl or large plastic freezer container. Pour the bourbon on top of the ice cream and mix well. Add the milk and stir to combine. Place the bowl in the freezer for 6 to 8 hours until frozen solid. Remove the bowl from the freezer 30 minutes to 1 hour before serving. The mixture should be slushy when you serve it. Serve in a large punch bowl. Sprinkle with nutmeg if desired. Leftovers can be refrozen.

▶ **Makes 20 servings**

Note: Button says that the frozen punch doesn't thaw evenly, so make and freeze the mixture a day or two ahead of time. Then thaw it for 30 minutes to 1 hour and chop and stir the mixture into chunks. Then refreeze. This extra step helps the punch thaw more evenly on party day.

Kathryn Tortorici and her husband always celebrate Valentine's Day with a very special date night, but Valentine's Day breakfast is a whole family celebration. "My children never know what surprises await them at the breakfast table. My menu changes from year to year as I strive to be more creative than the year before," says the Birmingham, Alabama, mother. However much she changes the menu, one item remains the same: Strawberry Milk. Its pink color and sweet flavor are just right for the day. Add Heart-Shaped Cheese Bites with Ham (page 66) and Strawberry Bread (page 88) for a menu full of love.

STRAWBERRY MILK

1 cup strawberries
1/2 cup sugar
1 cup water
1 1/2 cups whole milk

In a small saucepan bring the strawberries, sugar, and water to a boil. Boil for 10 minutes. Let stand for 10 minutes to thicken. Pour through a strainer into a jar or plastic storage container. (The pulp can be used as jam or topping for pancakes.)

Pour ¾ cup cold milk into each of two chilled glasses. Spoon in 3 tablespoons strawberry syrup and stir.

▶ Makes 2 servings

"I strive to be the hostess with the mostest!" says Shelly Collins of Durham, North Carolina. To her that means being prepared enough to enjoy her own party. "Preparing ahead as much as possible is what can make your hostess experience move from good to great. Paying attention to the finer details can put some oomph in your party, too." Her lemonade can be prepared more than a week ahead, and it's got that little bit extra from the addition of fresh fruit. "It is fresh, it is a crowd-pleaser, and it is versatile. You can freshen it up with some mint or make it fruity and super-Southern with peaches and blackberries in season. If you want to make it super-duper Southern, add bourbon," she says.

FRESH SQUEEZED LEMONADE WITH BLACKBERRIES AND PEACHES

Pour the water into a medium pot and bring to a boil over high heat. Add 2 cups of the sugar and remove the pot from the heat. Stir until the sugar dissolves. Let cool, then pour the sugar syrup into a 1-gallon pitcher.

Pour the lemon juice through a strainer into the pitcher. Stir to blend. Add the cold water and mix well.

In a medium bowl muddle the blackberries and peaches with the remaining ¼ cup sugar, crushing the fruit. Stir the fruit mixture into the lemonade. Serve over ice garnished with mint leaves.

▶ **Makes 16 servings**

Note: Fresh Squeezed Lemonade (without the peaches or blackberries) can be stored in the refrigerator for up to 2 weeks.

2 cups water

2 1/4 cups sugar, divided

2 cups fresh lemon juice

14 cups cold water

1 cup blackberries

1 cup diced, peeled peaches

Fresh mint leaves

The holiday cookie swap invitation from Angie Sarris of Johns Creek, Georgia, is one coveted invite. "I've had people RSVP before they've been invited!" she says. Friends bring decorative packages of three cookies to swap with others, plus extras to create cookie plates for shut-ins in their community. A pot of spiced punch provides a sweet sip for guests and smells as good as it tastes. Sarris tops off the fun with a hostess gift: a special apron for each guest printed with gingerbread men, Santas, or "Merry Christmas" in red and green, to reflect the party's theme.

2 1/4 cups pineapple juice

2 cups cranberry juice

1 3/4 cups cold water

1/2 cup firmly packed dark brown sugar

1 tablespoon whole allspice

1 tablespoon whole cloves

3 cinnamon sticks, broken into halves or thirds

HOLIDAY SPICE PUNCH

Combine the pineapple juice, cranberry juice, and water in an electric percolator. Place the sugar, allspice, cloves, and cinnamon sticks in the basket. Turn on the percolator and let it perk until it completes the cycle. When the cycle is done, the punch is ready. The percolator will keep it warm for hours.

▶ **Makes 6 servings**

Note: To make the punch on the stovetop, pour the pineapple juice, cranberry juice, and water into a 2-quart saucepan. Add the sugar and stir well. Tie the allspice, cloves, and cinnamon sticks in a cloth bag and add to the pot. Bring to a simmer over medium-low heat and simmer for 20 minutes. Remove the spices before serving. Pour into coffee cups or mugs.

Pam Zdenek's family in Houston, Texas, has held a very traditional Czech Christmas Eve dinner for the past 38 years: pork roast, sauerkraut, gravy, dumplings, potatoes, and apple pie or strudel. Though many Czech traditions have been lost by descendants living in America, she keeps the Christmas food ways alive by offering guests spiced teas laced with honey (for good luck), cookies, homemade fudge, spiced yeasted holiday bread, "and especially, the wonderful tradition of Czech kolache," a yeast bun filled with fruit or cream. Any time of year, her door is open to people who need a little hospitality. "We invite any and all: college kids, especially 'strays' who need some surrogate parenting, old friends, new friends. It's all about the storytelling, gathering hearts around home and hearth, and making sure guests always know they have a good hot meal and a safe harbor," she says.

WINTER HOT SPICED TEA

Bring 8 cups of water to a boil in a large pot over high heat. Remove the pan from the heat and add the tea bags. Brew the tea for about 5 minutes. Mix the cranberry juice, pineapple juice, orange juice concentrate, lemonade concentrate, and 10 ½ cups water in a large pot. Discard the tea bags and add the tea to the lemonade mixture. Add the sugars. Tie the cinnamon and cloves in a cloth bag or place in a metal tea strainer and add to the pot. Bring to a simmer over low heat and allow to simmer very gently for about 20 minutes. Do not boil. Remove the spices before serving.

▶ Makes about 24 cups

18 1/2 cups water, divided

6 or 7 peach-flavored or regular tea bags

2 cups cranberry juice, apple juice, or apple cider

3 cups unsweetened pineapple juice

1 (16-ounce) can frozen orange juice concentrate

1 (12-ounce) can frozen lemonade concentrate

3/4 cup white sugar, or to taste

1/4 cup brown sugar, or to taste

3 cinnamon sticks, broken into halves

1 1/2 teaspoons whole cloves

An unexpected snack served in an unexpected way becomes a clever conversation starter. Sheri Castle of Chapel Hill, North Carolina, offers guests this utterly Southern bar snack with drinks. She first had a version of fried field peas at Blackberry Farm, a luxurious and gracious resort in East Tennessee known for dreaming up creative ways to serve traditional Southern ingredients. Crunchy Fried Field Peas are served along with cocktails, "like very inventive bar nuts," says Castle. The special touch? They were served in tiny cast-iron skillets. Sometimes a small detail makes for a memorable gathering. These salty, smoky peas can also be the surprise topping for a salad, a platter of sliced tomatoes, or Tennessee Paella (page 131).

1 1/2 quarts water

1 tablespoon kosher salt, plus more for serving

2 cups shelled field peas

Vegetable oil for frying

1/2 teaspoon smoked paprika, or to taste

CRUNCHY FRIED FIELD PEAS

Bring the water to a boil in a large saucepan over high heat. Add 1 tablespoon of the salt. Add the peas and cook until crisp-tender, about 3 minutes. Use a slotted spoon or strainer to transfer them into a large bowl of ice water. Drain the peas well and spread them on paper towels. Let them dry completely.

Fill a large, deep skillet or heavy saucepan with oil to a depth of 2 inches. Heat the oil over medium-high heat until a deep-fry thermometer reaches 325 degrees. When the oil is hot, a pinch of flour sprinkled into it should sizzle immediately and slowly brown without popping.

Working in batches, carefully add the peas to the hot oil. Do not overfill the pan. The peas should be able to float freely in the oil. Fry for about 3 minutes until the peas are crisp. Transfer with a slotted spoon or strainer to paper towels to drain. Place the hot peas in a serving bowl. Sprinkle with additional salt to taste and smoked paprika and toss to coat. Serve the peas warm or at room temperature. Store any leftovers at room temperature in an airtight container.

▶ **Makes 2 cups, or 8 servings**

Tasia Malakasis of Belle Chevre Creamery, Elkmont, Alabama, makes this gracious appetizer for her guests. Malakasis often makes meal preparation part of the entertainment at her dinner parties to "*entertain* while entertaining and not be apart from it all," she says. She believes that guests want to see "what is going on around the stove." Her open kitchen floor plan accommodates her party style, allowing her to involve guests in the cooking process. "Engagement in the activity and action of cooking (sights, sounds, and smells) is as much a part of the appetizer as all the goodness yet to come," she says.

PICKLED SHRIMP

Heat the water in a large pot over high heat and bring to a rolling boil. Add 2 tablespoons of the salt and stir to dissolve. Add the shrimp and boil just until they turn pink, about 30 seconds. Drain.

Meanwhile, in a large bowl combine the onions, bay leaves, capers, lemon juice, vinegar, olive oil, garlic, remaining 1 teaspoon salt, celery seeds, pepper flakes, and parsley. Transfer the shrimp to the marinade. Cover tightly and refrigerate for 8 to 12 hours. When ready to serve, transfer to a serving bowl.

▶ Makes 8 to 10 servings

1 gallon water

2 tablespoons plus 1 teaspoon kosher salt, divided

2 pounds large (26-30 count) shrimp, peeled and deveined

1 cup thinly sliced onions

3 bay leaves

1/3 cup capers, drained

1/4 cup fresh lemon juice

1 cup cider vinegar

1/2 cup olive oil

1 teaspoon minced garlic

1 teaspoon celery seeds

1 teaspoon hot red pepper flakes

1/4 cup chopped fresh parsley

Who could have predicted that Southern food would be the darling of fusion cooking? As the region becomes more cosmopolitan, other influences are finding their way into traditional Southern dishes like spiced pecans. Exploring those influences is what keeps entertaining interesting for Tom Grose of Nashville, Tennessee. His version of spiced pecans is salty and slightly sweet, and still Southern enough to communicate a hearty "come on in and eat" to guests. It's just a bit of extra thought and effort that elevates an appetizer spread. Other ideas: go beyond carrots and celery for dips. Opt for unusual vegetables such as fennel, kohlrabi, daikon radish, and jicama. Similarly, look for interesting crackers and breads for spreads. Gourmet stores and ethnic markets offer seeded flatbreads, flavored crackers, and small-batch artisan crostini.

ASIAN GLAZED PECANS

In a small bowl mix the peanut oil, sesame oil, chili oil, and orange extract. In another small bowl combine the orange peel, sugar, salt, and pepper, and mash together with a fork.

Heat a wok or nonstick skillet over medium-high. Add the oil mixture and swirl to coat the bottom of the pan. Reduce the heat to medium and add the pecans, stirring to coat with the oil. When the pecans are fragrant, add a teaspoon of the sugar mixture and stir constantly. Continue adding 1 teaspoon of the sugar mixture at a time, and adjust the heat so the sugar glazes the pecans but does not burn.

When all the mixture has been stirred into the pecans, remove them from the pan and spread them on an oiled baking sheet to cool. If the pecans stick together, use two forks to separate them.

▶ Makes 2 cups, or 8 servings

1 1/2 teaspoons peanut oil

1/8 teaspoon toasted sesame oil

1/4 teaspoon chili oil

2 drops orange extract

Finely grated peel of 1 orange

4 teaspoons sugar

3/4 teaspoon kosher salt

1/4 teaspoon ground black pepper

2 cups whole raw pecan halves

As a personal chef in Nashville, Tennessee, Aly Armistead Greer gets a rare glimpse into many homes and admires how "these fantastic Southern hostesses prepare for their parties. I'm always amazed at how they pull it all together." One trick, she says, is to set the table the day before your party. "Figure out which serving pieces you will be using and pull them out. Put a little note in each one about what you'll be using it for. This is most helpful during the holidays when you're serving many, many dishes," she says. The takeaway: "If there's something I can do ahead of time, I do it. I don't leave anything until the end unless I have to."

PIMENTO CHEESE

4 cups shredded sharp Cheddar cheese

2 cloves garlic, finely chopped

3 tablespoons chopped canned pickled jalapeño pepper

1/2 cup mayonnaise (preferably Duke's)

2 tablespoons chopped pimentos

1 tablespoon Dijon-style mustard

Tabasco sauce, to taste

Salt and pepper, to taste

Splash of pickle juice

PINWHEELS

1 sheet frozen puff pastry (preferably Dufour brand), thawed

1 cup Pimento Cheese

PIMENTO CHEESE PINWHEELS

To make the Pimento Cheese, combine the cheese, garlic, jalapeño, mayonnaise, pimentos, mustard, Tabasco, salt, pepper, and pickle juice in a medium bowl and mix well. Taste and adjust seasoning as necessary. Refrigerate at least 1 hour, but preferably 8 to 12 hours to allow flavors to meld. Makes 2 cups. (You will have leftovers.)

To make the pinwheels, preheat the oven to 375 degrees. Lightly flour a work surface. Lay the puff pastry out on the work surface. Spread 1 cup of the Pimento Cheese evenly over the pastry, leaving a 1-inch border at the edges of the pastry. Carefully roll the pastry lengthwise to enclose the filling. Cut into ¼-inch pinwheels.

Place the pinwheels on a baking sheet lined with a silicone mat or parchment paper. Bake for 10 to 15 minutes, until golden and crispy. Place the pinwheels on a wire rack to drain and crisp for a few minutes.

▶ Makes about 40 pieces, or 20 servings

There's something about a porch that brings people together, and it was a porch that brought this recipe to Angela Roberts of Nashville, Tennessee. She was visiting a friend when that friend's neighbor dropped by for a visit and shared this zucchini fritter recipe with Roberts. Now Roberts uses the recipe, doubled for a big batch, to nourish and feed her own guests.

"Houses are now bigger than ever and supposed to make our lives better, but they come with entrances that require an invitation. I long for the times we used to sit on the front porch and neighbors would drop by for iced tea or coffee. Now we have more technology and we can text a friend on the other side of the world, but texting never tells the story," says Roberts. Her story shows that open-hearted hosting begins even before the front door opens.

5 large zucchini (about 2 1/2 pounds)

2 teaspoons salt, divided

3/4 cup all-purpose flour

1/2 teaspoon baking powder

1/2 cup Italian-seasoned bread crumbs

1/2 cup grated Pecorino Romano or Parmesan cheese

4 large eggs

Ground black pepper, to taste

1/2 cup grapeseed oil for frying

Sour cream, yogurt, or aioli for serving

ZUCCHINI FRITTERS FOR A CROWD

Shred the zucchini with a box grater or in a food processor. (A box grater yields a firmer texture, while the food processor yields wetter, mushier shreds.) Put the zucchini in a large bowl and sprinkle with 1 teaspoon of the salt. Let stand 10 minutes. Squeeze the zucchini with paper towels to remove as much liquid as possible.

Combine the flour, baking powder, bread crumbs, and the remaining 1 teaspoon salt in a large bowl. Add the cheese and mix well.

Beat the eggs in a small bowl. Pour the eggs over the zucchini. Add the flour mixture and stir to combine. Let the mixture stand 20 minutes. If it seems too wet, add enough flour to create a consistency that will hold its shape.

Heat the oil in a large skillet over medium-high heat. Cook a "test" fritter by spooning a teaspoon or tablespoon of the zucchini mixture into the oil. Flatten slightly and fry until well browned. Turn and cook until browned on the other side. Taste and add more cheese or salt to the zucchini mixture, if needed.

Fry the fritters in batches, using 1 teaspoon of the mixture for bite-size fritters and 1 tablespoon for larger fritters. Serve with sour cream, yogurt, or aioli.

▶ **Makes up to 60 small or 20 large fritters**

Note: It's important to use real Pecorino Romano cheese or high-quality Parmesan, such as Parmigiano-Reggiano cheese. Buy a block and grate it yourself for the best flavor.

The glories of pork sausage are well known outside the South. Exhibit A: these sausage pinwheels, familiar to Southerners but with a little West Coast addition of spinach and kale. Lori Miller, formerly of Tennessee, now of Chico, California, finds that the energy at a party can be boosted by simply re-arranging her living room. Rather than having chairs lined up against the wall or in a big circle, she creates clusters of three or four seats. This arrangement encourages conversation and even mingling, as most people won't stay in one seat all night.

1 pound bulk pork breakfast sausage

1 medium onion, chopped

3/4 teaspoon Tabasco sauce

1/2 teaspoon salt

1/2 teaspoon ground mace

1 (10-ounce) package frozen chopped spinach, thawed, drained, and squeezed dry

1 (10-ounce) package frozen chopped kale, thawed, drained, and squeezed dry

3 large eggs, divided

2 cups grated Gruyère cheese

2 sheets frozen puff pastry, thawed

SAUSAGE AND SPINACH PINWHEELS

Preheat the oven to 350 degrees. In a large skillet, brown the sausage over medium heat; add the onion and cook until browned, about 5 minutes. Stir in the Tabasco, salt, and mace and cook 2 minutes. In a large bowl combine the sausage mixture, spinach, kale, 2 of the eggs, and the cheese.

Gently unfold the pastry on a floured surface and roll each sheet with a rolling pin into an 18 x 8-inch rectangle. Spread half the sausage mixture over each rectangle, leaving a 1-inch border on the long side. Roll from the long edge to enclose the filling.

Beat the remaining egg and brush the border of the pastry with it; press to seal. Pinch the ends together. Brush the tops and sides of the roll with the remaining egg wash. Score the roll at 1-inch intervals. Place the roll on an ungreased baking sheet. Bake for 30 minutes. Let cool 15 minutes, then cut into pinwheels along the scores.

▶ Makes 36 pinwheels, or 18 servings

When Lisa Towery's husband served as deputy commandant of the U.S. Army War College at Carlisle Barracks, Pennsylvania, the couple had the opportunity to entertain large groups of people from outside the South, including military dignitaries, local leaders, and businessmen. "We almost always chose a theme to set the tone of our parties," says the Oxford, Mississippi, resident. At her Kentucky Derby Party, guests were greeted with a mint julep in a Jefferson cup, served from a silver punch bowl. A musician played cello, and silver and crystal service items were used. Fried Deviled Eggs were part of the menu, along with Fried Green Tomato Sliders with Aioli (page 47), pimento cheese with sweet pickled jalapeño peppers on spoon-shaped crackers, warm kettle potato chips with Gorgonzola, Kentucky Hot Browns (page 151), and mini sweet potato tarts.

FRIED DEVILED EGGS

14 large eggs, divided

1/4 cup mayonnaise

1 tablespoon spicy mustard

1 tablespoon chopped chives

1 tablespoon chopped pickled jalapeño peppers

Salt and ground black pepper, to taste

Oil for frying

1 cup all-purpose flour

1 cup panko or regular bread crumbs

Place 12 of the eggs in a large pot of water and bring to a boil over medium-high heat. Boil for 5 minutes. Remove the pot from the heat and let the water cool to room temperature. Peel the eggs and slice lengthwise. Remove the yolks and place in a medium bowl. Place the egg white halves on a large plate.

Add the mayonnaise, mustard, chives, jalapeños, salt, and pepper to the yolks, and mix well. Spoon the yolk mixture into the egg whites, pressing it firmly into the hollow.

Pour oil to a depth of about 2 inches in a deep frying pan and heat to 350 degrees. In a medium bowl, combine the flour and season with salt and pepper. In another medium bowl, beat the remaining 2 eggs. Pour the bread crumbs into a third medium bowl.

Dip the stuffed eggs into the flour, then into the beaten eggs, and finally into the crumbs. Slide them into the hot oil. Fry until golden brown, turning as needed to brown evenly, about 5 minutes. Remove and drain on paper towels. Sprinkle with salt and pepper.

▶ Makes 24 halves

Deviled eggs are having a moment in the culinary spotlight. Like other Southern home foods, they've moved to upscale restaurant menus and are getting makeovers all across the South. This version from Shamille Wharton of Nashville, Tennessee, gets a beautiful, brilliant pink exterior from beet juice.

After she's prepped the food, Wharton prepares herself to welcome and entertain guests by taking 15 minutes of quiet time before guests arrive. No prepping, no last-minute cleaning, only calm and quiet, because, she says, "It's up to you to set the tone of your event" and "if you're relaxed, your guests will be, too."

BEET PICKLED DEVILISH EGGS

Cut 1 of the serrano peppers into halves lengthwise, retaining the seeds. Place the pepper in a large saucepan and add the water, vinegar, sugar, beets, garlic, bay leaves, peppercorns, and salt. Bring to a boil over high heat, reduce the heat to low, and simmer until the beets are tender, about 20 minutes. Remove the pot from the heat and let cool completely.

Add the eggs to the beet liquid and refrigerate for at least 6 hours. Remove the eggs from the liquid and let them dry completely.

Cut the eggs into halves lengthwise and remove the yolks. Place the yolks in a medium bowl and place the whites on a large plate. Add the mayonnaise, olive oil, mustard, and Sriracha to the yolks. Mix and mash to combine thoroughly. Fill the whites with the yolk mixture. Slice the remaining serrano pepper into rounds. Top each egg with a slice of serrano and a sprinkle of curry powder, if desired.

▶ Makes 24 halves

2 serrano peppers, divided

3 cups water

1 cup white vinegar

1 1/2 cups sugar

2 small beets, peeled and sliced

3 cloves garlic, crushed

3 bay leaves

2 tablespoons whole black peppercorns

1 tablespoon kosher salt

12 large hard-boiled eggs, peeled

2 tablespoons mayonnaise

1 tablespoon extra-virgin olive oil

1 tablespoon Dijon-style mustard

1 tablespoon Sriracha sauce

Mild curry powder or smoked paprika for garnish, optional

The family of Sonia Chopra and her mother, Chandana Chopra, has always made batter-fried vegetables—they were a staple of their Indian-American kitchen. In Delhi, India, where the family visits, Pakoras are served as a snack alongside cups of chai tea, accompanied by cool chutney or ketchup for dipping. In this recipe, the Chopras replaced the traditional Indian fillings—spicy chili peppers, onions, and sliced potatoes—with local green tomatoes for "an excellent passed or plated appetizer," says Sonia. The Pakoras may be served with ketchup or a curry ketchup instead of the Mint Chutney in the recipe below.

PAKORAS

3/4 cup chickpea flour

1 tablespoon rice flour or all-purpose flour

1/2 teaspoon salt

1/2 teaspoon turmeric

1/2 teaspoon ajwain (oregano seeds), optional

1/4 teaspoon chili powder, or to taste

1/2 cup water

1 1/2 to 2 cups oil for frying

2 large green tomatoes, sliced 1/4-inch thick

MINT CHUTNEY

1/3 to 1/2 cup packed fresh mint leaves

1/4 cup fresh lemon juice

2 fresh green chilies, such as serranos or Thai chilies, or more to taste

1 medium Granny Smith apple, peeled, cored, and diced

1 medium orange, peeled, seeded, and cubed

1 teaspoon salt

GREEN TOMATO PAKORAS

To make the Pakoras, mix the chickpea flour, rice flour, salt, turmeric, ajwain (if using), and chili powder in a medium bowl. Add the water. Stir to make a thick batter, adding 1 teaspoon more water if needed.

In a wok or other deep pot heat the oil over medium heat until it is hot but not smoking. (To test, drop a small amount of batter into the oil. If it rises to the surface immediately and is bubbling, the oil is ready. If there aren't bubbles, the oil isn't ready.)

Coat a tomato slice with batter. Shake off the excess. Gently slide into the hot oil. Cook until golden brown, 2 to 3 minutes on each side. Remove with a large slotted spoon. Use the first tomato as a test. If it browns too quickly, the oil is too hot. Taste the Pakoras and adjust the spices in the batter if desired.

Repeat with the remaining tomato slices. You can cook more than one at a time, but don't overcrowd. Drain on paper towels. Let cool and firm up for a few minutes.

To make the chutney combine the mint, lemon juice, chilies, apple, orange, and salt in a food processor or blender and process until smooth. The chutney will keep in the refrigerator for a few weeks, though it will darken over time. It can be frozen in ice cube trays or small containers to be used later. Serve with the Pakoras.

▶ Makes 2 cups Mint Chutney and about 16 Pakoras, or 6 to 8 servings

Note: Pakoras are best served immediately but can be reheated in a toaster oven at 350 degrees for a few minutes, or held on a pan in an oven on low heat until guests arrive.

Helen Waddle's most memorable party was the one she threw at her Shreveport, Louisiana, home for her and husband Paul's fiftieth wedding anniversary. "I wanted to share the event with friends and family, and I knew I wanted some sort of program," she says. "So I invited a local woman to play piano for us after dinner. I kept it a surprise from Paul, and it was such a delight when the pianist came out to play popular songs from the 1940s, as well as some classical pieces. It made the event unforgettable." Take a cue from Waddle and bring in musicians to play tunes that suit your party's theme, whether a chamber group, swing dance, or bluegrass band.

1/2 cup chopped green onion

1 (2-ounce) can sliced black olives

1 1/2 cups shredded Cheddar cheese

1/2 cup mayonnaise

1/2 teaspoon salt

1/4 teaspoon black pepper

1/2 teaspoon curry powder

Crackers or cocktail rye bread for serving

BLACK OLIVE CURRY CANAPÉ

Preheat the oven to 350 degrees. Combine the green onion, olives, cheese, mayonnaise, salt, pepper, and curry powder in a bowl and mix well. Spoon into a small casserole dish and bake for 15 minutes, or until the cheese is melted. Spread on crackers or cocktail rye bread.

▶ Makes about 2 cups, or 8 servings

This dip, also known as Ro-Tel dip after the brand of tomatoes with chilies most frequently used, is an Arkansas invention that's common at parties all across the South. But it's new to Kath Hansen's friends in her Brooklyn, New York, apartment building. "They go crazy for it," says Hansen, who lived in the South for decades. It's an easy trick to emulate—dig out recipes that are unfamiliar to guests, but familiar to you. There are lots of possible additions to the classic formulation: ground beef or sausage, jalapeño peppers, or black beans. Hansen sticks with the original, "straight up, Southern-style" dip.

CLASSIC SOUTHERN QUESO DIP

1 pound processed American cheese loaf, cut into chunks

1 (10-ounce) can tomatoes with green chilies

Tortilla or corn chips for serving

Melt the cheese in a saucepan over low heat. Stir in the tomatoes and heat through. Keep warm in a slow cooker, if desired. Serve with tortilla or corn chips.

▶ Makes about 5 cups, or 20 servings

April McAnnally is from Birmingham, Alabama, where folks take college football very seriously. Her advice for SEC hosts is to have a roster of tailgate and game day recipes. This dip, based on the always-popular hot artichoke dip, will surely be near the top of the roster. The recipe makes a batch large enough for a crowd, it reheats well, and people love it. "And every time we share it with someone at a party, I wind up writing down the recipe," she says. She also warns, "If you have men at your house, get your bite early. Once they know it's out of the oven, it's gone." Having too much food at a party is better than running out too soon. Use this easy way to calculate servings of dips and spreads. Allow 1/4 cup or 2 ounces of dip or spread per person.

2 tablespoons butter

1 medium yellow onion, diced

1 (16-ounce) can black-eyed peas, rinsed and drained

1 (14-ounce) can artichoke hearts, drained and chopped

2 tablespoons grated Parmesan cheese

1/2 cup sour cream

1/2 cup mayonnaise (preferably Hellman's)

1 (.4-ounce) envelope buttermilk ranch salad dressing mix

1 cup shredded mozzarella cheese

Tortilla chips or pita chips for serving

HOT BLACK-EYED PEA AND ARTICHOKE DIP

Preheat the oven to 350 degrees. Melt the butter in a large skillet or saucepan over medium heat. Add the onion and cook until translucent. Add the peas, artichoke hearts, Parmesan cheese, sour cream, mayonnaise, dressing mix, and mozzarella cheese, and mix well. Spoon into a shallow 2-quart buttered baking dish. Bake for 30 minutes. Serve with tortilla or pita chips.

▶ Makes 6 to 7 cups, or about 24 servings

Genet Hogan moved from Louisiana to Woodstock, Georgia, but couldn't leave behind her passion for New Orleans Saints football. "Football parties, professional or college, are easy to plan and execute because you can center your menu on the regional specialties of the hometowns of the competing teams," she says. Her menus tend to include one light dish and two or three hearty ones. To keep the stress level down, she orders or buys one or two of the dishes on her menu. She asks guests to bring dessert. A typical game day menu includes Shoepeg Corn Dip, Chicken Sliders with Bacon and Avocado-Basil Cream (page 45), and Shrimp Etouffée (page 137). A veteran hostess, Genet has timelines for prepping and serving food during the game. Start the party with a dip (like this one), beer, and purchased snacks. At end of the first quarter, ask a guest to help assemble the sliders. Serve them in the second quarter. Follow up with etouffée in the third quarter. Serve dessert in the fourth quarter.

1 (12-ounce) can white shoepeg corn, drained

1 cup thinly sliced green onion

1 red bell pepper, seeded and finely chopped

1 jalapeño pepper, seeded and finely chopped

1 cup shredded sharp Cheddar cheese

1/4 cup grated Parmesan cheese

1 cup sour cream

1/4 cup mayonnaise

1 teaspoon dried parsley flakes

Salt and ground black pepper, to taste

Corn chips for serving

SHOEPEG CORN DIP

In a large bowl, combine the corn, green onion, bell pepper, jalapeño, Cheddar and Parmesan cheeses, sour cream, mayonnaise, and parsley flakes. Season with salt and pepper. Refrigerate at least 1 hour before serving. Serve with corn chips.

▶ Makes about 4 cups, or 16 servings

Randle Browning of Waco, Texas, says that parties in her state often include Mexican-inspired dips. She chooses Tex-Mex favorites like salsa and Lemon Guacamole (page 39) and serves them in small bowls before dinner. For a football party, she uses larger bowls and plenty of tortilla chips, pita chips, and celery and carrot sticks. Her version of hummus includes chipotle peppers for a little Tex-Mex accent.

CHIPOTLE-LIME HUMMUS WITH SOUR CREAM

In a food processor, puree the garbanzo beans with the garlic clove. Add the chipotle peppers one at a time and taste for heat. Process until the mixture appears grainy. Add the tahini and process until the mixture has the texture of clay.

Add the salt and pulse to blend. Add the lime juice a few tablespoons at a time, pulsing between each addition. Add the ice water, a few tablespoons at a time, processing between each addition until the mixture is smooth and lighter in texture. Add 3 tablespoons of the sour cream and process until just combined. Transfer the hummus to a serving bowl.

Mix the remaining 1 tablespoon sour cream with a small amount of water (about ½ teaspoon). Drizzle the mixture over the top of the hummus. Sprinkle with the cilantro. Serve at room temperature with pita chips, tortilla chips, or vegetable sticks.

▶ Makes 4 to 5 cups, or 16 to 20 servings

Note: Make this spread up to three days ahead and refrigerate in an airtight container. Let the spread come to room temperature before serving.

2 (15-ounce) cans garbanzo beans (chickpeas), drained

1 clove garlic

1 to 2 chipotle peppers from a can of chipotles in adobo sauce

3/4 cup tahini

1/2 tablespoon salt

6 to 8 tablespoons fresh lime juice

6 to 8 tablespoons ice water

4 tablespoons sour cream, divided

1/4 cup chopped fresh cilantro

Pita chips, tortilla chips, or vegetable sticks for serving

Queso dip and tortilla chips are an enduring favorite at Southern gatherings, from patio parties to pot-luck dinners. Tasia Malakasis uses goat cheese from her Elkmont, Alabama, creamery to dress up queso for a more formal get-together. Tangy goat cheese and rich cream plus a topping of fresh tomato and cilantro give the dip a fresh personality and good looks too. Malakasis pampers her guests by serving the dip with homemade tortilla chips. For this dip, be sure to chop ingredients extra-fine so they fit easily onto a chip.

2 tablespoons butter

1/2 cup minced onion

Salt and ground black pepper

1 tablespoon chopped garlic

1 jalapeño pepper, seeded and finely chopped

2 cups crumbled goat cheese

1/4 to 1/2 cup heavy cream

1/2 cup finely chopped tomato

2 to 3 tablespoons finely chopped cilantro

Homemade or store-bought tortilla chips for serving

GOAT CHEESE QUESO

Melt the butter in a saucepan over medium heat. Add the onion and cook for 2 minutes. Season with salt and pepper. Stir in the garlic, jalapeño, cheese, and cream. Cook until thickened, 3 to 5 minutes. Place in a serving dish and sprinkle with the tomato and cilantro. Serve with tortilla chips.

▶ Makes 2 cups, or 8 servings

A great way to keep warm dips heated during a party is to place them in a slow cooker set to the warm setting.

Guacamole may be Mexican in origin, but it was Texas that popularized it as party food. Randle Browning of Waco, Texas, makes her guacamole with an authentic Mexican border touch. "In Texas, many people who grew up in Mexico will tell you that they have always made guacamole with lemons," she says, and she prefers it to lime-flavored guacamole. For company, she makes her guacamole "tableside" for a little bit of a show. "They'll enjoy seeing you prepare the dip tableside, like it's prepared in restaurants in Texas," she says. To do a tableside guacamole service, prepare most of the ingredients several hours ahead and cover. Mix in the avocados, lemon, and Tabasco sauce as your guests arrive. Serve immediately with tortilla chips, vegetable sticks, and ice-cold beer.

LEMON GUACAMOLE

Combine the onion, tomato, jalapeño, cilantro, cumin, and paprika in a medium bowl. Add the avocados and 3 tablespoons of the lemon juice and stir with a fork, mashing some chunks of avocado against the side of the bowl. Season to taste with the remaining lemon juice, salt, pepper, and Tabasco. Serve immediately with tortilla chips or vegetable sticks.

▶ Makes 6 cups, or 24 servings

Note: Guacamole should be eaten immediately, but if there are leftovers, store in the refrigerator in an airtight container with plastic wrap pressed directly on the top of the dip to prevent contact with air.

1 cup diced red onion

1 large tomato, cut into halves, seeds and pulp squeezed out, diced

1 small jalapeño pepper, seeded and minced

1/4 cup chopped cilantro

1/4 teaspoon ground cumin

1/2 teaspoon paprika

4 cups cubed ripe avocado (5 to 6 avocados)

4 to 6 tablespoons fresh lemon juice

Salt and ground black pepper, to taste

1/2 teaspoon Tabasco sauce

Tortilla chips or vegetable sticks for serving

Sometimes the dish turns the occasion into a party, as Carolyn Ogleton of Nashville, Tennessee, has discovered. Salmon mousse is her all-purpose party dish, made when friends gather or for church suppers. It even transforms her work environment. The hair salon where Ogleton works can't say enough good things about it. "When the mousse arrives, it's a party," says a coworker. "You think you're just going to have one or two crackers with it, but it's just so good you can't stop." The 1950s look of salmon-shaped gelatin mold is poised to make a retro comeback. Cookbooks from the 1950s are chock-full of specialty mousse recipes. Salmon mousse usually has "scales" of thinly sliced cucumber and "eyes" of black or green olives.

Pick up party-themed canapé knives or spreaders inexpensively at discount shopping or party centers. The short handles offer precise handling and the short blades pick up the right amount of mousse for one cracker—easy for guests and no dropped blobs of dip.

SALMON MOUSSE

1 (8-ounce) package cream cheese, softened

1 (10-ounce) can cream of mushroom soup

1 (15-ounce) can pink salmon

Cold water

2 (.4-ounce) envelopes unflavored gelatin

1/2 cup chopped celery

1/2 cup chopped green onion

1 cup mayonnaise

1 tablespoon sea salt

1 tablespoon curry powder, optional

Cucumber slices and black olives for garnish

Crackers for serving

In a medium bowl, stir together the cream cheese and mushroom soup. Drain the salmon, reserving the liquid. Remove and discard the skin and bones.

Add enough water to the salmon liquid to make ½ cup. Combine the liquid with the gelatin in a medium bowl. Let stand 5 minutes to soften. Add the celery, onion, mayonnaise, and salt, and mix well. Add the cream cheese mixture and salmon and mix well.

Spoon into a mold, smoothing the top. Refrigerate until firm, 3 to 3 ½ hours. Unmold onto a serving platter. Garnish with cucumber slices and olives. Serve with crackers.

▶ Makes about 6 cups, or 24 servings

Hosting is much easier if you have the right tools for the job. That's the advice of Connie Crabtree Burritt, chef and director of the culinary arts program at Baltimore, Maryland, Outreach Services, a service organization for homeless people. A chafing dish is one way to keep hot dips hot so you can mingle instead of running around reheating party food. For an updated look, place a piece of clean flat slate rock on a riser and heat from beneath with gel chafing fuel. Set the hot casserole dish on the slate to keep it warm.

HOT MARYLAND CRAB DIP

Preheat the oven to 350 degrees. Combine the cream cheese, mayonnaise, mustard, lemon juice, Worcestershire sauce, Tabasco, and Old Bay, and mix well.

Check the crabmeat for shells. Fold the crabmeat into the cream cheese mixture, taking care not to break up the crab. The dip is best when the crab is still in lumps.

Spoon the dip into a 9-inch square ovenproof serving dish. Bake for 25 to 30 minutes until browned and bubbly. Serve with crostini, pita chips, or crackers.

▶ Makes 4 cups, or 16 servings

3 (8-ounce) packages cream cheese, softened

1/2 cup mayonnaise

1 tablespoon Dijon-style mustard

Juice of 1 lemon

1 teaspoon Worcestershire sauce

1/2 teaspoon Tabasco sauce

2 teaspoons Old Bay seasoning, or to taste

1 pound back-fin crabmeat

Crostini, pita chips, or crackers for serving

Kentucky-born Mindy Jacoway calls Benedictine "a Kentucky staple" in the repertoire of many Bluegrass hosts. Benedictine is named for Louisville tearoom hostess and caterer Jennie C. Benedict and dates back to at least 1910, when the recipe was published in *The Blue Ribbon Cookbook*. The creamy cucumber mixture works both as a sandwich filling and as a dip. Green food coloring is traditionally added to give the spread a mint green tint for a cool and refreshing look.

Jacoway's special touch for guests at her Nashville, Tennessee, home is to treat food as part of the décor: Halloween crudités arranged in a skeleton shape, with a white bowl of dip for the skull, red pepper ribs, and cucumber vertebrae; or a red-and-green soup course of Italian tomato, spinach, and tortellini soup for a holiday dinner party.

1 medium cucumber, grated, juice reserved

1 small onion, grated, juice reserved

1 (8-ounce) package cream cheese, softened

Pinch of salt

Pinch of cayenne pepper

2 drops green food coloring

Slices of white bread, crusts removed

Tomato slices or bacon crumbles

BENEDICTINE SPREAD

Wrap the grated cucumber in cheesecloth and drain the liquid into a bowl. Repeat with the onion. Discard the solids. Add the cream cheese, salt, pepper, and green food coloring to the liquid and mix well. Spread on bread and top with a tomato slice or bacon crumbles.

▶ Makes 2 cups, or 8 servings

Note: To make a dip instead of a spread, drain and discard the cucumber and onion juices. Add the solids to the cream cheese, along with the salt, pepper, and green food coloring. Add 1 tablespoon mayonnaise and 1 tablespoon sour cream. Serve with fresh vegetables or crackers.

Where would a Southern party be without these soft, sweet, mustardy, buttery, speckled ham rolls? Or open-hearted hostesses like Debbie Young of Nashville, Tennessee? Young worked for years in restaurants and cafeterias. She recommends serving these rolls on a buffet with other pick-up foods like artichoke crostini, vegetables and dip, prosciutto-wrapped asparagus, chicken wings, cheese straws, and bacon-wrapped chicken bites. Young suggests offering lots of beverage options. A special tea is nice for the non-imbibers—her usual is tea punch, or fruit tea like raspberry or peach. Craft beer for the beer drinkers, "mixed drinks for the hard core," and a bottle each of red and white wine keep the party flowing.

POLKA-DOT PARTY HAM AND SWISS ROLLS

Preheat the oven to 350 degrees. Melt the butter in a skillet or saucepan over medium heat. Add the onion and cook until tender. Stir in the mustard and poppy seeds. Turn the rolls out of their packages. Slice the whole slab horizontally into two halves. Remove the top. Spread the bottom layer with the onion mixture. Layer on the cheese and ham. Set the top layer of the rolls back on top and carefully return the rolls to their baking trays. Bake for 10 to 15 minutes. Turn the rolls out of the trays and cut into individual rolls. Serve warm or at room temperature.

▶ Makes 24 servings

1/2 cup (1 stick) butter

1 large yellow onion, diced

3 tablespoons yellow mustard

3 tablespoons poppy seeds

2 (15-ounce, 12-count) packages brown-and-serve rolls

3 cups shredded Swiss cheese

12 ounces ham, finely chopped, or 12 ounces good-quality thinly sliced deli ham

Genet Hogan of Woodstock, Georgia, simplifies her New Orleans-style football party menu by preparing some items ahead of time and making a mental timeline for completing each dish. For instance, the Avocado-Basil Cream here can be made the day before, while the blackened chicken can be prepared an hour before guests arrive. Keep the chicken warm in the oven until the end of the first quarter, then recruit a guest to help assemble the sliders so they're ready to serve at halftime. Ask a guest who doesn't seem to be mingling well—an attentive host knows that sometimes people are more comfortable when they have a "role" at a party.

CHICKEN SLIDERS WITH BACON AND AVOCADO-BASIL CREAM

AVOCADO-BASIL CREAM

1 large avocado, cut into halves and pitted

15 large fresh basil leaves

1 small clove garlic

1/4 cup sour cream

1 teaspoon fresh lemon juice

Salt and ground black pepper, to taste

SLIDERS

3 boneless, skinless chicken breasts

1/2 cup (1 stick) unsalted butter, melted, divided

1/4 cup blackening seasoning

1 (12-ounce) package sweet dinner rolls (such as King's Hawaiian)

1 cup shredded Monterey Jack cheese

12 slices bacon, crisply cooked and cut into halves

To make the Avocado-Basil Cream, scoop the avocado flesh into a blender or food processor. Add the basil, garlic, sour cream, lemon juice, salt, and pepper, and process until smooth. This may be prepared up to one day ahead, covered, and refrigerated. Stir before serving. Serve cold.

To make the sliders, place the chicken between sheets of waxed paper. With the flat side of a meat mallet, pound each breast until

it is about ½- to ¾-inch thick. Cut each breast into 4 equal portions.

Heat a large cast-iron skillet over high heat until it begins to smoke.*

Pour 4 tablespoons of the melted butter into a wide, shallow dish. Place the blackening seasoning in a separate wide, shallow dish.

_____

* Turn on the stove's exhaust fan or open the windows for ventilation.

Working in batches of 4, dip the chicken in the butter, then dredge in the seasoning. Place in the hot skillet. Cook, uncovered, until the bottom appears charred, 2 to 3 minutes. Turn the chicken over and cook until done, about 3 minutes longer. Add a small amount of additional melted butter to the pan as needed to prevent the chicken from sticking. Transfer the cooked chicken to a baking sheet. Repeat with the remaining chicken. The chicken may be kept warm in a 200-degree oven until ready to assemble.

To assemble the sliders, preheat the oven to 375 degrees. Turn the rolls out of their packages. Slice the whole slab horizontally into two halves and place them on a large baking sheet. Bake about 3 minutes, until lightly toasted. Separate the rolls. Place one piece of chicken on each bottom half of roll. Top with a tablespoon of cheese. Return to the oven until the cheese is melted. Finish each slider with 2 pieces of bacon, a dollop of Avocado-Basil Cream, and the top half of the roll.

▶ Makes 1 1/2 cups Avocado-Basil Cream and 12 sliders, or 6 servings

Lisa Towery, an experienced hostess of elaborate functions now living in Oxford, Mississippi, recommends hiring helpers. She employs restaurant workers and college students for prep, service, and clean up. Three people worked with her at her Kentucky Derby-themed party for 24, serving mint juleps, working action stations assembling Kentucky Hot Browns (page 151) and cherries jubilee, and cleaning up after the party. Extra hands open up lots of possibilities for expanding the food, service, and entertainment at any party.

FRIED GREEN TOMATO SLIDERS WITH AIOLI

To make the sauce mix the mayonnaise, garlic, lemon juice, salt, and pepper in a medium bowl. Cover and refrigerate for at least 30 minutes before using.

To make the sliders whisk together the eggs and milk in a small bowl. In another small bowl mix the cornmeal and flour.

Pour olive oil to a depth of ¼ inch into a large skillet. Heat the oil over medium heat.

Coat the tomato slices with the egg mixture, then the cornmeal mixture. Carefully place the slices in the hot oil. Fry, turning once, until browned on both sides. Drain on paper towels.

Arrange the tomatoes on the rolls. Top each with 1 tablespoon of the Garlic Aioli Sauce.

▶ Makes about 1 cup Garlic Aioli Sauce and 24 sliders, or 12 servings

GARLIC AIOLI SAUCE

3/4 cup mayonnaise

3 cloves garlic, finely chopped

2 1/2 tablespoons fresh lemon juice

3/4 teaspoon salt

1/2 teaspoon ground black pepper

SLIDERS

2 large eggs

1/2 cup milk

2 cups cornmeal

2 cups all-purpose flour

Olive oil for frying

5 to 6 medium green tomatoes, sliced

24 small rolls, such as slider buns or small ciabatta rolls

Larissa Arnault of Nashville, Tennessee, says her Cheesy Sausage Wontons are always on the guest list, at her parties and others'. "Each year a friend hosts a pumpkin carving party, and she always asks me, 'Will you make those wontons?' They never fail to be a filling hit!" she says. They're ideal on an appetizer buffet. She recommends making enough for each guest to have three, and making some lighter options for a balanced menu. "They're rich and heavy, so I offer them with some lighter, fresher things like crudités. They're great with a crisp drink that cuts through the richness," she says, such as lemon-spiked tea, citrus soft drinks, or dry white wine. The wontons are best right out of the oven. Time the baking so you can bring them out when guests are gathering around the buffet.

1 pound bulk pork breakfast sausage

1 1/2 to 2 cups shredded sharp Cheddar cheese

1 1/2 to 2 cups shredded Monterey Jack cheese

1 cup ranch dressing

1 red bell pepper, diced

1 (2-ounce) can chopped black olives

1 (48-count) package wonton wrappers

Vegetable oil

CHEESY SAUSAGE WONTONS

Preheat the oven to 350 degrees. Brown the sausage in a skillet over medium heat. Drain well. Place the sausage in a large bowl and add the Cheddar cheese, Jack cheese, dressing, bell pepper, and olives. Mix well.

Place a spoonful of the sausage mixture on each wonton wrapper. Brush the edges with water and fold over to seal. Set the wontons on a baking sheet. Brush the wontons with vegetable oil. Bake about 5 minutes, until the cheese is melted and the filling is bubbly. Serve immediately. Store leftovers in the refrigerator and reheat in a toaster oven.

▶ Makes 48 pieces, or 16 servings

Lucky and talented Anna Ginsberg of Austin, Texas, competed in the Pillsbury Bake-Off twice and says one of the best parts was tasting the entries of all the competitors. "During my first Bake-Off in 2004, one contestant introduced me to a spice that became my new favorite—smoked paprika," she says. "These days it is fairly common, but back then the 'smoked' type was a little more novel. I began using it in many dishes for entertaining, to introduce others to the taste. This chicken dish is one I created shortly after the Bake-Off."

Ginsberg says these quesadillas can be used as an appetizer or an entrée. They're right at home at a card or board game party. Offer a simple menu of vegetables and dip, quesadillas and sandwiches, and non-crumbly cookies—finger foods that free up guests' hands to play. To carry on the game-night theme, place old game boards at the buffet and drink stations. To make the party festive, Ginsberg recommends Spanish red wine to match the sweet and smoky flavor of the Spanish paprika.

SMOKY CHICKEN QUESADILLAS

1 tablespoon butter

1/4 cup regular or light sour cream

1/4 cup regular or light mayonnaise

1 teaspoon smoked paprika

1 tablespoon fresh lime juice

2 teaspoons honey

1 tablespoon chopped cilantro

8 (7-inch) flour tortillas

2 cups shredded sharp Cheddar cheese

2 cups chopped cooked chicken breast

Salsa for serving

Preheat the oven to 200 degrees. Grease a large skillet with the butter. In a small bowl, stir together the sour cream, mayonnaise, paprika, lime juice, honey, and cilantro.

Spread 1 tablespoon of the sour cream mixture on one half of each of the tortillas. Top with ¼ cup of the cheese and about ¼ cup of the chicken chunks. Fold the tortillas in half to make quesadillas, then place two or three (as many as you can fit) in the skillet.

Cook the quesadillas on the stove top over medium-high heat until hot and bubbly, about 2 minutes on each side. When the first few are done, set them on a baking sheet and keep them warm in the oven.

Slice each quesadilla into two wedges and serve with salsa on the side.

▶ Makes 8 servings

Don't underestimate your guests' sense of culinary adventure, counsels Wendy Perry, of Zebulon, North Carolina. Surprise them with something unusual. Chicken gizzards aren't for every kind of party, but in the right setting, like a North Carolina "pig pickin'," or traditional pig roast, they lend an authentic farm-to-table flavor. Perry cooks up to 50 pounds of chicken gizzards at a time and says "there is never a bit left."

For a mealtime gathering, plan on serving around 1 pound of food per guest. That's roughly 2 cups (32 tablespoons, if you're measuring soft foods like dips and spreads) per guest.

2 pounds chicken gizzards

1 cup apple juice or water

1 cup cider vinegar

1 tablespoon kosher salt

6 tablespoons brown sugar

1 teaspoon hot red pepper flakes

1 teaspoon finely ground black pepper

1 large sweet onion, cut into halves and thinly sliced

1/2 cup (1 stick) butter

WENDY'S BARBECUED CHICKEN GIZZARDS

Combine the gizzards, juice, vinegar, salt, sugar, pepper flakes, black pepper, and onion in a large, heavy pot. Cover and bring to a boil over high heat. Boil for 10 minutes, then reduce the heat to low. Simmer, covered, for 1 hour, stirring occasionally. Check for tenderness. If the gizzards are large, you may need to cook them an additional 20 to 30 minutes.

Uncover, add the butter, and return to a boil. Cook 5 to 15 minutes to reduce and thicken the sauce. Watch closely and stir to prevent sticking and reducing too much.

Serve the gizzards in a warming pan or chafing dish as part of an appetizer buffet, with toothpicks or with forks and cocktail plates.

To serve the gizzards as an entrée over grits, use two chafing dishes, one for the gizzards and another for the grits.

▶ Makes 8 appetizer servings or 6 to 8 entrée servings with grits

Mimi Manzler's entertaining style is pick-up food in a casual atmosphere. "I like for people to be able to 'free-range'—eat, drink, mingle—so I choose foods that can be held in the hand," she says.

At her Chicago home, her table typically includes half a dozen offerings. She depends on a warming tray to keep dishes hot so she can focus on socializing rather than reheating. A warming tray doesn't dry out foods, which can happen in a chafing dish, and feels safer than the open-flame of a gel chafing fuel. Vintage warming trays have a wonderfully retro look and evoke the style of her mother-in-law, Marg, who gave her this meatball recipe.

COCKTAIL MEATBALLS

Preheat the oven to 375 degrees. In a large bowl, mix the beef, sausage, eggs, cracker crumbs, and cheese. Shape into bite-size meatballs.

Arrange the meatballs in a roasting pan or shallow baking dish. Bake for 20 minutes, shaking the pan or turning the meatballs after about 10 minutes. Drain on paper towels.

Meanwhile, in a large saucepan or Dutch oven, combine the dressing mix, ketchup, brown sugar, grape jelly, and garlic powder. Bring to a simmer over low heat.

Place the meatballs in the sauce. Cover the pan and simmer the meatballs in the sauce. Serve with toothpicks.

▶ Makes about 40 meatballs, or 10 servings

1 pound ground chuck

1 pound Italian sausage (regular, hot, or a combination), casings removed

2 large eggs, beaten

1 1/2 cups cracker crumbs

1/4 cup Parmesan cheese

1/4 envelope dry French or Italian salad dressing mix

1 2/3 cups ketchup

1/2 cup brown sugar

1 1/2 cups grape jelly

Garlic powder, to taste

Patricia Hall, a native of Hendersonville, Tennessee, wants guests to savor dinner rather than fill up on appetizers. Her solution is to offer a pre-dinner tidbit like Bacon-Date Bites. "It's a great little cocktail bite," she says. "It has a bit of elegance without the effort. And you don't fill up on it like other heavy appetizers." Hall says that when you're serving a small appetizer, plan on serving dinner within 30 minutes. Have dinner mostly prepared as guests arrive, then set out the Bacon-Date Bites. They take the edge off your guests' appetites while you put together last-minute details like tossing a salad or heating bread.

BACON-DATE BITES

12 pitted dates

1/4 cup cream cheese

6 slices bacon (center cut works best)

Ground black pepper, to taste

Cut a slit lengthwise in each date. Fill each date with 1 teaspoon of the cream cheese. Press to close the date over the filling.

Cut the bacon slices crosswise into halves and trim the excess fat. The key to the flavor is using mostly bacon meat with little fat. Wrap each date with a piece of the bacon, making sure there is overlap. Sprinkle generously with pepper.

Heat a nonstick skillet over medium-high heat. Place the dates in the pan and cook, turning once, for about 2 minutes per side. Let cool slightly before serving.

▶ Makes 12 pieces, or 6 servings

BRUNCH, BREAKFAST, AND BREAD

The idea of brunch may have originated in England, but Southerners have made it a cornerstone of entertaining. A morning get-together catches guests when they're rested, in the hours before the busyness of the day begins. Mornings work well for entertaining families with young children, before the little ones grow tired and grumpy. Brunch can fuel a full day, or just segue right into a nap on a lazy weekend day. It's good for hosts, too, since many brunch dishes can be made the night before and baked or reheated. A morning guest is a hungry guest, so plan generously for big appetites.

Breads are the centerpiece of many satisfying brunch menus, but the Southern tradition of hot bread is more than a century older than brunch. After the popularity of hot biscuits and rolls languished for a generation of cooks, they've been embraced by a new generation of bakers enhancing traditional recipes and finding new ways to use old favorites to please company.

Ham with angel biscuits are "a must for receptions, holidays, and other special celebrations," says Nell Wallace of Cadiz, Kentucky. Angel biscuits are a little unusual—they use both baking powder and yeast, and they are absolutely "no fail"—perfect for the curious, cautious host.

ANGEL BISCUITS AND HAM SLICES

Combine the yeast and water in a small cup. Let stand 5 to 10 minutes for the yeast to activate.

In a large bowl sift together the flour, sugar, baking powder, baking soda, and salt. Add the shortening and blend with a pastry blender or your fingers until the shortening is in pea-size lumps. Add 1 cup of the buttermilk. Use a wooden spoon to stir. Add the yeast and the remaining 1 cup buttermilk. Mix thoroughly. Place the dough on a floured board and knead a few times. Store the dough in an airtight container in the refrigerator for several hours.

Preheat the oven to 400 degrees. Roll the dough to ½-inch thickness. Cut with a small biscuit cutter. Dip the biscuits into the butter and place on a baking sheet. Bake for about 10 minutes, until slightly browned. Split the biscuits and stuff with sliced country ham.

▶ Makes 24 biscuits

1 (.25-ounce) package active dry yeast

2 tablespoons lukewarm water

5 cups all-purpose flour

1/2 cup sugar

1 tablespoon baking powder

1 teaspoon baking soda

1 1/2 teaspoons salt

3/4 cup shortening

2 cups buttermilk

Melted butter, for dipping

24 thin slices Boiled or Baked Country Ham (page 57)

In all its beautiful abundance, a baked or boiled country ham is the glory of the table across the South. At Nell Wallace's Cadiz, Kentucky, home, ham is the start of many celebratory gatherings around her table.

"A fresh, pretty tablecloth with a seasonal centerpiece always says, 'welcome,'" says Wallace. "Centerpieces need not be expensive. In the spring and summer, you can use fresh flowers from your own garden to create a simple display. Colorful fall leaves and nuts make an attractive display in autumn, and in winter, candles and evergreen sprigs are the perfect finishing touch to your table."

BOILED HAM

1 (13- to 17-pound) country ham

1 cup vinegar

1 cup firmly packed brown sugar

TRIGG COUNTY BOILED AND BAKED HAM

Scrub the outside of the ham. (Mold on the outside of a country ham is not an indication of spoilage.) Cut off the hock. Put the ham into a large pot and cover with cold water. Add the vinegar and brown sugar. For a 13- to 15-pound ham, let it soak for at least 12 hours. Larger hams (15 to 17 pounds) will need to soak at least 15 hours.

Drain and discard the liquid. Cover the ham with fresh cold water. Cover with a lid, bring to a boil, and boil for 30 minutes.

Remove the pot from the heat. Wrap the pot in old quilts or newspaper to hold the heat in. Let stand for 24 hours. (The water will still be very warm.) Drain the ham. Trim off the skin and large areas of fat. Refrigerate the ham until ready to slice and serve.

▶ Makes 40 to 60 servings

Scrub the outside of the ham. (Mold on the outside of a country ham is not an indication of spoilage.) Cut off the hock. Put the ham into a large pot and cover with cold water. Add the vinegar and 1 cup of the brown sugar. For a 13- to 15-pound ham, let it soak for at least 12 hours. Larger hams (15 to 17 pounds) will need to soak at least 15 hours.

Preheat the oven to 300 degrees. Drain the ham. Line a deep roasting pan with heavy-duty aluminum foil, leaving enough overhang to fold over the ham to cover. Place the ham, skin side down, in the pan. Be sure not to puncture the foil.

Pour 1 quart of water into the pan. Pat the remaining 1 cup brown sugar on top of ham. Seal by double folding the foil over the top tightly. Bake for 15 minutes per pound. Leave the ham in the oven without opening the door until it is completely cold.

Trim off the skin and large areas of fat. Refrigerate the ham until ready to slice and serve.

▶ Makes 40 to 50 servings

BAKED COUNTRY HAM

1 (13- to 17-pound) country ham

1 cup vinegar

2 cups firmly packed brown sugar, divided

1 quart water

Pat Goodyear's guests at her Baltimore, Maryland, home are fortunate in high summer, when tomato quiche is on the lunch or brunch menu. To keep the quiche from being too watery and to make the slices neater, Goodyear fries the tomatoes lightly to firm them up before assembling the quiche. "It's a good brunch or lunch choice and can easily be served on a buffet, in the pie plate that it was baked in," she says. Cut the quiche before putting it on the buffet—don't make guests cut their own slices of most dishes, including dessert. If your pie plate is embarrassingly battered or stained, invest in a pretty one for the occasion, or just make up all the guests' plates in the kitchen, where the old pie plates can remain hidden. To complete the menu, add a lightly dressed salad and sweet tea.

FRIED TOMATO QUICHE

1 (9-inch) piecrust, store-bought or homemade

2 tablespoons vegetable oil

1/4 cup all-purpose flour

Salt and ground black pepper

2 large tomatoes, sliced 1/2 inch thick

1 cup minced green onions

3 to 4 ounces provolone cheese, sliced

2 large eggs

1 cup shredded Cheddar cheese

1 cup heavy cream

Preheat the oven to 425 degrees. Place the piecrust in a 9-inch pie pan. Line the crust with aluminum foil and place pie weights on top. Bake the crust for 8 minutes. Place on a wire rack to cool and reduce the oven temperature to 375 degrees.

Heat the vegetable oil in a large skillet over medium-high heat. Place the flour in a medium bowl. Season with the salt and pepper. Dip each tomato slice in the flour, then place in the hot oil and cook until nicely browned on both sides.

Scatter the green onion evenly over the bottom of the piecrust. Layer the tomatoes on top and cover with the provolone cheese. Beat the eggs in a small bowl and add the Cheddar cheese and cream. Pour the egg mixture into the piecrust, place the pie on a baking sheet, and bake for 45 minutes. Place on a wire rack to cool 5 minutes before slicing. Serve warm.

▶ Makes 6 servings

Dani Meyer and her husband, Kevin, of Oregon, then Georgia, and now Bend, Oregon, lived in a house that was being remodeled for months. They were determined to entertain friends despite a ripped out ceiling, no flooring, and only a single room available for gathering. "We are raised in such a perfectionist culture that it's difficult to let that stuff go," says Dani Meyer, "but you have to, or you'll just make yourself and everyone around you miserable. Remember that very few people are willing to open their homes to those around them; this alone makes a huge impression." They held big dinners when their living room served as their bedroom and invited their whole church congregation over for a friend's surprise party. She says that a simple evening of beer and board games "will do you a heck of a lot more good than hating your house because you can't have friends over until it's finished."

6 large eggs

1 cup milk

1/2 cup half-and-half

2 tablespoons oat flour

2 teaspoons baking soda

1/2 teaspoon ground cumin

Dash of cayenne pepper

Salt and ground black pepper, to taste

1/4 cup salsa, plus more for serving

1/2 cup diced tomatoes, drained

1/2 to 1 cup frozen or fresh corn

7 to 8 corn tortillas

1/2 cup shredded Mexican-blend cheese, plus more for the top, optional

Sour cream and cilantro for serving

MEXICAN QUICHE

Preheat the oven to 350 degrees. Combine the eggs, milk, half-and-half, oat flour, baking soda, cumin, cayenne, and salt and pepper in a blender. Blend until combined. Use a spoon to stir in the salsa, tomatoes, and corn.

Line a pie pan with the corn tortillas. Sprinkle with the cheese. Pour the egg mixture over the cheese. Sprinkle more cheese on top if using. Bake for 50 minutes. Serve warm or at room temperature with additional salsa, sour cream, and cilantro.

▶ Makes 6 servings

This whimsical (and useful) recipe is from Grant Johnson of Nashville, Tennessee. Johnson was a prep cook in a sorority house during college. His advice, naturally, is to get all the prep out of the way before guests arrive, along with most of the cooking and some of the cleaning. When your guests arrive, serve lots of good drinks and snacks so they start out happy.

TATER TOT SQUASH FRITTATA

Preheat the oven to 350 degrees. Heat a large, heavy skillet over medium heat. Cook the bacon until mostly crisp. Remove the bacon and drain on paper towels. Crumble the bacon. Leave the bacon fat in the pan. Add the onion, garlic, squash, and mushrooms to the pan. Cook and stir over medium heat until tender, about 10 minutes.

Beat the eggs and milk in a medium bowl. Add the salt and pepper. Pour over the vegetables in the pan. Cook until the eggs are partially set, about 3 minutes. Add the bacon crumbles and tater tots. Spread the cheese on the top. Put the pan in the oven and bake for 5 to 7 minutes, until the eggs are set.

Turn the oven to broil and broil the frittata until the top is slightly brown and bubbly. Remove from oven and let stand for 5 minutes before serving.

▶ Makes 3 servings

2 slices thick-cut bacon, chopped

1 large Vidalia onion, chopped

3 cloves garlic, finely chopped

2 small yellow crookneck squash, cut into 1/4-inch rounds

5 or 6 mushrooms, sliced

6 large eggs

Splash of milk

Sea salt and ground black pepper, to taste

1 cup tater tots, baked according to package instructions

1/2 cup shredded sharp Cheddar cheese

For Renee Flynn, a native of Pine Bluff, Arkansas, surprise was the element of memorable parties. Among her friends, the Come-As-You-Are breakfast was one popular way to entertain. Guests were awakened at dawn, and wearing their pajamas and curlers, without makeup, they were driven to the hostess's house for a brunch. What better way to cherish friends just as they are than to gather them in their pajamas for a hearty wake-up? A menu of Baked Egg and Bacon Cups and Baked French Toast (page 76) pleases both those who like a savory breakfast and those who prefer sweeter fare.

BAKED EGG AND BACON CUPS

12 slices bacon

Butter for the pan and dotting the eggs

12 large eggs

Salt and ground black pepper, to taste

Preheat the oven to 350 degrees. Fry the bacon in a skillet over medium heat until barely crisp, then drain on paper towels. Lightly grease a 12-cup muffin pan with butter. Wrap a piece of bacon inside each muffin cup. Crack 1 egg into each muffin cup. Sprinkle with salt and pepper, and dot with a small pat of butter. Bake for 15 minutes or until the egg whites are set but the yolks are still runny. Gently slide the bacon-egg cups onto serving plates.

▶ Makes 12 servings

At her family Valentine's breakfast bash, Kathryn Tortorici decorates her Birmingham, Alabama, kitchen table with fun items she collects all year just for the occasion. "Everything must be something unexpected," she says. Another special touch: Tortorici uses cookie cutters to cut different shapes from strawberry toaster pastries to create sweet tidbits for her children. There might be other heart-shaped foods, too, like these little baked ham and cheese sandwiches.

1 loaf day-old white bread, sliced

1 pound thick-sliced honey ham

2 (5-ounce) jars cheese spread

1 cup (2 sticks) butter, softened

1/2 teaspoon cayenne pepper

HEART-SHAPED CHEESE BITES WITH HAM

Use a small heart-shaped cookie cutter to cut two hearts out of each slice of bread, making sure not to get any of the crust. Cut the ham slices with the cookie cutter.

Combine the cheese and butter in a bowl. The mixture should be about the consistency of cake icing. Add the pepper.

Spread about half of the cheese mixture on half of the bread pieces. Add a slice of ham on top of the cheese mixture. Top with the remaining bread pieces. Spread the remaining cheese mixture on the tops and sides of the hearts.

Arrange the hearts on a baking sheet lined with parchment paper or aluminum foil. Freeze for at least 1 hour. Preheat the oven to 400 degrees. Bake for 15 minutes or until slightly brown.

▶ Makes 20 pieces

Marirae Mathis, of Who Cooks for You? personal chef services in Nashville, Tennessee, just can't stay up for the "ball drop" on New Year's Eve, so she and her husband, Bob, began holding a New Year's Day open house in their home. On the menu: egg-and-bread strata, a tray of artisan cheeses and fruit, and sauerkraut, a German New Year's tradition. One popular menu item is this sweet and spicy, super crunchy bacon. She offers a signature cocktail or two in pitchers and asks guests to bring along a dish to share. It's a true open house: no clock, no pressure, just an open door, warm food, a little something bracing, and friends to share best wishes for a happy, healthy, and prosperous New Year.

BROWN SUGAR AND SPICE BACON BLISS

2 pounds bacon

3/4 cup firmly packed brown sugar

2 teaspoons Dijon-style mustard

1 teaspoon Worcestershire sauce

1/2 teaspoon Sriracha or other hot pepper sauce

1/2 teaspoon ground cinnamon

Preheat the oven to 425 degrees. Line 2 rimmed baking sheets with parchment paper. Spread the bacon out on the sheets and bake for 15 to 20 minutes, until light brown but not crisp.

Combine the brown sugar, mustard, Worcestershire sauce, Sriracha, and cinnamon in a small saucepan. Cook over medium-low heat, stirring, until the sugar is dissolved.

Remove the bacon from the oven and brush with the brown sugar mixture. Return the bacon to the oven and bake about 7 minutes, or to desired crispness. Drain on paper towels.

▶ Makes 8 to 10 servings

Grillades (pronounced gree-yahds) is a common brunch recipe in Louisiana where Jean Button grew up. She and her friends turned party prep into party time by gathering a group to cook the grillades. "I've made this dish many times with a small group of friends. There are usually four or five of us, and we divide the prep work. Then we gather to do the cooking. Everyone arrives with their assigned sliced meat, chopped veggies, etc. Since we all work during the day, it saves us from having to pull a marathon cooking event. We make a fun evening of it, and it's done way ahead of the party." Grillades and grits were the staple of Louisiana Mardi Gras brunches, and Button imported the tradition to her Fayetteville, Arkansas, home. "Everyone comes in costume. The kids loved it and looked forward to it. They grew up understanding what Mardi Gras was. I wouldn't have come to school in Arkansas if I had realized they didn't have Mardi Gras everywhere!" she says. Grillades can be made well ahead of time and frozen. Grillades served over Gruyère grits is a little "gilding the lily" that Button says is memorably delicious.

GRILLADES

3 1/4 cups all-purpose flour, divided

Garlic powder, to taste

Ground black pepper, to taste

8 pounds beef round steak, cut into 2-inch strips

2 cups peanut oil, divided

3 cups chopped onion

2 cups chopped celery

3 cups chopped bell pepper

2 teaspoons minced garlic

1 cup chopped green onions

4 cups sliced mushrooms, optional

1 (15-ounce) can tomato sauce

2 teaspoons dried thyme

1 tablespoon salt

1 teaspoon pepper

1 cup water

2 cups burgundy or other dry red wine

1 tablespoon Tabasco sauce

1/4 cup Worcestershire sauce

6 bay leaves

1 1/2 cups chopped parsley

Cheese grits or rice for serving

Combine 2 cups of the flour with the garlic powder and black pepper in a large zip-top bag. Add the beef strips to the bag, seal, and gently shake to coat.

Heat 1 cup of the oil in a large pan over medium-high heat. Use a pair of tongs to remove the beef from the bag, shaking off the excess flour, and place in the hot oil. Brown the meat in batches to avoid overcrowding the pan. Drain the cooked meat on paper towels.

Make a roux by adding the remaining 1 cup of peanut oil to the pan. Stir in the remaining 1 ¼ cups flour, and cook over medium-high heat, stirring constantly, until a dark caramel color develops, about 15 minutes. Remove the pan from the heat and let the roux cool for 10 to 15 minutes, then return the pan to the heat. Add the onion, celery, bell pepper, garlic, green onions, and mushrooms. Cook and stir until tender. Add the tomato sauce, thyme, salt, and pepper. Cook over medium-low heat, stirring, until the color of the tomato sauce starts to fade, about 20 minutes.

Stir in the water, wine, Tabasco, Worcestershire sauce, bay leaves, and parsley, and mix well. Add the meat and any accumulated juices back to the pan, cover, and simmer over low heat for 2 hours. Serve over cheese grits or rice.

▶ Makes 30 to 35 servings

Note: You can use thinly sliced leftover cooked meat (smoked brisket is delicious) and skip the dredging and cooking steps.

Hush puppies are the classic deep South accompaniment to fried seafood, and like many fried foods, they taste so much better when made at home and served fresh from the fryer. In the hands of Connie Crabtree Burritt of Baltimore, Maryland, they get a dose of crabmeat or shrimp, transforming them into luxurious little bites that star anywhere from brunch to side dish to cocktails to snack. To serve them hot, you'll likely be frying as guests arrive. To multitask successfully, read and memorize the recipe before-hand so you can chat with your guests while you tend to the hushpuppies. If you prefer to fry solo, warn guests you're a nervous fryer, or direct them to drinks, snacks, or entertainment in another room.

HUSH PUPPIES WITH CRAB OR SHRIMP

Heat the oil to 375 degrees in a Dutch oven. Combine the cornmeal, flour, baking powder, cayenne, sugar, and salt in a medium bowl.

In a small bowl beat the egg, milk, onion, and jalapeño until well blended. Add to the cornmeal mixture and mix well. Stir in the cheese and crabmeat. The batter should be thick enough to hold its shape when dropped from a spoon.

Slide spoonsful of batter into the hot oil. Do not overcrowd the pan. Cook for about 5 minutes until the hush puppies are golden brown and rise to the top. Drain on paper towels. Serve warm.

▶ Makes 8 to 10 servings

4 cups vegetable oil

1 cup yellow cornmeal

1/2 cup all-purpose flour

2 teaspoons baking powder

1/4 teaspoon cayenne pepper

1 teaspoon sugar

1/2 teaspoon salt

1 large egg

3/4 cup milk

1/2 cup minced onion

Diced jalapeño peppers, to taste, optional

1 cup shredded sharp Cheddar cheese

3/4 pound crabmeat or peeled, chopped, cooked shrimp

Jocelyn Ruggiero's go-to meal for easy entertaining in her Madison, Connecticut, home is brunch. "It's easy to prepare in advance and somehow, the expectations are more casual," she says. Hosting just a few people gives guests the gift of leisurely time in one another's company. "I threw a memorable brunch just before Christmas a few years ago as a reunion for my cousins. We hadn't all been in the same room for many years and wanted plenty of time to talk. That day, my cousin Anne Marie brought a French toast casserole made with cinnamon bread that was a hit. We all sat at my dining room table for hours—eating, laughing, reminiscing, and sharing news of our grown-up lives. My casserole draws on classic Southern flavors and is a tribute to my cousin Marylou who passed away shortly after that day." Don't wait for a big occasion—entertain the people you enjoy however you can, whenever you can.

FRENCH TOAST CASSEROLE WITH PEACHES, BACON, AND MAPLE BOURBON PECANS

2 tablespoons butter, divided

6 large eggs

1/2 cup heavy cream

1 cup milk

1/4 cup white sugar

1 teaspoon vanilla extract

1/2 teaspoon ground cinnamon

1 pound French bread, cut into 1-inch cubes

1/2 cup pecans

1/4 cup maple syrup, plus more for serving

1 tablespoon bourbon

2 1/2 cups canned sliced peaches packed in juice

1 cup firmly packed light brown sugar

4 slices bacon

The night before grease a 9 x 13-inch baking pan with 1 tablespoon of the butter. In a large bowl whisk the eggs. Add the cream, milk, sugar, vanilla, and cinnamon, and mix well. Add the bread cubes and mix gently. Pour the mixture into the pan. Cover with plastic wrap and refrigerate for at least 8 hours.

When ready to bake preheat the oven to 350 degrees. Heat the remaining 1 tablespoon butter in a medium skillet over medium-high heat. Add the pecans and stir to coat. Add the maple syrup and bourbon. Cook until most of the liquid is reduced, about 3 minutes. Spread the pecans on a dish to dry. (Do not clean the pan.)

Dip the peach slices in brown sugar, then arrange in a single layer over the bread. Sprinkle the pecans evenly over the top. Bake for 45 minutes or until a knife inserted in the center comes out clean. While the casserole is baking, cook the bacon over low heat in the pan the pecans were toasted in until well browned.

Drain on paper towels. Let cool. Crumble the bacon.

Turn the oven to broil. Broil the casserole for about 2 minutes, or until the peaches and pecans are golden. Cut into individual servings. Serve with the bacon crumbles and warm maple syrup.

▶ Makes 8 to 10 servings

Melissa Denchak of Princeton, New Jersey, starts at the end of the meal when entertaining: she makes dessert first. No matter what happens, you'll have a sweet way to end the party, and that last taste is what people remember the most as they head out the door. Her Blueberry-Pecan Crumb Cake will be a welcome addition to any brunch menu.

BLUEBERRY-PECAN CRUMB CAKE WITH BOURBON GLAZE

TOPPING

1 cup all-purpose flour

6 tablespoons unsalted butter, softened

1/2 cup finely chopped toasted pecans

1/4 cup firmly packed light brown sugar

1/4 teaspoon kosher salt

CAKE

1/2 cup (1 stick) unsalted butter, softened, plus more for greasing the pan

1 cup white sugar

1 teaspoon finely grated lemon peel

2 large eggs

1 tablespoon fresh lemon juice

1 teaspoon vanilla extract

1 1/2 cups, plus 2 tablespoons, all-purpose flour, divided

1 1/2 teaspoons baking powder

1/2 teaspoon salt

1/2 cup sour cream

2 1/2 cups blueberries, divided

GLAZE

1/4 cup powdered sugar

3/4 teaspoon milk

3/4 teaspoon bourbon

Preheat the oven to 350 degrees. Butter and flour an 10 x 8-inch baking pan.

To make the topping, combine the flour, butter, pecans, brown sugar, and salt in a medium bowl. Refrigerate.

To make the cake, combine the butter, sugar, and lemon peel in a large mixing bowl. Using an electric mixer or a hand mixer, beat on medium speed until fluffy, 1 to 2 minutes. Add the eggs one at a time, mixing until just incorporated. Add the lemon juice and vanilla, and mix until just incorporated. (The batter may look curdled.)

In a medium bowl combine 1 1/2 cups of the flour, baking powder, and salt. Add half the flour mixture to the butter mixture, mixing until just combined. Add the sour cream and the remaining flour mixture, mixing after each addition, until just combined.

In a medium bowl toss 2 cups of the

blueberries with the remaining 2 tablespoons flour. Fold the blueberries into the batter. Do not overmix.

Scrape the batter into the prepared pan. Sprinkle the crumb topping and the remaining ½ cup blueberries over the top. Bake 45 to 50 minutes, until golden and a wooden pick inserted into the center comes out with just a few crumbs. Let cool.

To make the glaze, combine the powdered sugar, milk, and bourbon in a small bowl. Drizzle the glaze over the cake.

▶ Makes 10 servings

A well-planned breakfast spread for guests takes into account all kinds of morning appetites. A savory dish, a sweet dish, and a light dish hit all the right notes. Renee Flynn of Pine Bluff, Arkansas, serves Egg and Bacon Cups (page 65) alongside this lightly sweet, puffy French toast. Add coffee, juice, and a fruit salad in a beautiful bowl and everyone—the big eater, the sweet tooth, and the light appetite—has an appealing option.

5 tablespoons unsalted butter, divided

1 (13-inch) loaf soft-crust Italian bread

2 large eggs

1 2/3 cups milk

1/4 teaspoon salt

1 teaspoon vanilla extract

3 tablespoons sugar

Maple syrup for serving

BAKED FRENCH TOAST

Grease a 9 x 13-inch baking pan with 1 tablespoon of the butter. Cut the bread into 1-inch slices and arrange in the pan. Melt the remaining 4 tablespoons butter and drizzle over the bread. In a medium bowl whisk together the eggs, milk, salt, and vanilla until well combined. Pour evenly over the bread. Press the bread down into the milk mixture. Cover and refrigerate for at least 1 hour and up to 1 day, until the bread has absorbed all of the milk mixture.

When ready to bake preheat the oven to 425 degrees. Bring the casserole to room temperature and sprinkle with sugar. Bake, uncovered, for 20 to 25 minutes, until the bread is puffed and golden on top. Serve warm with maple syrup.

▶ Makes 12 servings

Note: The bread may be cut into cubes instead. Increase the amount of milk by ½ cup and add an egg. The result is like a breakfast bread pudding.

When Martha Hopkins was new to Austin, Texas, she hosted a come-as-you-are weekend breakfast. The invitations read, "Come in your running clothes, from farmers' market, don't even have to brush your hair." She invited cookbook authors and food writers, with one hitch: "I wanted it to be people who didn't know each other," she says. She served a biscuit breakfast including Rosemary Manchego Scones and fruit. Her solution to morning libations is worth remembering: a cocktail made with grapefruit juice is refreshing enough for people to drink one, but they don't typically overindulge as they might with a sweeter drink.

ROSEMARY MANCHEGO SCONES

3 cups self-rising flour (preferably Martha White or White Lily)

1 teaspoon salt

1 tablespoon ground black pepper

2 to 3 tablespoons finely chopped fresh rosemary

1 tablespoon sugar

1/2 cup lard, chilled

1 cup grated Manchego cheese

1 cup buttermilk

Melted butter or cream for brushing the scones

Preheat the oven to 400 degrees. Line a baking sheet with parchment paper.

Combine the flour, salt, pepper, rosemary, and sugar in a food processor and pulse until just combined. Add the lard and pulse until the mixture resembles coarse meal, but with some large pieces of lard still remaining. (Alternatively, use your hands and work the lard into the flour mixture.) Scrape the dough into a large mixing bowl and add the cheese, stirring to combine.

Add the buttermilk and stir until just combined. Turn the dough out onto a floured work surface. Pat the dough into an 8-inch circle about 1 inch high. Cut the circle into 8 wedges with a sharp knife.

Place the wedges on the pan and brush with melted butter or cream. Bake for 13 to 18 minutes, until golden brown.

▶ Makes 8 scones

Notes: The scones are best eaten immediately, split open and smeared thickly with softened butter. You also can use them to make mini-sandwiches with Serrano ham, sliced Manchego cheese, and a touch of mayonnaise.

Angela Roberts, a transplant to Nashville, Tennessee, says, "The single most important thing in entertaining is making guests feel welcome, and having time to greet them and introduce them. I never leave guests unattended or allow them to go unnoticed when they arrive." This recipe is very popular with readers of her food and home blog, spinachtiger.com

BACON CHEDDAR CHIVE BISCUITS

2 cups soft wheat all-purpose flour or all-purpose flour

1 tablespoon baking powder

1 teaspoon chopped fresh chives

1/2 teaspoon salt

6 tablespoons unsalted butter, cubed, frozen

3 slices bacon, cooked and crumbled

1 1/2 cups shredded sharp Cheddar cheese

3/4 cup full-fat buttermilk

Melted butter for brushing the biscuits

Preheat the oven to 450 degrees. Mix the flour, baking powder, chives, and salt in a large bowl. Work the butter into the flour with a pastry blender or your hands until the mixture resembles coarse meal. Add the bacon and cheese.

Add the buttermilk and mix with a spoon. Use a little extra flour if needed to make a dough that will form a mound. Turn the dough out onto a floured work surface. Pat into a circle about 1 inch high. Cut out biscuits with a biscuit cutter.

Arrange the biscuits in a cast-iron skillet or on a baking sheet with their sides touching. Bake for 15 minutes. Remove from the oven and brush with melted butter. Serve warm.

▶ Makes 10 servings

When using a biscuit cutter, be sure to cut straight down through the dough and then remove the cutter in a straight-up motion. Twisting the cutter will result in flat or uneven biscuits.

When you make a dish that becomes famous in your social circle, keep making it. Hot rolls were a feature of tables across the South for decades but are rare these days. "I'm from Mississippi, and we always had rolls growing up," says Angie Sarris, who now lives in John's Creek, Georgia. "I miss my grandmother—she always had them on her table." Sarris began making rolls for her parties, and now everyone, from her friends to her son's college buddies to the guests at the local mission, expects her rolls. "Now I'm the Roll Lady," she laughs. She embraces the name and bakes them often for guests and potluck dinners. Soft and sweet when hot, these rolls firm up after a day to become the base for another Southern party favorite: mini sandwiches filled with chicken salad or tenderloin.

3 1/4 cups bread flour

1/4 cup sugar

1 teaspoon salt

2 large eggs

1 cup whole milk

8 tablespoons butter, divided

2 1/2 teaspoons instant active dry yeast (bread machine yeast)

4 tablespoons butter, melted

HOMEMADE YEAST ROLLS IN A BREAD MACHINE

Place the flour, sugar, salt, eggs, milk, 4 tablespoons of the butter, and the yeast in the bowl of a bread machine. Prepare according to the manufacturer's recommendations for the dough setting. Let the dough rest in the machine until doubled in size.

Melt the remaining 4 tablespoons butter. Pull off pieces of dough and roll into balls. For lunch-size rolls, use 2 tablespoons of dough. For dinner rolls, use 3 tablespoons. For hamburger buns, use ½ cup. Arrange rolls on baking sheets lined with parchment paper. Brush some of the melted butter on top of the rolls. Let rise for 1 hour.

Preheat the oven to 325 degrees. Bake the rolls for 12 minutes or until golden brown. Brush with melted butter again.

▶ Makes 36 lunch rolls or 24 dinner rolls or 8 to 10 buns

Note: To make ahead, shape the dough into balls, brush with melted butter, and arrange on the baking sheet. Refrigerate 8 to 12 hours. Remove from refrigerator and let rise 30 minutes, then bake as directed.

As you think about what to serve at a breakfast or brunch function, include a few items that can be made a day before the meal and then reheated. Offer just one or two hot dishes, preferably ones that serve a lot of people. An adventurous host with an indestructible kitchen space might bring out the waffle iron and let guests make their own. Otherwise skip the foods that must be cooked one or two at a time— you'll drive yourself crazy poaching eggs or making cinnamon toast at the last minute. This recipe from Janie Burke Ledyard of Nashville, Tennessee, can be made a day ahead. Pile the cooked muffins in a large baking dish, cover with aluminum foil, and warm in a 250-degree oven.

PEACHES AND CREAM MUFFINS

Preheat the oven to 350 degrees. Coat 12 muffin cups with cooking spray, or grease and flour them. If you use paper liners, be sure to grease them, as these muffins stick.

Combine the flour, baking powder, sugar, salt, and cinnamon in a large bowl. Stir in the sour cream, butter, vanilla, and almond extract, if using, and mix gently. The batter may be lumpy. Fold in the peaches.

Fill the muffin cups two-thirds full of batter. Bake for 30 to 35 minutes, until lightly browned on top.

▶ Makes 12 muffins

Cooking spray

2 cups all-purpose flour

1 tablespoon baking powder

1/2 cup sugar, or to taste

1/4 teaspoon salt

1/4 teaspoon ground cinnamon

1 cup sour cream

1 cup (2 sticks) butter, melted

1 teaspoon vanilla extract

1/4 teaspoon almond extract, optional

1 1/2 cups chopped fresh ripe peaches, or frozen peaches, thawed and drained

Let the season and your instincts lead your party impulses. Kathryn Mitchell Johnson of Nashville, Tennessee, gives guests the gift of fresh, seasonal ingredients and plans gatherings around foods that make a big batch, "something that requires a lot of people to help us eat it." Both characterize this recipe. As any herb gardener knows, basil is super abundant in summer, and the search is always on for ways to use it. Tiny biscuits are a perfect way to satisfy large groups of people—hot fresh bread is always welcome, as is a recipe that makes a big batch quickly. Piled on a large serving tray, little biscuits are as beautiful as any centerpiece and tempting as a dinner side dish or paired with herbed butter for breakfast.

3 cups all-purpose flour

2 tablespoons baking powder

1 teaspoon sea salt

1/2 teaspoon ground black pepper

1 cup grated Parmesan cheese

1/4 cup chopped fresh basil

10 tablespoons cold unsalted butter, cut into 1/2-inch pieces

1 1/4 cups buttermilk

PARMESAN BASIL MINI BISCUITS

Preheat the oven to 450 degrees. Mix the flour, baking powder, salt, and pepper in a large bowl. Add the cheese and basil, and mix well. Work the butter into the flour with a pastry blender or your hands until the butter pieces are a little smaller than peas. Work quickly so that the heat of your hands won't melt the butter.

Add the buttermilk, and gently fold the mixture a few times until it holds together. Do not overmix. It is important to work the dough as little as possible.

Turn the dough out onto a floured work surface and fold it quickly and gently 4 or 5 times. Sprinkle a little more flour under the dough so that it won't stick to the surface and lightly dust the top with flour. Roll the dough out to about ½-inch thickness. Cut with a 1-inch biscuit cutter. Arrange the biscuits on an ungreased baking sheet. Bake for 11 to 12 minutes, until the tops are light golden.

▶ Makes about 36 mini biscuits

Music helps Amy Hooper of Nashville, Tennessee, set the tone for her dinner parties, whether she's having two or twenty guests. She burns several CDs with her song selections, for different points in the evening. "It's important to have something upbeat at the start, when people are arriving," she says. "Too slow and everyone just sits down and loses energy. When it's time to eat, I'll have a selection of more mellow music. After dinner, I'll switch to dance music or some old favorites." This cornbread is the perfect partner for chili and soup eaten while listening to most any kind of soundtrack. Heating the cast-iron skillet in the oven before adding the batter ensures a dark brown, crispy crust.

1 cup stone-ground yellow cornmeal

1 cup whole wheat flour

1/4 cup sugar

1 tablespoon baking powder

1/2 teaspoon baking soda

1 teaspoon kosher salt

1 large egg

1 cup buttermilk

1/4 cup, plus 2 tablespoons, olive oil, divided

WHOLE GRAIN SKILLET CORNBREAD

Place an 8-inch cast-iron skillet in the oven and preheat the oven to 400 degrees.

In a medium bowl whisk together the cornmeal, flour, sugar, baking powder, baking soda, and salt. In a small bowl combine the egg, buttermilk, and ¼ cup of the olive oil. Mix well. Fold the egg mixture into the cornmeal mixture and mix until just combined. Don't overmix.

Remove the pan from the oven. Pour the remaining 2 tablespoons olive oil into the hot pan, swirling to coat the bottom. Pour in the batter and smooth the top with a spatula. Bake 20 to 25 minutes, until golden brown. Cut into wedges to serve.

▶ Makes 8 servings

Catherine Mayhew of Brentwood, Tennessee, whips up corn cakes to go with her Pulled Smoked Pork (page 93). Many other meals also call for a hot corn cake on the side, including an all-vegetable lunch or dinner, a leisurely weekend breakfast, or a big pot of chili or soup. Unlike cornbread, which loses its appeal as it cools, corn cakes hold their texture and flavor for a while. Pile hot, freshly cooked corn cakes into a large baking pan and cover with aluminum foil to keep warm for up to an hour, or put the pan into a warm oven until serving time.

CORN CAKES

Combine the cornmeal, flour, baking powder, sugar, and salt in a medium bowl. Add the milk, eggs, and vegetable oil, and mix well.

Heat a griddle or cast-iron skillet over medium heat. For each small corn cake, ladle about ¼ cup of the cornmeal mixture into the pan. Cook until bubbles form on the edges. Flip and cook until both sides are brown.

▶ Makes about 20 small or 10 large corn cakes

- 2 cups cornmeal
- 1 cup all-purpose flour
- 2 tablespoons baking powder
- 2 tablespoons sugar
- 1 teaspoon salt
- 1 cup milk
- 2 large eggs, beaten
- 1/4 cup vegetable oil

The best company dishes are familiar but festive, like Raspberry Cornbread. Serve it as part of a brunch buffet, says chef Connie Crabtree Burritt of Baltimore, Maryland. Serving simple food you are already comfortable making is much less stressful than trying something new or complicated. Bonus: you won't have to keep glancing at a cookbook because you know the recipe by heart. Though this cornbread recipe is straightforward, it won't fail to impress guests. If you prefer blueberries, use them instead of raspberries.

RASPBERRY CORNBREAD

Preheat the oven to 400 degrees. Place 2 tablespoons of the melted butter in an 8-inch skillet. Combine 1 ¼ cups of the cornmeal, flour, sugar, baking powder, and salt in a medium bowl. Mix the remaining 6 tablespoons melted butter, milk, and eggs together in a small bowl, then stir into the dry ingredients. Fold in the raspberries.

Sprinkle the remaining ½ tablespoon cornmeal over the butter in the skillet. Pour in the batter. Bake for 30 minutes or until golden brown on top. Let stand for about 10 minutes before turning onto a plate to serve.

▶ Makes 8 to 10 servings

8 tablespoons butter, melted, divided

1 1/4 cups, plus 1/2 tablespoon, white cornmeal, divided

3/4 cup, plus 1 tablespoon, flour

3 tablespoons sugar

1 tablespoon baking powder

1 teaspoon salt

1 cup evaporated milk

2 large eggs

1 cup fresh raspberries

For better conversations with children, whether your own or children at parties, skip the question "How's school?" The answer is inevitably the conversation-ending "Fine." Instead, ask an engaging question, such as, "What toy or book would you take to a desert island?" or "What superpower would you rather have: invisibility or the power of flight?" Kathryn Tortorici of Birmingham, Alabama, serves this bread with Heart-Shaped Cheese Bites with Ham (page 66) and Strawberry Milk (page 13) for a Valentine's Day family breakfast.

3 cups all-purpose flour

1 teaspoon salt

1 teaspoon baking soda

1 tablespoon ground cinnamon

2 cups sugar

3 large eggs, well beaten

1 1/4 cups canola oil

2 cups sliced fresh strawberries

STRAWBERRY BREAD

Preheat the oven to 350 degrees. Lightly grease 2 (8 x 4-inch) loaf pans. In a large bowl combine the flour, salt, baking soda, cinnamon, and sugar. Make a well in the center of the dry ingredients. Add the eggs and oil. Stir until the dry ingredients are just moistened. Stir in the strawberries. Spoon the batter into the loaf pans. Bake for 1 hour. Let the bread cool in the pans 10 minutes, then invert onto a wire rack to cool at least 8 hours before slicing.

▶ Makes 2 loaves

There's no need for an "occasion" to invite someone over. Most Sundays, Teresa Blackburn of Nashville, Tennessee, has a friend over for a mid-morning meal and the *New York Times* crossword. One Sunday, Blackburn invented this spoon bread, a sweeter, softer, and more cake-like dish than traditional spoon bread. The recipe made four to six servings, but she and her friend ate the whole thing. If a host can't lavish a friend with an indulgent treat on a Sunday morning, when can she?

SLIGHTLY SWEET BLUEBERRY SPOON BREAD

1 1/2 cups buttermilk

1/2 cup raw sugar

1/2 cup yellow self-rising cornmeal

3 large eggs, separated

1 teaspoon salt

2 tablespoons butter, softened

1 tablespoon vanilla extract

2 tablespoons heavy cream

2 cups blueberries

Powdered sugar for serving

Preheat the oven to 375 degrees. Place the buttermilk and sugar in a medium saucepan and heat over low heat. When the buttermilk begins to bubble around the edges of the pan, slowly whisk in the cornmeal. Stir with a whisk for about 8 minutes. The mixture should be mushy. Remove the pan from the heat. Let cool slightly.

In a small bowl beat the egg whites with the salt until stiff peaks form.

Whisk the butter and vanilla into the slightly cooled cornmeal mixture. Add the egg yolks and whisk until well blended. Whisk in the cream.

Gently fold in the beaten egg whites. Pour half of the mixture into a buttered 2-quart baking dish. Top with half of the blueberries. Spread the remainder of the cornmeal mixture over the blueberries. Top with the remaining blueberries.

Bake for 30 to 35 minutes, until top is golden brown and firm but wobbly in the center. This spoon bread will be somewhat like a soufflé in puffiness. Let stand for about 5 minutes. Serve hot with a dusting of powdered sugar.

▶ Makes 4 to 6 servings

MAIN DISHES

$\mathcal{J}$ust as an event has a personality, so does the entrée. Some entrées are traditional and deeply rooted in the culture. Others represent a welcome change. Some are quietly soul-satisfying, while others are fresh and unexpected. Elaborate projects, outdoorsy meals, refined, down-home, or uptown—all styles of main dishes are welcome when there's pleasant company to share them with.

"Barbecue" in the South means something different than in the North. In the North, "barbecue" is a verb, while in the South, it's an iconic food for outdoor gatherings. Catherine Mayhew of Brentwood, Tennessee, smokes a pork butt all day, then invites friends to the feast. "I am a fan of the round table with place cards so spouses or significant others don't sit together," she says. She also doesn't object to guests helping in the kitchen. "Someone can pull the pork while another guest makes the corn cakes on the griddle," she says. Guests will always ask, "What can I do to help?" and putting them to work in the kitchen or at the grill "is a conversation starter." Mayhew got the idea for the pork, Mustard Slaw (page 169), and Corn Cakes (page 85) combination from Lodge Manufacturing, maker of iron skillets, another iconic symbol of Southern cooking.

PULLED SMOKED PORK

1 bone-in pork butt (about 5 pounds)

1/4 cup plain yellow mustard

Your favorite sweet barbecue spice rub

Rub the pork all over with the mustard. Season liberally with the spice rub.

Prepare a lump charcoal fire in a smoker and monitor the temperature until it is 225 to 250 degrees. Add several chunks of pecan or other fruit wood, or hickory (but not mesquite) to the hot coals.

Place the butt in the smoker, close the lid, and smoke for 4 hours. (When the meat reaches an internal temperature of 140 degrees, it will not accept any more smoke so there's no need to add more wood).

Remove the butt, wrap tightly in heavy-duty aluminum foil, and return to the smoker. Continue cooking for 2 to 4 more hours, until the internal temperature reaches 200 degrees and the bone is easily removed. Let the meat rest for 30 minutes before pulling the pork into shreds with two forks.

▶ Makes 10 to 15 servings

Note: You can keep the pork warm for 3 to 4 hours by wrapping it in heavy-duty foil and then in a clean towel, and placing it in an insulated cooler.

When Cristina Stewart, of Charleston, South Carolina, and Nashville, Tennessee, gathers friends to lavish them with attention, she also remembers to take care of herself. "Always come back to you. Take care of yourself because at the end of the day, though you are making memories for everyone else, you are most important. I make lots of lists and check off things as I go during the week, and I always, always schedule time for myself to get a nice bubble bath, a mani-pedi, or a massage before a big event or party so I can be the best I can be for myself and my guests!" She found that adding a Southern accent to her native Cuban food made it familiar to Southern guests. Cuban *lechon*, or roast pork, is not usually served with a sauce. "But since Southerners love a good sauce with their barbecue," she says, she developed a delicious, tangy, herb-scented mixture that's true to both its Cuban and Southern heritage. She serves it with black beans, fried plantains, and coconut rice, though cornbread works nicely, too.

CUBAN-SOUTHERN PORK ROAST WITH CHIMICHURRI "BARBECUE" SAUCE

PORK

1 (20-pound) pork shoulder, skin on

1/4 cup chopped garlic

1/4 cup vegetable oil

2 tablespoons original sazon (such as Goya brand)

2 tablespoons original adobo seasoning, to taste (such as Goya brand)

1 teaspoon ground cumin

1 teaspoon dried oregano

MOJO MARINADE

1 cup fresh orange juice

1/2 cup fresh lime juice

5 cloves garlic, peeled and finely chopped

2 teaspoons ground cumin

2 teaspoons dried oregano

2 dried bay leaves

Salt and pepper, to taste

CHIMICHURRI SAUCE

2 cups olive oil

1/4 to 1/3 cup red wine vinegar, or to taste

1 1/2 cups chopped fresh parsley

2 tablespoons chopped garlic

Pinch of cumin

1/2 teaspoon dried oregano

Pinch of hot red pepper flakes, or to taste

1/2 teaspoon original sazon (such as Goya brand)

Juice of 2 to 3 limes

Salt and pepper, to taste

CARAMELIZED ONIONS

4 to 5 tablespoons olive oil

3 to 5 large onions, chopped

To make the pork preheat the oven to 300 degrees. Place the meat fat side down in a large baking pan. Use a large knife to make large, deep slits all over the meat. Combine the garlic and vegetable oil and pack it into the slits. Pat the roast dry. Sprinkle the meat with sazon, adobo, cumin, and oregano.

To make the marinade combine the orange juice, lime juice, garlic, cumin, oregano, bay leaves, salt, and pepper in a small bowl and mix well. Pour the sauce over the meat. Roast the meat for 6 to 7 hours, until fork tender inside, with crispy bits outside.

Use a large fork and knife to cut the meat away from the fat side. Pull or shred the meat, discarding the fatty pieces.

To make the sauce combine the oil, vinegar, parsley, garlic, cumin, oregano, pepper flakes, sazon, lime juice, salt, and pepper in a medium bowl and whisk to blend.

To make the onions heat the olive oil in a large skillet (you may have to use two skillets) over low heat. Add the onions and cook, stirring infrequently, until they are a deep caramel color, about 30 minutes.

Arrange the meat on a serving platter. Top with the onions and Chimichurri Sauce.

▶ Makes 3 1/2 cups of Chimichurri Sauce and about 30 servings of pork

Cold, dreary weather is a great time for a party—it's true! Winter gatherings are much appreciated and often the best attended. Folks are eager to get out of the house, and schedules are usually less full in cold weather. Connecticut transplant to Nashville, Tennessee, Lisa Waddle says using smoked salt and smoked paprika helps replicate the flavor of a backyard barbecue, no matter the weather. Serve the pork on soft white buns with additional hot pepper sauce, so diners can adjust the heat.

SLOW COOKER PULLED PORK

2 teaspoons smoked salt

2 tablespoons smoked paprika

4 tablespoons light brown sugar, divided

2 teaspoons chili powder

1/2 teaspoon ground black pepper

2 1/2 pounds boneless pork shoulder

2 tablespoons vegetable oil

3/4 cup cider vinegar

2 teaspoons hot pepper sauce

In a medium bowl, mix the salt, paprika, 1 tablespoon of the brown sugar, the chili powder, and black pepper. Reserve 1 tablespoon of the spice mix; rub the remaining spice mix over the pork. Put the pork in a bowl, cover, and refrigerate for at least 4 hours, or up to 12 hours.

In a large skillet, heat the oil over medium-high heat. Brown the pork on all sides. Put the pork into a 4- to 5-quart slow cooker.

Add the vinegar, the reserved tablespoon of the spice mix, and the remaining 3 tablespoons of brown sugar to the same skillet. Heat on medium-high until it boils. Scrape up any browned bits from the bottom of the pan, and then pour the mixture into the slow cooker. Cover and cook the pork on low for 6 to 10 hours, until it shreds easily with a fork.

To serve, remove the pork from the slow cooker and shred using two forks. Pour the hot pepper sauce into the liquid remaining in the cooker and return the shredded pork. Toss to coat. Serve warm, or keep warm for up to several hours.

▶ Makes 6 servings

"Clean the stove, the kitchen sink, and the bathroom sink. Put out clean hand towels and don't worry about the rest," counseled my Southern mother, Sylvia Pendleton of Nashville, Tennessee. That's great advice for hosts who issue impulsive, last-minute invitations. Another true friend of the last-minute host: pork chops. If you've got wine and jelly (and let's face it—who doesn't have a jar of jelly with no clear purpose in the back of the pantry?), juicy chops with a sweet, garlicky glaze are about 20 minutes away.—Nicki Pendleton Wood

GLAZED PORK CHOPS WITH WINE AND JELLY

Heat the butter and oil in a large skillet over medium-high heat until hot but not smoking. Season the chops generously with salt and pepper. Place the flour in a shallow dish and dredge the chops in the flour, shaking to remove any excess. Add the chops to the hot pan and cook until browned, about 5 minutes. Turn and cook for 5 minutes longer.

Reduce the heat to medium. Remove the chops from the pan. Add the garlic and cook for 1 to 2 minutes. Add the wine and stir to loosen the brown bits from the bottom of the pan. Add the jelly and cook, stirring, until it melts. Return the chops to the pan and cook, turning occasionally, until the liquid reduces to a glaze that clings to the chops.

▶ Makes 4 servings

2 tablespoons butter

2 tablespoons vegetable oil

4 pork chops, 1- to 1 1/4-inches thick

Salt and ground black pepper, to taste

2 tablespoons all-purpose flour

1 clove garlic, minced

1/2 cup white wine

1/4 cup muscadine, hot pepper, crabapple or other clear jelly

Southern barbecue and slaw meet Chinese pork and moo shu-style pancakes. Tom Grose of Nashville, Tennessee, says in a pinch you can substitute flour tortillas for the pancakes. Since it's company, go for the pancakes—guests deserve the best.

Save yourself the work of compiling a playlist for the party—just stream one from an online music service like Spotify or Pandora. Both have playlists for lots of occasions, from graduation celebrations to Chinese New Year to bachelor parties. The playlist will be a surprise for you and guests alike and is a great way to discover new music.

BBQ PORK MOO SHU STYLE

BRINE AND PORK

2 quarts water

1/2 cup firmly packed dark brown sugar

12 ounces kosher salt

1 (6- to 8-pound) Boston butt

SPICE MIXTURE

1 teaspoon cumin seeds

1 teaspoon fennel seeds

1 teaspoon coriander seeds

1/2 teaspoon Szechuan peppercorns

1 tablespoon onion powder

1 tablespoon chili powder

1 tablespoon paprika

PANCAKES

1 cup water

1 cup whole milk

4 large eggs

1/2 teaspoon salt

2 cups all-purpose flour

4 tablespoons melted butter, plus more for greasing the pan

Pinch of saffron powder or turmeric

1 tablespoon black sesame seeds

SAUCE

6 cloves garlic, peeled and minced

1 teaspoon kosher salt

1 teaspoon chili oil

1 tablespoon toasted sesame oil

1/4 cup soy sauce

1/4 cup rice vinegar

1/2 cup hoisin sauce

1/2 teaspoon sugar

SLAW

2 1/2 cups shredded Napa cabbage

2 teaspoons grated, peeled fresh ginger

8 green onions, sliced

1 cup bean sprouts

1/4 cup rice vinegar

To make the brined pork combine the water, brown sugar, and salt in a large pot, stirring to dissolve the sugar and salt. Put the pork into the brine, cover, and refrigerate 8 to 12 hours.

To make the rub grind the cumin, fennel, coriander, and Szechuan peppercorns in an electric spice grinder or with a mortar and pestle. Add the onion powder, chili powder, and paprika, and mix well.

To make the pancake batter combine the water, milk, eggs, and salt in a blender. Add the flour and blend on high. Add the butter and blend again. Refrigerate the batter for 2 hours.

Preheat the oven to 210 degrees. Remove the pork from the brine and pat dry. Rub with the spice mixture. Place the pork in a roasting pan and bake (or smoke) for 10 hours, or until the meat pulls into shreds when raked with a fork. Let the pork rest 1 hour before shredding it with two forks. Cover until ready to serve.

Check the pancake batter—it should be thick enough to just coat the back of a spoon; if too thick, add water. Divide the batter between two bowls; add saffron or turmeric to one bowl and mix until the batter is light yellow.

Heat a nonstick 8-inch skillet over medium heat. Coat the pan with a little butter. Pour in just enough yellow batter to thinly coat the bottom after swirling. Cook about 1 minute, then flip the pancake and cook 30 seconds longer. Remove the pancake to a plate and cover to keep warm. Repeat with the remaining yellow batter.

Use the non-saffron batter to make sesame pancakes in the same manner. Sprinkle a few sesame seeds on the batter right after swirling it in the pan.

To make the sauce combine the garlic, salt, chili oil, sesame oil, soy sauce, vinegar, hoisin, and sugar in a small bowl and mix well.

To make the slaw toss the cabbage with the ginger, onions, sprouts, and rice vinegar in a large bowl.

Serve the pork with pancakes, sauce, and cabbage.

▶ Makes 12 servings

"This recipe reminds me of growing up on a farm in New Jersey, where we employed a family called Ellis to help out," says Warren Bobrow of Morristown, New Jersey. "They were from Georgia, and through their guidance I learned a thing or two about Southern recipes and cooking techniques. My cast-iron pan dates back to this time, and the thick crust of memories that coats it speaks clearly of the past." When cast iron is on the stove, something good is coming to the table. Bobrow fancies up this homey main dish for company by using rib chops and panko bread crumbs.

FRIED PORK CHOPS

Preheat the oven to 300 degrees. Heat a cast-iron pan over medium-high heat until it's almost smoking.

In a shallow bowl mix the flour, salt, pepper, and cayenne. Place the egg in another shallow dish. Spread the panko on waxed paper or a plate. Dredge each pork chop in the flour, then dip it in the egg, then coat with panko.

Add the bacon drippings to the hot pan. Sear the pork chops for 3 to 4 minutes on each side. Put the pan in the oven for 10 minutes, or until the chops are cooked through.

▶ Makes 3 servings

1 cup all-purpose flour

Salt and ground black pepper, to taste

1 teaspoon cayenne pepper

1 large egg, beaten

2 cups panko or other bread crumbs

6 (1/2-inch thick) rib pork chops

1/4 cup bacon drippings

A "company" meal in Texas often includes flavors, colors, and traditions of Mexican cooking. Pam Zdenek of Houston says there's more to a Tex-Mex meal than the food. This Texan takes a cue from her Mexican neighbors and includes some bright serving platters to serve this Tex-Mex dish. "I want my table to represent a culture, not just a meal. It is always about how much the company will get into the food and the culture," she says. Fajitas, also known as "tacos al carbon," can be served on a platter or, more authentically, sizzling in an iron skillet.

AUTHENTIC TEXAS FAJITAS

MARINADE AND BEEF

1/2 cup olive oil

6 to 7 tablespoons minced garlic, divided

1/2 cup minced red, yellow, or white onion

1 tablespoon fajita seasoning mix

3 tablespoons vegetable oil

4 to 5 tablespoons good tequila, optional

6 tablespoons fresh lime juice

1 1/2 teaspoons kosher salt

1 1/2 teaspoons ground cumin

1 1/2 teaspoons black pepper

2 tablespoons mesquite seasoning (such as Goode Company Mesquite Shake)

1/2 cup finely chopped fresh cilantro

3/4 cup minced green onions

1 tablespoon minced serrano or jalapeño pepper, optional

2 pounds skirt steak, trimmed and tenderized

VEGETABLES

4 tablespoons vegetable oil

1 cup thinly sliced quarter rings white onion

3/4 cup thinly sliced quarter rings green pepper

6 to 8 green onions, sliced once lengthwise

FOR SERVING

Flour tortillas, sour cream, fresh cilantro, chopped green onions, pico de gallo, pickled jalapeño pepper, sliced or cubed avocados, shredded sharp Cheddar or Monterey Jack cheese, and lime wedges

To make the marinade heat the olive oil in a saucepan over low heat. Add 4 or 5 tablespoons of the garlic and the onion. Cook and stir for 5 minutes. Add the seasoning mix and cook for 2 to 3 minutes. Let cool slightly.

In a medium bowl combine the vegetable oil, tequila, lime juice, salt, cumin, pepper, and mesquite seasoning, and whisk to blend. Add the cilantro, green onions, the remaining 2 tablespoons garlic, and the serrano, and mix well. Add the onion mixture and mix well.

Put the meat in a dish just large enough to

hold it. (You may have to cut the meat to fit.) Pour the marinade over the meat, making sure it is completely covered. Marinate for at least 2 hours. (Most Texas cooks marinate 24 hours for tenderized, flavorful meat.)

To cook in a cast-iron skillet heat the skillet over medium-high heat. When sizzling hot, sear the steak until medium-rare or medium, 8 to 10 minutes. Fajita meat should be slightly crusty on the outside and tender on the inside. Slice across the grain into thin strips.

To cook on the grill remove the meat from the marinade and pat dry. Grill over high heat for 2 to 3 minutes per side for medium rare. For the best flavor, use mesquite wood chips.

To make the vegetables heat the oil in a saucepan over medium heat. Stir in the onions, peppers, and green onions, and cook and stir until slightly tender.

Pile the sliced meat on a platter or in the hot skillet. Top with the vegetables. Serve with warm flour tortillas and bowls of sour cream, cilantro, onions, pico de gallo, jalapeños, avocado, cheese, and lime wedges.

▶ Makes 6 to 8 servings

Manchester, Tennessee, native Vivek Surti learned his warm, confident hosting style from his parents. "My mom never really got overwhelmed with anything, even when Dad would invite people over for dinner with just a couple of days' notice. She's so good in the kitchen—she can crank out food for 10 people with about 2 hours' notice. When people come to the house, she's already got the food ready, so she can sit back and relax," he says. He brings that spirit to the occasional supper clubs he hosts to gather friends old and new together for a unique meal. "I want to tell a story through food, especially my story, which was growing up as an Indian kid in the South," he says. "I use it as a way to challenge myself to see what kind of dishes I can create." In this recipe, pork, the South's favorite meat, is mixed with Indian spices, then drizzled with a mint and cilantro sauce flavored with curry leaves.

PORK KABOBS WITH GREEN CHUTNEY

GREEN CHUTNEY

1/2 cup packed fresh cilantro leaves

1/2 cup packed fresh mint leaves

4 sprigs curry leaves (usually available at south Asian markets)

1/2 teaspoon minced fresh garlic

2 teaspoons minced, peeled fresh ginger

2 small fresh hot chilies, such as Thai bird chilies

Juice of 1/2 lime

1/4 cup canola oil

Kosher salt, to taste

KABOBS

1 tablespoon coriander seed

2 teaspoons cumin seed

2 teaspoons fennel seed

2 teaspoons ground black pepper

2 star anise pods

4 cloves garlic

1/2 red onion

1 (2-inch) piece fresh ginger, peeled and roughly chopped

2 tablespoons cilantro leaves

1 to 2 tablespoons water

2 pounds ground pork shoulder

Kosher salt

Canola oil

To make the chutney combine the cilantro, mint, curry leaves, minced garlic, minced ginger, chilies, lime juice, oil, and salt in a blender. Blend until pureed, 2 to 3 minutes.

To make the kabobs place the coriander seed, cumin seed, fennel seed, black pepper, and star anise pods in a small skillet and cook over medium heat until the spices are slightly browned and fragrant, 4 to 5 minutes. Grind the spices to a fine powder in an electric spice grinder or with a mortar and pestle.

In a food processor combine the garlic,

onion, ginger, cilantro, and water. Pulse until a smooth paste forms. Add the ground spices and pulse to combine.

Combine the paste with the pork. Form the mixture into meatballs or around wooden skewers that have been soaked in water to make kabobs. Season with salt and drizzle with canola oil.

Preheat the oven to 400 degrees. Heat a grill pan or a large cast-iron pan over medium-high heat until it is almost smoking. Sear the kabobs a few at a time, taking care not to crowd the pan. Remove the kabobs to a large baking sheet, preferably fitted with a wire rack. Place in the oven and bake for about 5 minutes, until the internal temperature is 150 degrees. Plate two kabobs for each serving. Drizzle with Green Chutney.

▶ **Makes 1 cup chutney and 6 servings of kabobs**

Brian Geiger of Charlottesville, Virginia, learned a basic math lesson once when cooking for a crowd, and it has served him well ever since. "Remember that increasing the amount of food is likely going to increase the cooking time significantly," he says. "When I made a barbecued brisket for a party once, I figured that, since we were cooking two briskets instead of one larger one, it would be easier than cooking a larger brisket. But it still added hours to the cooking time. There was an emergency run to the store to get additional ready-to-eat food while we finished cooking the briskets one at a time. Unless you have two ovens, don't expect a doubled recipe to take the same amount of time as the original."

PAN-FRIED CHICKEN

Place the chicken in a large bowl and cover with the buttermilk. Soak for about 1 hour. Combine the flour, salt, garlic powder, chili powder, and oregano in a shallow bowl.

Set up a wire rack over a baking sheet. Remove a piece of chicken from the buttermilk and let most of the buttermilk drip back into the bowl. Dredge the chicken piece in the flour mixture, tapping off any excess. Place the chicken piece on the rack. Repeat with the remaining chicken pieces.

Heat the shortening in a heavy frying pan or Dutch oven over medium-high heat until it reaches 365 degrees. Carefully place the chicken in the oil. Fry until golden brown, about 10 minutes. Turn and cook 10 minutes longer, or until cooked through. Drain on a clean rack set over newspaper or paper towels.

▶ Makes 4 to 5 servings

1 (4- to 6-pound) chicken, cut into pieces, or the equivalent

2 cups buttermilk, more as needed

1 cup all-purpose flour

1 tablespoon kosher salt

2 teaspoons garlic powder

2 teaspoons chipotle chili powder

1 teaspoon dried oregano

About 1 1/2 cups shortening for frying

Kat Riehle says it helps the flow of entertaining to assign roles for herself and her husband when they have guests over to their small New York City apartment. So when Riehle cooks, her husband takes the coats and fills drink orders, and vice versa. "I think it makes everyone feel welcome to be greeted with a drink, rather than walking in on two crazy people bumping into each other in a tiny kitchen, frantically attempting to get food on a table," she says.

BACON AND KALE POT PIES

DOUGH

2 cups all-purpose flour

1/2 teaspoon salt

13 tablespoons (1 stick plus 5 tablespoons) cold unsalted butter, diced

6 tablespoons sour cream

1 tablespoon white wine vinegar

1/4 cup ice water

1 large egg, beaten with 1 tablespoon water

FILLING

Olive oil

1/2 to 3/4 cup diced thick-cut bacon

1 onion, finely chopped

1 carrot, finely chopped

1 celery stalk, finely chopped

Pinch of hot red pepper flakes

Salt to taste

2 cloves garlic, minced

4 cups thinly sliced kale leaves

Ground black pepper to taste

SAUCE

3 1/2 tablespoons butter

3 1/2 tablespoons all-purpose flour

3 1/2 cups sodium-free or low-sodium chicken or vegetable broth

Salt and pepper to taste

2 cups cooked or canned white beans

To make the dough combine the flour and salt in a large bowl. Add the butter and work it into the flour with a pastry blender or your hands until the mixture resembles small pebbles. Break up the pebbles, and keep rubbing in the butter bits until they are tiny.

In a small bowl mix the sour cream, vinegar, and water. Add to the flour mixture. Knead the dough until it forms a ball. Wrap in plastic wrap, flatten a bit, and refrigerate for at least 40 minutes.

To make the filling heat a splash of olive oil in a large saucepan over medium heat. Add the bacon and cook until crisp. Drain on paper towels and crumble. Place the bacon in a medium bowl. Add more olive oil to the pan. Add the onions, carrot, celery, pepper flakes, and a pinch of salt, and cook until the vegetables are tender, about 8 minutes. Add the garlic and cook 1 minute longer. Add the kale and cook until it is wilted. Season with more salt and pepper. Add the vegetables to the bacon.

To make the sauce, melt the butter in a medium saucepan over medium-high heat. Add the flour and cook, stirring constantly, until the flour is browned. Whisk in the broth, a little at a time, mixing completely between additions. Scrape up any bits from the bottom of the pan and mix in. Bring the mixture to a boil. Reduce the heat to low and simmer the sauce until it thickens, about 10 minutes. Season with salt and pepper. Add the beans, vegetables, and bacon, and mix well.

Preheat the oven to 375 degrees. Set 4 ovenproof bowls on a baking sheet. Divide the filling among the bowls. Divide the dough into four pieces, and roll into rounds that will cover the bowls with a little overhang. Brush the rims of the bowls with some of the egg-water mixture. Drape a pastry round over the top of each bowl, pressing it gently so it will adhere. Brush the dough rounds with the egg-water mixture. Use a small, sharp knife to cut a few vents in the dough.

Bake for 30 to 35 minutes, until the tops are lightly browned and the filling is bubbling.

▶ Makes 4 servings

One of Beverly Mai's most memorable dinner parties at her Kirkwood, Missouri, home was during the brief recession in the 1960s. "I made big pots of vegetable, beef, and bean soup. We held the party in our basement, where we have a small kitchen, and served the soup from the pots on the stove. Everyone lined up and ladled out their portion. We lit some antique oil lamps and put out red-checked paper tablecloths. Everyone had a good time, which just shows you don't have to spend a lot to entertain," she says.

SOUTHERN SMOTHERED CHICKEN

Preheat the oven to 400 degrees. In a large bowl mix together ¼ cup of the flour, the salt, curry powder, paprika, and pepper. Dredge the chicken in the flour mixture, shaking to remove excess flour. Heat 4 tablespoons of the butter in an ovenproof skillet. Add the chicken to the pan and brown on both sides. Put the pan in the oven and bake for 30 minutes. Remove the pan from the oven and reduce the heat to 325 degrees.

Arrange the onions, tomatoes, and mushrooms over the chicken in the pan.

Heat the remaining 3 tablespoons butter in a small saucepan. Stir in the remaining 3 tablespoons flour. Add the reserved mushroom liquid and bouillon. Cook, stirring, until slightly thickened. Pour the sauce over the chicken and vegetables. Bake 25 minutes longer. Serve over hot cooked rice.

▶ Makes 4 servings

1/4 cup, plus 3 tablespoons, all-purpose flour, divided

1 teaspoon salt

1/2 teaspoon curry powder

1/2 teaspoon paprika

1/4 teaspoon ground black pepper

4 boneless, skinless chicken breast halves

7 tablespoons butter, divided

1/4 cup chopped green onion

2 medium tomatoes, sliced

1 (4-ounce) jar button mushrooms, drained (reserve liquid)

1 cup boiling chicken bouillon

Hot cooked rice

A thoughtful host weighs guests' preferences when putting together a menu. Sheri Castle's solution is to cook something that everyone can enjoy, including picky eaters and guests with dietary restrictions. That's the beauty of BLT Chicken. The Birmingham, Alabama, host "customizes" each piece by leaving off the tomato, adding extra bacon, or leaving the chicken plain for purists.

BLT CHICKEN

Place the chicken in a large bowl or zip-top plastic bag. Pour in enough of the buttermilk to submerge and coat the chicken, cover or close, and refrigerate for at least 1 hour or up to overnight.

Preheat the oven to 400 degrees. Set a wire rack inside a large rimmed baking sheet lined with aluminum foil. Mist the rack with cooking spray.

Pour the bread crumbs into a shallow plate and season with the salt and pepper. Working with one piece at a time, remove the chicken from the buttermilk, letting excess buttermilk drip off, and coat with the crumbs. Place in a single layer on the rack and drizzle with the butter.

Bake for 20 to 25 minutes, until the chicken is cooked through and the crumbs are golden. The chicken is done when an instant-read thermometer inserted into the thickest part of a breast registers 165 degrees and the juices show no traces of pink.

Place a tomato slice on each piece of chicken. Top the tomato with some of the bacon, followed by a slice of cheese. Return the pan to the oven for about 2 minutes, until the cheese melts.

Toss the lettuce with the dressing and arrange on a serving platter. Top with the warm chicken.

▶ Makes 6 servings

6 (6-ounce) boneless, skinless chicken breast halves

2 cups buttermilk

Cooking spray

1 cup dry plain or Italian-flavored bread crumbs

2 teaspoons kosher salt

1/2 teaspoon ground black pepper

1 to 2 tablespoons melted butter or extra-virgin olive oil

6 large slices fresh tomato

6 slices bacon, cooked and diced

6 slices Cheddar cheese

6 to 8 cups shredded romaine lettuce or other crunchy lettuce

1 cup bottled creamy Italian or ranch dressing, or to taste

"Nothing is ever ready to go at the start time of your gathering. It just never is," says event planner Natalie Dietz Raines of Nashville, Tennessee. Timing is one of the toughest issues facing a host. "That means you will probably be tied up in the kitchen for a bit as guests start to arrive," she says. "The best first line of defense for this is to set out some snacks on the coffee table or other available flat surface. If you have a partner, roommate, or other willing party, have them greet guests and pour beverages. If you're going it solo, throw some options out with ice, glassware, and beverage napkins or coasters and encourage guests to help themselves. These two things will buy you at least 15 minutes to finish up in the kitchen."

CHIPOTLE CHICKEN "COBBLER"

FILLING

2 (15-ounce) cans crushed tomatoes

2 to 4 chipotle chilies in adobo

2 tablespoons vegetable oil

2 pounds boneless, skinless chicken thighs, cubed

2 teaspoons original-flavor adobo seasoning (such as Goya brand)

1 medium onion, diced

3 medium cloves garlic, finely chopped

2 (4-ounce) cans diced roasted green chilies

2 tablespoons tequila, optional

CHEESE CORNMEAL BISCUIT DOUGH

1 cup all-purpose flour

1 cup cornmeal (not cornbread mix)

1 tablespoon baking powder

1 teaspoon salt

1/4 cup (1/2 stick) cold butter, cut into small pieces

1 cup shredded Monterey Jack cheese, divided

1 cup shredded sharp Cheddar cheese, divided

3/4 cup buttermilk, plus 1 tablespoon if needed

Grease a 2- to 2 ½-quart baking dish. To make the filling, puree the tomatoes with the chipotle chilies in a blender or food processor.

Heat the oil in a Dutch oven over medium-high heat. Add the chicken and sprinkle with the adobo seasoning. Cook, stirring, until the chicken is well browned on all sides, about 5 minutes. Remove from the pan. Add the onion to the pan and cook until it begins to brown, 2 to 3 minutes. Add the garlic and green chilies and cook for 2 to 3 minutes longer. Return the chicken with any accumulated juices to the pan. Add the tequila to the pan and stir to scrape up any browned bits from the bottom of the pan.

Stir the tomato chipotle puree into the chicken. Bring to a low boil over medium heat, then reduce heat to low and simmer until the sauce thickens, about 10 minutes. Taste and adjust the seasoning as needed. Pour the chicken mixture into the baking dish.

Preheat the oven to 400 degrees. To make the biscuits, combine the flour, cornmeal, baking powder, and salt in the bowl of a food processor. Pulse twice. Add the butter and pulse 3 or 4 times. Add half the cheeses (about ½ cup of each) and pulse 3 or 4 more times. Blend in the buttermilk until the mixture forms a cohesive and slightly sticky dough. Be careful not to overwork the dough.

Use a spoon or your hands to form 10 to 12 biscuits. Lay them on top of the chicken. Sprinkle with the remaining cheese. Bake for 25 to 30 minutes, until the biscuits and cheeses are browned.

▶ **Makes 6 to 8 servings**

Anna Watson Carl is a recipe developer, tester, cookbook author, and serial hostess of dinner parties around a yellow dinner table she brought to New York City from her childhood home in Brentwood, Tennessee. "With dinner parties, I'm a list-keeper," she says. "First, there's the menu, then the shopping list. Then there's the to-do list (errands, cleaning, cooking, table, music, etc.), and finally the day of, the cooking prep list. I like to check things off and know where I stand in the process."

INDIVIDUAL CHICKEN POT PIES WITH WHOLE WHEAT CRUST AND KALE

CRUST

1 cup whole wheat flour

1/2 cup all-purpose flour

1/2 teaspoon salt

1/2 cup (1 stick) cold unsalted butter, cut into small pieces

8 tablespoons ice water

1 large egg, beaten with 1 teaspoon water

Sea salt

FILLING

1/4 cup (1/2 stick) unsalted butter

1/2 cup diced carrot

1/2 cup diced celery

1/2 cup diced onion

2 teaspoons fresh thyme leaves

Salt and ground black pepper, to taste

1/4 cup all-purpose flour

1/4 cup white wine

3 cups chicken broth

2 cups shredded rotisserie chicken

1/2 pound kale, torn into 1-inch pieces (about 2 cups)

To make the crust combine the whole wheat flour, all-purpose flour, and salt in the bowl of a food processor. Add the butter and pulse until the butter pieces are the size of peas. With the motor running, add the water slowly, just until the dough begins to come together. Dump the dough onto a floured surface, knead a few times, and shape into a round disc. Wrap tightly in plastic wrap and place in the refrigerator at least 1 hour.

Preheat the oven to 375 degrees. To make the filling heat the butter in a large pot or Dutch oven over medium heat. Add the carrot, celery, onion, and thyme, and cook until the vegetables are softened and the onion is translucent, 6 to 8 minutes. Season with salt and pepper. Add the flour and continue to cook over medium heat, stirring constantly, until the mixture is lightly browned, with a nutty smell, 2 to 3 minutes. Add the wine and simmer for 2 minutes to absorb. Add the chicken broth and bring the mixture to a boil. Reduce the heat to low and simmer until thickened, 8 to 10 minutes. Season with additional salt and pepper to taste. Stir in the chicken and kale and cook until the kale wilts, 2 to 3 minutes. Remove the pan from the heat and let the mixture cool slightly.

Remove the dough from the refrigerator. Let stand for about 10 minutes before rolling it out. Roll the dough on a floured surface to about ¼-inch thickness. Cut the dough into four 7-inch circles. (You can use a 6-inch ramekin as a guide, cutting the dough ½ inch beyond the rim of the ramekin all around.)

Fill four 6-inch ramekins with the chicken mixture. Place a dough circle on top of each ramekin and gently press the dough into the sides of the ramekin. Cut several small slits in the top of each crust.

Set the pot pies on a baking sheet and brush the tops with the egg mixture. Sprinkle the tops with sea salt. Bake for 30 minutes, or until the crust is golden brown and the filling is bubbly. Let cool for at least 15 minutes before serving.

▶ **Makes 4 servings**

The size and shape of the event space can determine the type of party and the menu, says Pam Erbes of Denver, Colorado. "That determines what I will serve, whether it needs to be finger food or maybe a little messier," she says. A summertime backyard event would fit more people and allow everyone to sit down and eat, while a winter cocktail party might find most guests standing to eat finger food. Potato Chip Chicken is a plate-and-fork entrée for a seated meal, whether outdoors or indoors. Erbes says it is perfect for tailgating and can be served warm, cold, or at room temperature.

2 cups crushed potato chips

1/4 teaspoon garlic salt

Dash of ground black pepper

1 (2 1/2-pound) chicken, cut into pieces

1/3 cup melted butter

POTATO CHIP CHICKEN

Preheat the oven to 375 degrees. Combine the potato chips, garlic salt, and pepper on a plate or waxed paper. Dip the chicken pieces in the butter and roll in the potato chip mixture. Arrange the meat skin-side up in a shallow pan. Bake the chicken for 1 hour, or until tender.

▶ Makes 4 servings

Better to keep it simple and have people over than not entertain because you feel you can't make it special enough. Heather Kokubun of Ponca City, Oklahoma, counsels, "Just having people over should be cherished." This reliable and easy entrée is based on Chicken-Fried Steak. Add Farm-Style Green Beans (page 184), Twice-Baked Sweet Potatoes (page 192), sweet tea, and pecan pie and call your dinner party "Southern Cafeteria Nite."

BAKED "CHICKEN-FRIED" CHICKEN

Preheat the oven to 400 degrees. Coat a rimmed baking sheet with cooking spray. Spread the flour in a shallow bowl. Beat the egg in another shallow bowl. In a large bowl mix the cracker crumbs, bread crumbs, salt, and pepper.

Dip each chicken piece in the flour, then in the egg, then in the bread crumb mixture, and place on the baking sheet. Bake for 8 minutes, then use tongs to flip each piece over. Bake for another 8 minutes, or until the chicken is cooked through.

▶ Makes 2 to 4 servings

Cooking spray

1/2 cup all-purpose flour

1 large egg

1/4 cup crushed round butter crackers

1/4 cup bread crumbs

1/8 teaspoon salt

1/8 teaspoon ground black pepper

4 boneless, skinless chicken breast halves, pounded thin

Jessica Pendergrass of Louisville, Kentucky, says, "I've found you can be the best host when you're at ease in your own space. Plan a menu with dishes that you are comfortable making. If they can be prepared in advance, or put in the oven to bake as your guests arrive, even better. This will give you the flexibility to greet guests, fix them a drink, and get them settled in. Keep appetizers and drinks in an open space where people can talk and mingle. People tend to gravitate toward the kitchen in any house (no matter how small) so be prepared for that. If you need to prepare dishes fresh while people arrive, you can make it work. As a cook, I've found my friends and family really enjoy watching me do my thing. I can stand at the stove making batches of fried chicken for an hour while having some of the best conversations of my life."

FRIED CHICKEN NUGGETS WITH HONEY-MUSTARD DIPPING SAUCE

CHICKEN

1 1/2 cups shortening

1 1/2 cups buttermilk

2 pounds chicken breast tenderloin, cut into bite-size pieces

2 cups self-rising flour (such as White Lily)

1 teaspoon cayenne pepper

1 teaspoon paprika

Sea salt and ground black pepper, to taste

HONEY-MUSTARD DIPPING SAUCE

1/4 cup Dijon-style mustard

2 tablespoons Worcestershire sauce

1 tablespoon fresh lemon juice

1/3 cup honey

To make the chicken, in a large nonstick or cast-iron skillet heat the shortening over medium heat until bubbles form at the bottom, but it is not smoking.

Pour the buttermilk into a large bowl. Place half of the chicken pieces in the buttermilk. In a paper bag or large zip-top plastic bag, shake together the flour, cayenne, paprika,

salt, and pepper. Remove the chicken from the buttermilk and place in the bag, taking care that the pieces don't stick together. Close the bag and shake to coat the chicken with the flour mixture.

Remove the chicken from the bag and carefully place in the skillet. Work in batches so the pan is not overcrowded. The chicken should sizzle and bubble and start to brown quickly when placed in the pan. Fry the chicken until golden brown, 4 to 5 minutes. Turn and fry until cooked through, another 3 to 4 minutes. Do not move it around or flip it more than once. Drain the chicken on paper towels.

Soak, coat, and cook the remaining chicken.

To make the sauce, in a small bowl whisk together the mustard, Worcestershire sauce, lemon juice, and honey. Serve with the warm chicken.

▶ Makes 4 to 6 servings

Note: You can keep leftovers in the refrigerator and reheat in a 350-degree oven. The chicken won't be as crispy, but it'll still be super tasty.

At their Sweet Potatoes Café in Winston-Salem, North Carolina, owners Stephanie Tyson and Vivián Joyner's greatest joy is for guests to ask one another, "What did you order?" Food is community, and the couple welcomes people of all sorts and conditions at the Sweet Potatoes table. "When we break bread together, the barriers are lowered for at least a moment, and all things seem possible," says Tyson. "Good friends, good conversation, and great food—an extension of our living room." A one-pot meal like Chicken Country Captain is a simple solution for a casual evening meal. There's no need to fuss over side dishes, unless you feel up to making a fruit salad. Serve the chicken right from the dish to close friends, or transfer it to a big bowl to serve at the table for a more "formal" dinner.

1/4 cup all-purpose flour

1/2 teaspoon salt

1/2 teaspoon ground black pepper

2 to 4 teaspoons smoked paprika

3 slices bacon

4 chicken leg quarters, cut into legs and thighs

1/4 cup vegetable oil

2 green bell peppers, diced

1 medium onion, diced

2 celery stalks, diced

1 teaspoon chopped garlic

1 tablespoon curry powder

1 (15-ounce) can diced tomatoes

1 cup chicken broth

1/2 cup dried cranberries

1 cup chopped toasted pecans

1/4 cup chopped fresh cilantro, optional

4 cups cooked white rice

CHICKEN COUNTRY CAPTAIN

Combine the flour, salt, pepper, and paprika in a bowl. Cook the bacon in a large skillet over medium heat, turning occasionally, until crisp. Drain on paper towels and crumble. Discard the bacon drippings or save for another recipe.

Preheat the oven to 425 degrees. Dredge the chicken pieces in the flour mixture, tapping to remove excess flour. Heat the oil in the skillet over medium heat. Add the chicken and brown for about 8 minutes on each side. Remove to a large baking dish.

Add the peppers, onion, and celery to the pan and cook until the onion is translucent, about 5 minutes. Add the garlic and curry powder and cook until the curry powder is fragrant, 2 to 3 minutes. Add the tomatoes and broth and bring to a simmer. Pour the sauce over the chicken. Sprinkle cranberries over the chicken. Cover with aluminum foil and bake for 20 to 30 minutes, until the chicken is cooked through and the sauce has thickened. Uncover and top with the bacon, pecans, and cilantro. Serve over the cooked white rice.

▶ Makes 4 servings

Growing up in Pine Bluff, Arkansas, Renee Flynn learned a lot about entertaining. There were parties for every occasion and for hardly any reason at all. "We threw types of parties that I don't think they had elsewhere," she says. Chicken Spaghetti has reliably fed many a Southern guest at countless parties over the years. Flynn's family has served it at christening luncheons for generations.

1 (5- to 6-pound) chicken

3/4 cup diced green bell pepper

3 cloves garlic, crushed

3/4 cup diced onion

3/4 cup diced celery

1 (10-ounce) can cream of mushroom soup

1 (10-ounce) can tomato soup

3/4 teaspoon dried oregano

1 1/2 tablespoons soy sauce

1 tablespoon Worcestershire sauce

1 1/2 cups chicken broth

1 pound vermicelli

1 (6-ounce) can sliced mushrooms

3/4 cup grated Parmesan cheese

1 (8-ounce) can sliced water chestnuts

1/2 cup sliced black olives

2 cups shredded sharp Cheddar cheese

Salt and ground black pepper, to taste

CHICKEN SPAGHETTI

Place the chicken in a large pot and cover with water. Bring to a boil over medium-high heat. Cover, reduce the heat to low, and simmer for 1 hour. Turn off the heat and let the chicken cool in the broth. Remove the meat from the bones and chop the meat.

Combine the bell pepper, garlic, onion, celery, mushroom soup, tomato soup, oregano, soy sauce, Worcestershire sauce, and chicken broth in a saucepan. Bring to a boil over medium-high heat. Reduce the heat to low and simmer for about 20 minutes.

Preheat the oven to 300 degrees. Bring a large pot of salted water to a boil over high heat. Add the vermicelli and cook over medium-high heat 1 minute less than the package directions. Drain well.

In a rectangular 3-quart baking dish, layer half the vermicelli, half the chicken, half the mushrooms, half the Parmesan, half the water chestnuts, half the olives, half the sauce, and half the Cheddar cheese. Then layer on the remaining vermicelli, chicken, mushrooms, water chestnuts, olives, and sauce. Top with the remaining Parmesan cheese.

Cover with aluminum foil and bake for 10 minutes. Uncover and sprinkle with the remaining 1 cup Cheddar cheese. Cook, uncovered, for 10 minutes longer, or until bubbly and lightly browned on top.

▶ Makes 8 to 10 servings

Charlotte, North Carolina, pastor Ann Gibert says she's come to accept that part of caring for people is feeding them, and that cooking is part of her ministry. She even has a bumper sticker that reads, "Love People/Cook Them Tasty Food." Her "company" version of a chicken casserole looks like a lot of work but couldn't be easier. Gibert uses it as a go-to recipe for simple entertaining at home or for taking to someone. The little bundles of creamy chicken in crescent roll dough look appealing and don't contain any ingredients that challenge picky eaters.

CHICKEN ROBIN

2 cups chopped cooked chicken

2 to 3 tablespoons reduced-fat cream cheese, softened

Minced fresh sage, to taste

1 (8-ounce) can reduced-fat crescent rolls

Melted butter or cooking spray

Dry bread crumbs or stuffing mix

Cranberry sauce for serving

Preheat the oven to 350 degrees. Grease an 8-inch baking pan. Combine the chicken, cream cheese, and sage in a medium bowl.

Unroll the crescent rolls and separate the triangles. Put a triangle of dough in your palm. Scoop up about one-eighth of the chicken mixture and place it in the middle of the dough. Fold, pull, flatten, and pinch the dough to enclose the filling.

Arrange the "robins" very close together in the pan, squeezing them in. Press them down a little to flatten. Drizzle with melted butter or spray lightly with cooking spray. Sprinkle with bread crumbs.

Bake for 30 minutes, or until nicely browned. Serve with cranberry sauce.

▶ Makes 4 servings

Note: For an Indian-inspired version, use mayonnaise instead of cream cheese. Add a little curry powder and chopped onion to the mayonnaise. Shape and bake as directed. Serve with chutney.

Since 2000, Ann Wells Parrish's book club in Nashville, Tennessee, has gathered for friendship, book talk, and a safe place to experiment with party food. "The host provides beverages and everyone else brings a dish to share—usually an hors d'oeuvre or finger food," she says. "One great thing about being in a group you know really well, and where there will be a plethora of foods, is that you can experiment. At least one person will arrive at a meeting saying, 'I've never made this before and have no idea if it will be any good.' It is usually wonderful, of course, but we allow for mistakes, too. This recipe was definitely not a mistake. The biscuits were assembled at my house, then bundled up and taken to the meeting." The filling keeps the biscuits warm, which is the trickiest thing about transporting or holding biscuits.

BUFFALO BLUE CHEESE BUTTERMILK BISCUITS WITH CREAMY BUFFALO CHICKEN FILLING

BUFFALO BLUE CHEESE BUTTERMILK BISCUITS

3 cups self-rising flour (such as White Lily)

1 teaspoon celery seed

3 tablespoons sugar

1/4 cup (1/2 stick) butter, frozen

1 cup blue cheese crumbles

3/4 cup buttermilk

1/4 cup hot pepper sauce

1/4 cup nonfat Greek yogurt

1/4 cup all-purpose flour

BUFFALO CHICKEN FILLING

4 ounces cream cheese, softened

1/2 cup sour cream

2 tablespoons buttermilk

1/4 cup hot pepper sauce

1/4 cup blue cheese crumbles

1/4 teaspoon celery seed

1 green onion, sliced

2 cups shredded roast chicken

Preheat the oven to 425 degrees. Cover a baking sheet with parchment paper.

To make the biscuits combine the flour, celery seeds, and sugar in a medium bowl. Grate the frozen butter into the bowl. Toss to coat the butter with flour. Add the cheese and toss to coat.

Whisk the buttermilk, hot pepper sauce, and yogurt in a small bowl until combined.

Make a well in the center of the flour

mixture and add the buttermilk mixture. Mix quickly with a large spoon or your hands, turning the bowl and gently scooping the dry ingredients into the wet. Add more buttermilk, if needed, to make the dough moist but not too wet. It will be somewhat sticky.

Sprinkle some of the all-purpose flour onto a work surface. Turn the dough out of the bowl onto the flour. Sprinkle more flour on the dough and onto your hands. Knead the dough a few times. Pat the dough to make a 1/2-inch thick disc. Fold the dough in half. A pastry scraper can be helpful here to lift up the dough.

Transfer the dough to the baking sheet. Press the dough into a ½-inch thick rectangle. Using a pastry scraper, knife, spatula, or other metal edge, cut the dough into 1 ½-inch squares. You do not need to move the dough after cutting. Bake for 15 to 17 minutes, until the tops of the biscuits are slightly browned. Remove the baking sheet from the oven and let the biscuits cool for a few minutes before breaking them apart.

To make the filling reduce the oven temperature to 350 degrees. Combine the cream cheese, sour cream, buttermilk, hot pepper sauce, blue cheese, celery seeds, green onion, and chicken in a bowl and mix well. Spoon into a small baking dish. Bake for 20 minutes. Split or tear apart the biscuits and fill with the chicken mixture. Serve warm.

▶ **Makes about 24 biscuits, or 12 servings**

Mary Anne Parker of Parker Homestead in Harrisburg, Arkansas, says, "Outdoor entertaining is a must. That's the great thing about the South: We are able to enjoy the outdoors almost year-round. A fire is always inviting. Add some lights, food, drinks, and music, and whether you are hosting the T-ball team or a wine tasting, everyone will be happy." Whether there's a hunter in the family or you purchase the bird, goose breast rolled with cream cheese, bacon, and jalapeño pepper is an entrée guests will never forget. Parker uses the white-fronted goose, commonly known as "specklebelly goose."

SPECKLEBELLY GOOSE BREAST WITH BACON, JALAPEÑOS, AND CREAM CHEESE

8 to 10 specklebelly goose breasts

Salt

1 (8-ounce) package cream cheese, cut into 8 to 10 slices, softened

8 to 10 jalapeño pepper slices

8 to 10 slices bacon

Pinch of seasoned salt for each piece, or to taste

Pinch of Greek seasoning for each piece, or to taste

Dash or two of Worcestershire sauce for each piece, or to taste

Salt, ground black pepper, and garlic salt, to taste

Wash the meat, then salt it. Cover with water in a bowl or dish and refrigerate for 8 hours or more.

Preheat a smoker or grill to 325 degrees. Cut the breasts lengthwise without cutting through the other side and open like a book. Put a piece of cream cheese and a slice of jalapeño onto the meat. Roll the meat to enclose the ingredients. Wrap the bundle with bacon and secure with a toothpick or two.

Season with the seasoned salt, Greek seasoning, Worcestershire sauce, salt, pepper, and garlic salt.

Put a few chunks of hickory or applewood on the fire if you like a smoky flavor. Grill the breasts, turning once or twice, for 8 to 12 minutes, until the bacon is cooked through.

▶ Makes 8 to 10 servings

At Lisa Cascio Mays's paella parties in Nashville, Tennessee, the food is the entertainment. "A paella party is a perfect way to entertain for a party, especially outdoors using your grill. It is the original communal dish meant to be shared," she says. She makes paella with a Southern accent using local ingredients from farmers' markets and butchers: green beans, tomatoes, and onions grown nearby; chicken, pork, and sausage from farmers in her area; Southern shrimp from Florida or Georgia; and clams from South Carolina. Sometimes she tops the finished dish with fried black-eyed peas or Crunchy Fried Field Peas (page 18).

For outdoor cooking, a smaller paella pan can fit on a grill. Ask guests to bring a Spanish-style appetizer and a bottle of Spanish wine.

TENNESSEE PAELLA

4 tablespoons olive oil, or more as needed

1 (5-pound) chicken, cut into pieces

Salt and ground black pepper, to taste

1 pound smoked ham, cut into bite-size pieces

4 links fresh sausage (chorizo, Italian, or other type)

1 1/2 to 2 cups diced white or yellow onions

4 cloves garlic, finely chopped

2 teaspoons dried oregano

2 teaspoons dried thyme

1 tablespoon smoked paprika

1/4 teaspoon saffron threads

2 bay leaves

1 pound Spanish chorizo, thinly sliced

2 cups Spanish bomba rice (you can use other rice varieties but the result will be different)

4 1/2 to 5 1/2 cups chicken broth, plus more if needed

Juice of 1 lemon

1 dozen fresh clams, washed

1 dozen fresh mussels

1/2 pound shell-on shrimp

1 cup green peas, cooked lima beans, cooked green beans, or cooked or canned garbanzo beans

2 roasted red bell peppers, julienned

2 lemons, sliced into wedges

1/4 cup chopped fresh flat-leaf parsley

Heat a paella pan over medium heat. Add the olive oil. Season the chicken with salt and pepper. Place the chicken in the pan and cook until browned, about 10 minutes. Add the ham and sausage, and cook until browned. Remove the meats from the pan.

Add more olive oil if necessary. Add the onions. Cook and stir until translucent. Add the garlic, oregano, thyme, paprika, saffron, bay leaves, and chorizo. Cook for 2 to 3 minutes. Add the rice and cook another 2 to 3 minutes, stirring to coat each grain with oil.

131

Spread the rice over the bottom of the pan. Add the broth and lemon juice and bring to a boil over medium heat. Taste and adjust seasonings. Add more broth if needed. Reduce the heat to low. Place the chicken, sausage, ham, clams, mussels, and shrimp in the rice. Do not stir once the ingredients are arranged.

Loosely cover the pan with aluminum foil to ensure that the shellfish open and shrimp turn pink. Simmer for 10 to 15 minutes. Check the rice and seafood for doneness.

Sprinkle the peas over the top. Arrange pepper strips over the top. Garnish with lemon wedges and parsley.

▶ Makes 10 servings

Note: Spanish chorizo and bomba rice are available at some specialty markets, or online at tienda.com

A new or rediscovered cooking gadget is a great excuse to invite friends over, as Mindy Merrell and R. B. Quinn of Nashville, Tennessee, discovered when they dusted off the rarely used turkey fryer. "Suddenly, we were heating vats of oil, frying all kinds of things, and saying 'come on over' more often," says Merrell. One favorite use for the "party pot" is to fry piles of catfish fingers and French fries. The frying is part of the spectacle, and watching makes guests hungry for hot catfish and fries. No seated dinner here: "It's a grazing, grab-a-handful-while-they're-hot, pour-another-beer party," says Merrell. Serve the catfish plain, or stuff it into rolls topped with Merrell's famous Tartar Slaw. Don't have a turkey-size party pot? A heavy pot on the kitchen stove works fine too, even if it doesn't exactly shout "party!"

FRIED CATFISH FINGERS WITH TARTAR SLAW

To make the fried catfish fingers, heat 2 to 3 inches (or even 6 inches in a large pot) of oil in a heavy pot or deep skillet over medium-high heat to 365 degrees. Place a wire rack on a baking sheet. Place the cornmeal in a shallow bowl and roll the catfish fingers in the cornmeal. Place on the wire rack to dry a few minutes so the cornmeal adheres well.

Fry a few pieces of fish at a time (don't overcrowd the pan) in the hot oil until golden brown on all sides, 3 to 5 minutes. Test for doneness by piercing the thickest part of the fish with a fork or the tip of a knife. The fish is cooked through if the center is opaque and the flesh flakes easily. Season with salt and pepper while the fish is hot.

To make the tartar slaw, whisk together the mayonnaise and lemon juice in a large bowl until well blended. Stir in the pickle relish. Sprinkle with salt. Add the cabbage and toss to coat. Taste for seasoning and add more salt as necessary. Serve immediately or refrigerate.

▶ Makes 8 to 10 servings

FRIED CATFISH FINGERS

Vegetable oil for frying

1 to 1 1/2 cups self-rising cornmeal mix

6 to 10 catfish fillets, cut into 1 1/2- to 2-inch wide strips

Salt and ground black pepper, to taste

TARTAR SLAW

1/2 cup mayonnaise

2 tablespoons fresh lemon juice

1/2 cup sweet pickle relish

Salt to taste

6 cups finely shredded green cabbage

Crab cakes are a luxurious food for guests at Kat Riehle's home in New York City, whether they're served as an appetizer or entrée. Pairing seafood and wine can be a little tricky, so do your homework and ask the staff at the wine store. When guests offer to bring wine, let them know that seafood is on the menu. If a guest brings a bottle as a gift for you personally, don't feel compelled to serve it. Ask if they wish to open it and share, and if not it's fine to set it aside to enjoy later.

2 slices dried bread, crusts removed

2 to 4 tablespoons milk

1 tablespoon mayonnaise

1 tablespoon Worcestershire sauce

1 tablespoon chopped fresh flat-leaf parsley

1 tablespoon baking powder

1 teaspoon fish and seafood seasoning (such as Old Bay)

1/4 teaspoon salt

1 large egg, beaten

1 pound fresh lump crabmeat, cleaned, shells and cartilage removed

Butter for sautéeing

Lemon slices for serving

MISS JOY'S SOUTH CAROLINA CRAB CAKES

In a large bowl break the bread into small pieces and moisten with the milk. Remove the bread from the liquid.

In a medium bowl mix the bread, mayonnaise, Worcestershire sauce, parsley, baking powder, seafood seasoning, salt, egg, and crabmeat gently with your hands. Form into 4 patties and place on a baking sheet or large plate. Cover with waxed paper and refrigerate for 30 minutes.

Sauté the crab cakes in butter in a large cast-iron skillet over medium-high heat for 3 to 4 minutes on each side until golden. Serve with the lemon slices.

▶ Makes 4 servings

Lucy Mercer of Atlanta, Georgia, says the nice things she received for wedding gifts—crystal, silver, and china—languish unused in storage now. She still likes to entertain, because making people feel comfortable and welcome never goes out of fashion. Mercer seats guests at round tables (for better conversation) on a big, deep porch and offers big bowls and pots of good things, like Seafood Creole, that people can serve themselves to keep it simple for the cook and easy for guests. When company's coming, Lucy recommends using good-quality Gulf Coast seafood and really taking your time with the roux for the richest, deepest flavor.

SEAFOOD CREOLE

In a large pot or Dutch oven over medium heat, heat the butter and cook until foamy. Stir in the flour and cook over medium heat, stirring often, until dark brown, about 20 minutes. The smell will be like nearly burned buttered popcorn and the color will be like milk chocolate.

Add the onion, garlic, celery, bell pepper, wine, tomatoes with liquid, salt, black pepper, paprika, bay leaf, and thyme. Stir well. Bring to a low boil over medium-high heat, then reduce heat to low, cover, and simmer for 10 minutes. Uncover and continue simmering until the celery and bell pepper are tender.

Remove the bay leaf. Season to taste with Creole seasoning and hot pepper sauce. Add the fish, shrimp, and scallops, and simmer for 3 to 5 minutes until the fish is opaque and shrimp are pink. Remember that the seafood will continue to cook after being removed from the heat from the residual heat of the stew. Serve over a bed of hot rice.

▶ Makes 6 to 8 servings

Note: When the vegetables are tender, you can continue cooking the base, either on the stovetop or covered in a 300-degree oven. Check frequently to make sure the liquid level doesn't get too low. Remove the bay leaf and add the Creole seasoning, hot pepper sauce, fish, shrimp and scallops 3 to 5 minutes before serving time.

4 tablespoons unsalted butter

4 tablespoons all-purpose flour

1 large onion, diced

3 cloves garlic, finely chopped

3 celery stalks, diced

1 medium red bell pepper, diced

1/2 cup white wine

2 (16-ounce) cans whole tomatoes, undrained

1 teaspoon salt

1/2 teaspoon ground black pepper

1/2 teaspoon paprika

1 dried bay leaf

1/2 teaspoon dried thyme or 1 teaspoon chopped fresh

1/4 teaspoon Creole seasoning (such as Tony Chachère's)

1/2 teaspoon hot pepper sauce, or to taste

2 pounds of a combination of mild fish (such as flounder); peeled, deveined shrimp; and bay scallops

4 to 6 cups hot cooked rice

Genet Hogan of Woodstock, Georgia, moved away from New Orleans but keeps the flame for Saints football on game day. She serves Shoepeg Corn Dip (page 36), Chicken Sliders (page 45), and Shrimp Etouffée. Although that menu may sound ambitious, much of the work for the etouffée can be done long before kick-off. The day before, make the etouffée base and peel and devein the shrimp. About an hour before guests arrive, make the rice for the etouffée. At half time, reheat the etouffée base and finish the dish so it's ready for the third quarter. Hogan says she's not a baker, so she asks guests to bring desserts, which are set out at the beginning of the fourth quarter.

SHRIMP ETOUFFÉE

SEASONING MIX AND SHRIMP

1 dried bay leaf

1 tablespoon dried parsley flakes

1 tablespoon kosher salt

1 teaspoon dried basil leaves

1 teaspoon dried thyme

1 teaspoon ground black pepper

1 teaspoon ground white pepper

1/2 teaspoon cayenne pepper

3 pounds medium (26-40 count) shrimp, peeled, deveined

ETOUFFÉE

1/2 cup canola oil

1/2 cup all-purpose flour

1 cup chopped onions

1/2 cup chopped celery

1/2 cup chopped green bell pepper

2 cloves garlic, finely chopped

3 cups seafood stock or chicken stock

1/4 cup thinly sliced green onions

1/2 cup (1 stick) unsalted butter

1 teaspoon filé powder

Hot cooked rice

To make the seasoning mix, in a small bowl thoroughly combine the bay leaf, parsley, salt, basil, thyme, black pepper, white pepper, and cayenne. In a large bowl toss the shrimp with at least 1 teaspoon of the seasoning mixture. Cover and refrigerate for 15 minutes to 12 hours. Set aside the remaining seasoning mix.

To make the etouffée, in a large, heavy skillet (preferably cast-iron) heat the oil over high heat until it begins to smoke. Gradually add the flour, whisking vigorously after each addition until smooth. Cook, whisking continually, until the roux is the color of peanut butter. Add the onions, celery, and bell pepper. Cook, stirring constantly until the vegetables begin to soften, about 5 minutes. Add the garlic and cook 2 minutes longer. Remove the pan from the heat.

In a large saucepan or Dutch oven, bring the stock to a boil. Gradually add the roux mixture to the boiling stock, whisking after each addition until dissolved. Return to a boil, stirring often, until the sauce begins to thicken. Reduce the heat to low and cook, stirring occasionally, for 30 minutes. The dish can be made up to this point and kept warm until ready to serve.

Add the seasoned shrimp, green onions, butter, reserved seasoning mixture, and filé powder 10 minutes before serving time. Cook, stirring occasionally, until the shrimp are cooked through, for 7 to 10 minutes. Be careful not to overcook the shrimp. Adjust the seasonings, if necessary. Remove the bay leaf and serve over hot cooked rice.

▶ Makes 6 to 8 servings

Juanita Traughber of Nashville, Tennessee, is also a triathlete and enthusiastic home cook. She says, "A good hostess serves a variety of food and beverages at her cocktail and dinner parties. Southern hospitality means knowing guests' food allergies and dietary restrictions before creating the menu." Brunch is her favorite meal, and Shrimp and Grits is a very popular brunch item that also works as a dinner entrée.

SOUTHERN SHRIMP AND GRITS

Bring the water to a boil in a medium saucepan over high heat. Stir in the grits. Cover and reduce the heat to low. Cook until thick, about 5 minutes. Remove the pan from the heat and stir in the cheese.

Heat the olive oil in a skillet over medium heat. Add the bacon and fry until crisp, 8 to 10 minutes. Remove the bacon and drain on paper towels. Add the onions to the pan and cook until tender, about 5 minutes. Add the diced tomatoes, wine, and hot pepper sauce. Bring to a boil, then reduce to low heat. Cook until the sauce begins to thicken, about 5 minutes.

Season the shrimp with the salt, pepper, and garlic powder. Add the shrimp to the pan and cook, tossing, until they turn pink, 2 to 3 minutes. Remove the pan from the heat. Crumble the bacon and add to the shrimp mixture.

Stir the grits and add a little water if they are too thick. Divide the grits among 4 bowls. Top with the shrimp mixture. Garnish with chives.

▶ Makes 4 servings

3 cups water

1 cup uncooked quick-cooking grits

1/3 cup shredded pepper jack cheese

2 teaspoons olive oil

4 slices turkey bacon, torn into pieces

1/2 onion, diced

2 medium tomatoes, diced

1/4 cup dry white wine

1 teaspoon hot pepper sauce

24 medium shrimp, peeled, deveined

Salt, pepper, and garlic powder, to taste

Chopped fresh chives for garnish

Pat Lile of Little Rock, Arkansas, cooks seasonally, and winter means ducks in her freezer. Her duck cooking skills earned her a place in *Southern Living* magazine. "When they showed up with a reporter and photographer, well, I had four children, and I did what I could to get the house in order, but it was too much, so I began throwing stuff in the laundry room. When they were taking pictures, a fuse blew. The fuse box is in the laundry room. We could hardly get the door open." The moral? When the food and company are good, don't work yourself into a "tizzy" about the condition of the house.

SMOKED DUCK AND OYSTER GUMBO

3 wild ducks, cleaned, or 1 (4- to 6-pound) farmed duck

1/2 cup (1 stick) butter

1/2 cup all-purpose flour

1 medium green bell pepper, chopped

1 large onion, chopped

1 large clove garlic, finely chopped

1/4 cup minced fresh parsley, plus more for garnish

1 (10-ounce) package frozen cut okra, or 8 ounces fresh okra, cut up

1 (16-ounce) can diced tomatoes, or 4 to 6 fresh tomatoes, diced

Salt, black pepper, paprika, and red pepper, to taste

1 pint fresh shucked oysters, drained (halved if huge)

Hot cooked rice

Smoke the ducks over indirect heat with hickory chips according to manufacturer's directions, for 4 hours or until cooked through.

In a Dutch oven combine the ducks with enough water to reach halfway up the ducks. Bring to a boil, reduce the heat to low, and simmer until the meat is very tender and almost falling from the bones, 2 to 3 hours. Strain the broth and return to the Dutch oven. Let the ducks cool. Pull the meat from the bones, checking for any small bones. Dice the meat.

Melt the butter in a large cast-iron skillet over low heat. Add the flour and cook, whisking, until the roux is dark golden. Add the bell pepper and onion, and cook, stirring, until tender. Add the garlic and cook 1 minute.

Heat the reserved broth to a simmer over medium heat. Whisk in the roux mixture and cook, stirring, until well blended and hot. Add the duck meat, cover, reduce the heat to low, and cook for about 30 minutes. Stir in the parsley, okra, tomatoes, salt, pepper, paprika, and red pepper. Simmer until the okra is tender. (The gumbo can be made ahead to this point and refrigerated.)

Add the drained oysters to the simmering gumbo. Cook until they are plump and opaque and their edges begin to curl, about 3 minutes. Taste and adjust seasonings.

Serve over hot cooked rice in large soup bowls and sprinkle with more minced fresh parsley.

▶ Makes about 8 servings

For football watching or a houseful of kids, a slow cooker of chili is a good fit, says Patsy Read of Austin, Texas. This bean-less chili is good served on its own with crackers or cornbread, but there's so much more it can do. Add it to queso dip instead of sausage or spoon it over tamales. Top hot dogs with it or serve it over corn chips for a corn chip pie. For company, create a make-your-own-bowl-of-chili station with sliced jalapeño peppers, sour cream, shredded cheese, and green onions. An avocado salad is a cool, fresh side dish, and "the Texas beverage of choice is beer," says Read. Sangria, Texas red wine, margarita, and pomegranate tea are all good choices too. Read says her best advice for remaining relaxed around guests is, "Never say it was a mistake. Just go with it!" And remember—try to be a guest at your own party. After all, it's a party!

TEXAS-STYLE CHILI

Cook the chuck and ground beef in a large pot over medium-high heat, stirring until browned and crumbly, about 10 minutes. Drain the grease. Add the onions to the pot and cook over medium heat until the onions are soft, about 5 minutes. Add the garlic and cook 2 minutes. Add the cumin, salt, pepper, cayenne, and chili powder, and mix well.

Hold the tomatoes over the pot and crush them by hand, so the juices will fall into the pan. Stir in the tomato sauce and enchilada sauce. Cook over low heat for 1 ½ hours. Add the water (or tomato sauce) and cook for 1 ½ hours longer. Let cool and skim off any grease that rises to the top. Reheat to serve.

▶ Makes 10 servings

3 pounds chuck roast, coarsely ground

2 pounds lean ground beef, chili grind

2 large onions, finely chopped

5 cloves garlic, finely chopped

3 tablespoons ground cumin or cumin seed

1 tablespoon salt

2 teaspoons ground black pepper

1/2 teaspoon cayenne pepper, or to taste

3 tablespoons chili powder

2 (28-ounce) cans whole tomatoes, undrained

1 (15-ounce) can tomato sauce

1 (14-ounce) can red enchilada sauce

1 1/2 cups water (or substitute a second can of tomato sauce)

Burgoo is a long-time staple at big outdoor gatherings in Kentucky. It's a meal associated with rural areas and is nearly always cooked and served outdoors, usually in a big kettle. Mindy Jacoway, a Kentucky native now living in Nashville, Tennessee, developed her recipe from a burgoo served at a burgoo festival and the one served at Keeneland Race Track. "A cup of burgoo kept us warm during brisk days at the race track," she says. The lamb gives it a deeper, almost gamey flavor. And don't skimp on the vegetables. "The more vegetables the better," she says. Jacoway's party planning includes meticulously calculating quantities. "Always plan for enough," she says. With a big pot of burgoo, you're well on the way to that goal.

KENTUCKY BURGOO

1 ham bone (preferably from a country ham)

2 pounds veal shank

2 pounds beef shank or chuck roast (cut chuck into 3- or 4-inch chunks)

1 pound pork shank or country ribs (cut ribs into sections to fit in the pot)

2 pounds lamb breast, cut into sections to fit into the pot

1 (4-pound) chicken, quartered

8 quarts cold water

1 1/2 pounds potatoes, cubed

1 1/2 pounds onions, chopped

1 pound carrots, peeled, cut into thick slices

2 large green bell peppers, chopped

2 cups chopped cabbage

1 (32-ounce) can crushed tomatoes, undrained

2 cups fresh or frozen corn kernels

2 cups fresh or frozen cut green beans

2 cups fresh or frozen okra, diced

2 cups fresh or frozen lima beans, butter beans, peas, or a combination

1 cup diced celery

2 cloves garlic, sliced

3/4 cup Kentucky bourbon

1/2 cup ketchup

2 1/2 tablespoons salt

2 tablespoons freshly ground black pepper

1/4 cup Worcestershire sauce, or to taste

Tabasco sauce

Combine the ham bone, veal, beef, pork, lamb, and chicken with the water in a 3- to 5-gallon pot. Slowly bring to a boil over high heat, then lower the heat to medium and simmer until the meat falls from the bones, 4 to 6 hours.

Remove the meat and bones from the broth and let them cool. Skim the foam off the broth. Discard the bones and the chicken skin. Chop all of the meat.

Return the meat to the broth. Add the potatoes to the pot and simmer for 1 hour. Add the onions, carrots, peppers, cabbage, tomatoes, corn, green beans, okra, lima beans, celery, garlic, bourbon, and ketchup. Simmer until the vegetables are tender and the stew is thick but still soupy, 3 to 6 hours. Season with salt, pepper, and Worcestershire sauce. Serve in mugs or Styrofoam cups with Tabasco on the side.

Note: This preparation is traditional, but Jacoway sometimes sears the meats before boiling, which gives the finished stew a richer, almost grilled flavor.

▶ Makes about 3 gallons, or 32 servings

Carrie Ferguson Weir has been in Tennessee for two decades, long enough to combine some of her Cuban favorites like picadillo with Tennessee ingredients like sweet potatoes. If coming up with a menu for company paralyzes you, go on and invite guests anyway. That creates a "deadline," which Ferguson, a resident of Nashville and a former reporter, says will motivate you to come up with something.

1 tablespoon vegetable oil

1 medium sweet potato, peeled, cut into 1/4-inch cubes

1 tablespoon olive oil

1 large yellow onion, chopped

3 cloves garlic, finely chopped

1 red bell pepper, chopped

1 pound lean ground beef

1/2 cup tomato sauce

1 tablespoon ground cumin

1/2 teaspoon dried oregano

Salt to taste

1 teaspoon capers, drained, or to taste

Hot pepper sauce or cayenne pepper, optional

Hot cooked rice

SWEET POTATO PICADILLO

Heat the vegetable oil in a skillet over medium-high heat. Add the sweet potato and cook, covered, until softened and lightly browned, about 20 minutes, checking regularly. Remove from the pan.

Heat the olive oil in the same pan over medium-high heat. Add the onion, garlic, and bell pepper and cook until the onion is translucent, about 5 minutes. Add the ground beef and cook until browned, 8 to 10 minutes. Drain any excess fat. Add the tomato sauce, sweet potato, cumin, oregano, and salt. Simmer for 10 minutes. Add the capers to the dish as it simmers, or use as a garnish after the picadillo is plated. Season with the hot pepper sauce or cayenne. Serve over rice with crusty bread and a simple green salad.

▶ Makes 4 servings

Note: Sweet Potato Picadillo also makes a good filling for empanadas, a type of turnover made throughout the Spanish-speaking world.

When all the "pretty" slices have been cut from a Boiled Country Ham (page 57) or Baked Country Ham (page 58), there is still lots of ham left in odd sizes and shapes. The solution? Ham salad. "It's a good way to use those scrappy pieces of ham," says Nell Wallace of Cadiz, Kentucky. She serves hers with Angel Biscuits (page 59) for a "pick up" bite that's good on a buffet or luncheon plate.

COUNTRY HAM SALAD

Combine the ham, salad dressing, sugar, and relish in a large bowl and mix well. Serve as a dip or use to fill Angel Biscuits.

▶ Makes 3 1/2 cups, or 6 to 8 servings

3 cups ground cooked country ham

6 to 8 tablespoons salad dressing (more as necessary to reach spreading consistency)

1/4 cup sugar

1/2 cup sweet pickle relish

Angela Roberts of Nashville, Tennessee, says it's worth taking time a day or two ahead of your event to focus on the table, chairs, and seating arrangements. "I set the table, arrange the chairs, add extra table leaves if needed," she says. She also makes place cards either the evening before or the morning of the event. "I find assigning seats is very helpful, and the guests seem to like to know where to sit. I think it makes them feel special when they see their name, and there are a lot of fun ways to do it, without being fancy. One of the cutest things I've ever seen done was a picture frame with name, which we got to keep," she says.

1 (1-pound) package lasagna noodles

3 large sweet potatoes, peeled

1 tablespoon unsalted butter

6 shallots, finely chopped

1 pound ricotta cheese

1 (4-ounce) log goat cheese, divided

2 tablespoons finely chopped fresh flat-leaf parsley

1 large egg

Sea salt and ground black pepper, to taste

1/4 teaspoon freshly ground nutmeg

1/2 cup freshly grated Parmigiano-Reggiano or pecorino cheese, divided

Fresh thyme

1 cup shredded mozzarella cheese

FOUR-CHEESE SWEET POTATO LASAGNA

Cook the lasagna noodles in boiling water in a large pot for 3 minutes less than the time called for in the package directions. Drain in a colander.

Use a mandoline to slice the potatoes to a medium thickness, about ¼ inch thick. You can either boil the slices for 2 to 3 minutes, then pat them dry, or roast them in a 375-degree oven for 10 minutes, turning once.

Preheat the oven to 375 degrees, if it isn't already on. In a small skillet heat the butter over medium-high heat. Add the shallots. Cook and stir until softened.

Combine the ricotta cheese, ¼ cup of the goat cheese, the parsley, egg, salt, pepper, nutmeg, and half of the Parmigiano-Reggiano cheese in a bowl and mix well.

In a 9 x 13-inch baking dish, make layers of the pasta, ricotta cheese mixture, sweet potatoes, a few of the shallots, a pinch of the thyme, and the mozzarella cheese. Repeat layers. Then make final layers of the remaining pasta, mozzarella cheese, goat cheese, sweet potatoes, and fresh thyme.

Bake for 30 minutes. Spread the remaining Parmigiano-Reggiano over the top. Bake 10 minutes longer.

▶ Makes 9 to 12 servings

What's more gracious than sharing a recipe? New Yorkers Kat Riehle and her fiancé sampled this heavenly tomato pie with its biscuit crust at a North Carolina friend's home during the height of tomato season. The crust is folded over the outer part of the filling, leaving a window on the beautiful ripe tomatoes. They begged for the recipe, which the host generously shared.

If your dining table is small, serve the plates from the kitchen to keep the table clear. Leave room for a pitcher or carafe of water or tea. Guests can refill their own glasses, so you don't have to keep getting up for refills. A big, dramatic pitcher is a nice flourish, while the footprint of a carafe is better for small tables.

BISCUIT CRUST TOMATO PIE

CRUST

2 cups all-purpose flour, plus extra for sprinkling

1 1/2 teaspoons baking powder

1/2 teaspoon baking soda

1/2 teaspoon kosher salt

6 tablespoons (3/4 stick) chilled unsalted butter, cut into 1/2-inch cubes

1 cup buttermilk

FILLING

1 1/2 pounds large ripe tomatoes, cored and cut into 1/4-inch slices

2 1/2 cups coarsely shredded extra-sharp Cheddar cheese

1/4 cup finely grated Parmesan cheese

1/2 cup sliced green onions

1/2 cup mayonnaise

2 tablespoons chopped fresh dill

1 teaspoon cider vinegar

2 teaspoons sugar

3/4 teaspoon kosher salt

1/2 teaspoon ground black pepper

2 tablespoons cornmeal

To make the crust whisk the flour, baking powder, baking soda, and salt in a medium bowl. Add the butter and using a pastry blender or your hands, rub it into the flour until the mixture resembles coarse meal and some small lumps remain. Stir in the buttermilk and knead gently with your hands, adding more flour if needed, until a soft biscuit dough forms. Wrap in plastic and refrigerate for 1 hour.

To make the filling lay the tomatoes in a single layer on a baking sheet lined with 2 layers of paper towels. Place another 2 layers of paper towels on top of the tomatoes. Let stand for 30 minutes to drain.

Preheat the oven to 425 degrees. On waxed paper, pat and gently roll out the dough to a 14-inch circle and fit into a 9-inch pie dish, allowing the dough to hang over the edges.

Place the Cheddar and Parmesan cheeses in a medium bowl. Stir to mix. Whisk together the green onion, mayonnaise, dill, vinegar, sugar, salt, and pepper in a small bowl.

Sprinkle the cornmeal evenly over the bottom of the crust, then top with ½ cup of the cheese mixture. Arrange one-third of the tomatoes on top. Spread half of the mayonnaise mix over the tomatoes. Repeat the layers with 1 cup cheese mixture, half of the remaining tomatoes, and the remaining mayonnaise mix. Cover with 1 cup cheese, then the remaining tomato slices. Top with the remaining ¼ cup cheese mixture. Fold overhanging dough over the tomatoes and cheese mixture.

Bake for 35 to 40 minutes, until the crust is golden and the cheese is golden brown. Check the pie halfway through the baking time and tent with aluminum foil if the crust is browning too quickly. Let cool at least 1 hour before slicing.

▶ **Makes 6 to 8 servings**

Making everyone feel well-served at the table is important to Kathy Masulis of Nashville, Tennessee. That can be tricky nowadays with so many people claiming dietary restrictions. Her solution is to pick dishes that can be flexible, with things like meat, cheese, and nuts added at serving time, or at the table. This vegetarian recipe works as a vegan, dairy-free entrée or side dish. Other ideas for "flexitarian" foods: add the meat to stir-fry dishes after a meatless portion is set aside; create meatless versions of pizzas to serve alongside the ones with meat; and offer shrimp and peanuts at the table for pad thai.

1 large sweet potato

1/2 cup quinoa, cooked according to package directions

1 large egg, slightly beaten

2 teaspoons minced fresh cilantro

1 small onion, diced

1 (2-inch) piece fresh ginger, peeled and minced

1 clove garlic, finely chopped

1/2 teaspoon sea salt

1/2 teaspoon garam masala

1/2 teaspoon curry powder

1/4 teaspoon mustard seed, optional

1/8 teaspoon cayenne pepper

Melted coconut oil, for brushing

LAURA'S SWEET POTATO AND QUINOA PATTIES

Preheat the oven to 400 degrees. Place the sweet potato on a small baking sheet. Pierce the potato several times with a fork. Bake 45 minutes, or until tender. Let cool slightly, then cut the potato into halves lengthwise. Scoop out the pulp and place in a large bowl.

Add the quinoa, egg, cilantro, onion, ginger, garlic, salt, garam masala, curry powder, mustard seed, and cayenne to the sweet potato, and mix well. Form into 8 patties.

Place the patties on a large parchment-lined baking sheet. Brush the tops of the patties with a little coconut oil. Bake for 15 minutes. Flip, brush again with coconut oil, and bake for another 15 minutes, or until golden brown. Serve as a meatless entrée or burger style with rolls or buns and fixings.

▶ Makes 4 servings

Lisa Towery of Oxford, Mississippi, likes to have an "action station" as a unique feature of her parties. For a Kentucky Derby-themed party she held while her husband was stationed in Carlisle Barracks, Pennsylvania, she served these Kentucky Hot Brown Sandwiches. "We assembled and served these sandwiches at a station with one wait staff prepping them using a griddle. The sauce, bacon, and mushrooms were made on our kitchen stove and taken to the assembly station. Guests loved watching their sandwiches made to order right in front of them. It was easier to do than it may sound and added a touch of class to our event," she says. This recipe makes four open-face sandwiches, so adjust the quantities to serve your crowd.

KENTUCKY HOT BROWN SANDWICHES

In a large skillet over medium heat, melt ½ cup of the butter. Stir in enough flour to absorb all of the butter. Slowly whisk in the milk. Stir in 6 tablespoons of the cheese. Add the egg and cook, stirring, until the sauce thickens, but do not let it boil. Remove from the heat and season with salt and pepper.

Heat the remaining 1 tablespoon butter in a small skillet over medium-high heat. Cook and stir the mushrooms until soft.

Preheat the broiler. For each sandwich, place two slices of toasted bread onto a broiler-proof dish or plate. Cover the toast with about ¼ cup of the cooked mushrooms and add a couple of tomato slices. Top with a generous amount (4 ounces) of turkey. Pour ¾ cup of the sauce over the sandwich. Sprinkle with a little of the remaining cheese. Repeat with the remaining ingredients to make 4 open-face sandwiches.

Place the dish under the broiler. Broil until the sauce is speckled brown and bubbly. Remove the dish from the broiler, and criss-cross two slices of bacon on top of each sandwich. Serve hot.

▶ Makes 4 servings

1/2 cup (1 stick), plus 1 tablespoon, butter, divided

About 6 tablespoons all-purpose flour

3 cups milk

1/2 cup freshly grated Parmesan cheese, divided

1 large egg, beaten

Salt and ground black pepper, to taste

2 cups sliced fresh mushrooms

8 slices bread, toasted

1 medium tomato, thinly sliced

1 pound thinly sliced cooked turkey

8 slices bacon, cooked

Cooking for people has always come naturally to cookbook author Sandra Gutierrez of Cary, North Carolina. And entertaining need not mean lots of work. "This is the kind of recipe that I fall back on when I want to entertain on a whim: easy, quick, and sensational. Wilted salads are simple to assemble and this one has a great twist that introduces Latin American flavors," says Gutierrez. Post-its are her best friends when entertaining, she says. She uses them to remind herself of "cooking times and temperatures, or the order in which different foods need to be baked in the oven, and when to turn the coffee maker on."

SANDRA'S SPINACH SALAD WITH HOT CHORIZO DRESSING

To make the dressing heat the oil in a medium skillet over medium heat. Add the chorizo and cook until all of the fat has been rendered and the chorizo is cooked through, 3 to 4 minutes. Drain all but 2 tablespoons of the rendered fat, leaving the sausage in the pan. Reduce the heat to low. Whisk in the vinegar, brown sugar, and mustard until dissolved. Taste and season with salt and pepper.

To make the salad, in a large bowl toss together the spinach, mushrooms, and onion. Pour the warm dressing over the salad and toss well to coat. Garnish with the hard-boiled eggs and serve immediately.

▶ Makes 3/4 cup dressing and 4 to 6 servings of salad

HOT CHORIZO DRESSING

3 tablespoons extra-virgin olive oil

5 ounces Mexican chorizo, casings removed

1/3 cup cider vinegar

2 tablespoons, plus 2 teaspoons, dark brown sugar

1 teaspoon Creole mustard

Salt and ground black pepper, to taste

SPINACH SALAD

6 ounces baby spinach leaves, washed and spun dry (about 6 cups)

2 cups sliced white mushrooms

1/2 cup very thinly sliced red onion

2 hard-boiled large eggs, peeled and sliced

From Betsy Watts Koch of Brentwood, Tennessee, comes a recipe for an utterly Southern salad loved across the region. It's popular with guests, but you may love it even more because it can be made up to a day ahead, freeing you up for all those last-minute hosting tasks. Koch served it as part of a salad buffet to the ladies at her church. In addition to Curried Chicken and Rice Salad, she served a broccoli salad and fruit salad, banana bread, and assorted sweets. "What I remember the most is how much all the ladies loved it. Beautiful weather didn't hurt!" she says. It's worth moving a party outside in nice weather for the difference it makes in the energy of the gathering. Group chairs around small tables, or if it's a "lap lunch," create clusters of four or five chairs. Keep food under wire bowl covers and plastic wrap until serving time.

CURRIED CHICKEN AND RICE SALAD

1 (10-ounce) package frozen snow peas

2 boneless, skinless chicken breast halves, cooked and cut into 1-inch pieces

4 large carrots, coarsely shredded

6 green onions, thinly sliced

1/2 cup golden raisins

3 cups cooked white rice, at room temperature

1 cup plain fat-free yogurt

2 tablespoons mayonnaise

1/4 cup milk

1 teaspoon curry powder

1/4 teaspoon salt

1/8 teaspoon ground black pepper

1/4 cup toasted slivered almonds

Cook the snow peas as directed on the package until crisp-tender. Drain. Slice the snow peas crosswise into 1-inch pieces. Combine with the chicken, carrots, green onions, raisins, and rice in a large bowl.

In a small bowl, whisk the yogurt with the mayonnaise, milk, curry powder, salt, and pepper until smooth. Pour over the chicken mixture and stir until well combined. Cover and refrigerate for at least 1 hour and up to 12 hours.

To serve sprinkle the salad with the almonds. Serve on a buffet, or plate a scoop on a bed of lettuce.

▶ Makes 4 to 6 servings

Deanna Larson of Nashville, Tennessee, simplifies the menu with quick dishes like this one that can be put together in the time it takes to cook the pasta.

When you're picking up flowers for the table, take their fragrance into account. A strongly fragrant arrangement might not appeal to every guest and could overwhelm even the bacon and collards in this recipe. Choose alstroemeria, tulips, daisies, dahlias, iris, or other unscented or lightly scented flowers for the table. Save the highly fragrant stephanotis and lilies for the entryway or guest bath.

PENNE WITH BACON AND BABY COLLARDS

Bring a large pot of lightly salted water to a boil over high heat. Add the pasta, and cook until tender, 8 to 10 minutes.

Meanwhile, heat 1 tablespoon of the olive oil in a skillet over medium heat. Cook the bacon until browned and crisp. Add the garlic and cook for about 1 minute. Stir in the tomatoes and cook until heated through.

Put the collards in a colander and drain the hot pasta over it so it will wilt. Transfer to a large serving bowl, and toss with the remaining olive oil and the tomato mixture.

▶ Makes 6 to 8 servings

1 (16-ounce) package penne pasta

2 tablespoons olive oil, divided

1 pound bacon, chopped

2 tablespoons minced garlic

1 (14-ounce) can diced roasted tomatoes, undrained

1 (16-ounce) bag baby collards

Shamille Wharton relies on pretty things to set a welcoming table at her Nashville, Tennessee, home. "Even if you can't boil water, invest in beautiful serving dishes and utensils—that way anything you serve your guests will look beautiful. Half of the dining experience is what your guests see." Her grandmother was her greatest inspiration for entertaining. She went out of her way to prepare each person's favorite dish, her "silent way to tell us that we were loved and thought of," says Wharton. Similarly, your guests will feel loved and thought of with this decadent and delicious version of macaroni and cheese.

1 (16-ounce) package cavatappi or other spiral pasta

1/2 cup (1 stick) unsalted butter

3 tablespoons all-purpose flour

1 quart heavy cream

1 cup shredded Swiss cheese

1 cup shredded Gruyère cheese

1 cup shredded Fontina cheese

Dash of freshly grated nutmeg

1 pound lump crabmeat

1 large shallot, diced

Finely grated peel of 1 small lemon

1 teaspoon hot pepper sauce, or to taste

1 teaspoon Dijon-style mustard

1 tablespoon white truffle oil

1 cup panko or dry bread crumbs

1 cup grated Parmesan cheese

1/2 cup chopped fresh flat-leaf parsley

Salt and pepper to taste

CRAB CAKE MAC AND CHEESE

Preheat the oven to 350 degrees. Grease a 9 x 12-inch baking dish or 6 to 8 individual baking dishes. Bring 2 quarts of salted water to a boil in a large pot over high heat. Add the pasta and cook according to package directions until al dente. Drain.

Melt the butter in a skillet over medium heat. Whisk in the flour. Gradually add the cream, whisking to combine. Reduce the heat to medium-low. Add the Swiss, Gruyère, and Fontina cheeses and the nutmeg. Cook until the cheeses melt.

In a large bowl combine the crabmeat, shallot, lemon peel, hot sauce, and mustard, and mix well.

In a medium bowl combine the truffle oil, panko, Parmesan, and parsley, and mix well.

Add the pasta to the crab mixture. Pour in the cheese sauce, add salt and pepper, and stir gently a few times to loosely combine. The mixture will be soupy. Pour the mixture into the baking dish or into individual serving dishes. Spread the panko mixture over the top. Gently pat down.

Bake for 20 to 25 minutes, until the panko topping is slightly browned and the pasta mixture is bubbling at the sides. Let stand 10 minutes before serving.

▶ Makes 10 to 12 servings

When her children were small, Betsy Watts Koch of Brentwood, Tennessee, used to have a Christmas Day party around 4 or 5 in the afternoon "to give us all something to do when the Christmas morning present buzz wore off," she says. "Our children were in single digits then, and we invited families with children to hang out with us. One of the great things about having a party on Christmas Day is that people expect a certain amount of post-present clutter, so having a spotless house doesn't really matter." The party started as a chili party, but evolved into a three-soup party as the children grew. The chili and soups stayed on the stove on low, and guests served themselves one or more. The Christmas meal ended with a birthday cake for baby Jesus "complete with candles," says Koch. Football was watched, beer and wine consumed, children played, and parents talked and laughed.

CORN CHOWDER WITH CHILIES

Heat the butter in a large pot or Dutch oven over medium heat. Add the onions and cook for 3 to 4 minutes. Add the corn and cook, stirring, for 1 minute. Add the potatoes, chipotles, and green chilies, and mix well. Stir in the broth, cream, and salt. Bring to a boil. Reduce the heat to low. Add the bacon.

Add the cornmeal and water mixture to thicken the soup. Stir to combine. Cover and cook for 15 minutes over low heat. If the chowder needs more thickening, add another tablespoon of cornmeal mixed with water. Cook for 10 minutes longer.

▶ Makes about 12 servings

2 tablespoons butter or olive oil

1 1/2 sweet onions, diced, or 1 (12-ounce) bag frozen chopped onions

4 cups corn cut from 5 ears, or 1 (2-pound) bag frozen corn

1 (24-ounce) bag frozen diced potatoes

2 whole chipotle peppers in adobo sauce, finely diced, or to taste

2 (4-ounce) cans diced green chilies

1 (32-ounce) container low-sodium chicken broth, or to taste

1 1/2 cups half-and-half or heavy cream

1/2 teaspoon kosher salt, or to taste

1/2 to 1 cup crumbled cooked bacon (8 to 16 slices)

3 tablespoons cornmeal or masa mixed with 1/4 cup water, optional

There's nothing like live music to energize an occasion. Helen Waddle of Shreveport, Louisiana, asked a friend to play piano for her 50th anniversary party. If you don't have a musical friend, ask around for a referral. And there's always Craigslist or nextdoor.com. From string duos to dance DJs to bluegrass bands, if musicians are near you, they're probably online. Be sure to check any musician's references to avoid surprises. And if the budget is tight, a community quartet, church choir, or talented music student might be the solution.

CRAWFISH FETTUCCINE

3/4 cup (1 1/2 sticks) butter

1 green bell pepper, chopped

4 cloves garlic, crushed

5 or 6 green onions, chopped (1/4 pound)

1/3 cup all-purpose flour

1/2 cup water

2 pounds crawfish tail meat or 2 1/2 pounds shrimp, peeled

1/4 cup chopped fresh parsley

18 ounces fettuccine pasta*

1 pound Mexican processed cheese spread, cut into cubes

1 pint half-and-half

Salt and ground black pepper, to taste

Parmesan cheese, to taste

Preheat the oven to 350 degrees. Grease a 5- to 6-quart baking dish. Bring a large pot of salted water to a boil over high heat.

In a large skillet over medium heat, melt the butter and add the bell pepper, garlic, and green onions. Cook until the pepper begins to soften, about 10 minutes. Stir in the flour. Add the water, reduce the heat to low, and simmer for about 5 minutes. Add the crawfish and parsley. Cook, stirring frequently, for about 15 minutes.

Add the pasta to the boiling water and cook for 2 minutes less than the package directions. Drain.

Add the cheese, half-and-half, salt, and pepper to the skillet. Add the pasta to the sauce and mix well. (The sauce will appear thin but the noodles will absorb it.)

Pour the mixture into the baking dish and top with Parmesan cheese. Bake for 20 to 25 minutes, until hot and bubbly.

▶ Makes 10 to 12 servings

*If you can find spinach fettuccini, swap out half of the regular for a more colorful dish.

Plan a "post-holiday leftovers" potluck to spread the love and share the bounty. Let guests bring their holiday leftovers (or whatever they've made from leftovers) to share. Guests without leftovers can be asked to bring drinks and bread. This creamy, chilie-warmed soup from Anna Ginsberg of Austin, Texas, will tempt even the turkey-weary.

TURKEY POBLANO SOUP

1 poblano pepper

4 (5- to 6-inch) corn tortillas, chopped

2 tablespoons all-purpose flour

1/2 teaspoon chili powder

3/4 teaspoon ground cumin

1/8 teaspoon salt, or to taste

1/2 teaspoon ground black pepper

2 tablespoons vegetable oil

1/2 cup chopped onions

1 clove garlic, finely chopped

2 tablespoons butter

3 cups chicken broth

1/2 cup half-and-half (or 1/4 cup each milk and heavy cream)

1 to 2 cups chopped cooked turkey

Shredded Monterey Jack cheese or shredded Mexican-style cheese

Heat the broiler. Wash the poblano, cut into halves lengthwise, and remove the stem and seeds. Place the poblano on a baking sheet and broil about 5 inches from the heat until blistered and soft. Put in a plastic bag and seal; let cool. Remove from the bag, peel off the skin, and chop to make ½ cup.

Combine the chopped tortillas, flour, chili powder, cumin, salt, and pepper in the bowl of a food processor and process until the mixture is the consistency of very coarse cornmeal.

Heat the oil in a large pot over medium heat. Add the onion and poblano, and cook until the onion is tender. Add the garlic and cook 1 minute. Add the butter and let it melt. Add the tortilla mixture to the pot and mix to form a roux. Slowly add the broth (about 1 cup at a time), stirring to make a thick soup. Cook 4 to 5 minutes, stirring constantly. Taste and adjust the salt if necessary. Add the half-and-half and bring to a slow simmer. Reduce the heat to low and cook until the soup is hot. Do not let it boil. Remove from the heat and add the turkey. Ladle into bowls and top each serving with cheese.

▶ Makes about 4 servings

Among the many guests at Pat Lile's table when she lived in Little Rock, Arkansas, were the nice people from church, Hillary Clinton and her little daughter, Chelsea, and Hillary's husband, Bill, who attended a different church. "I worked with Hillary on a children's advocacy program at that time. Bill had lost the election for his second term for governor and was virtually counted out. I always felt great rapport with him because I, too, was raised by grandparents. My grandparents and his grandparents both ran small stores in Hope, Arkansas. When he lost the election, I was crushed for him so I invited them to Easter Sunday lunch," she recalls. Lile served asparagus, homemade rolls, and ham with her grandmother-in-law's sauce to the future president of the United States that day, but the real gift was an afternoon of kindness and refuge at a troubling time for the family.

GRAM'S HAM SAUCE

3 large egg yolks

1 tablespoon all-purpose flour

1/2 cup undiluted canned tomato soup

1/2 cup prepared yellow mustard

1/2 cup cider vinegar

1/2 cup vegetable oil

1/2 cup sugar

Combine the egg yolks and flour in a heavy 1-quart saucepan and stir with a whisk over very low heat until slightly warmed and well mixed.

Whisk in the soup, mustard, vinegar, oil, and sugar. Cook, stirring, over low heat until thickened. Serve warm in a gravy boat or pitcher, or spoon over plated ham slices.

▶ Makes about 2 1/2 cups

Note: The sauce may be made ahead of time and refrigerated. Reheat before serving.

For years Mindy Jacoway and friends attended the Derby Brunch at the Pendennis Club in Louisville, Kentucky, a place where Derby hospitality has been offered for decades (and, by the way, where the Old Fashioned cocktail was invented). "When you enter, you've got a Bloody Mary or Mimosa in your hand within seconds, along with the day's Racing Program and Daily Racing Form," she says. Patrons love the traditional feel of the occasion: the brass band features the same musicians since the early 1970s, and the buffet menu hasn't changed much either. Henry Bain was an employee of the club when he created this boldly flavored sauce nearly 100 years ago. In her Nashville, Tennessee, home, Jacoway uses an adapted version of it for game such as duck, pheasant, and venison. It's good with beef, too. Like the Derby, it's a Kentucky original.

HENRY BAIN SAUCE

Combine the chutney, walnuts, ketchup, steak sauce, Worcestershire sauce, chili sauce, and Tabasco in a large bowl and mix well. Serve over cooked game or beef, or in a small cup alongside as a condiment.

▶ Makes about 8 cups

*Mindy uses Major Grey's mango chutney.

1 (17-ounce) jar mango chutney*

1/2 of 9-ounce jar imported pickled walnuts, optional (available from online gourmet retailers)

1 (14-ounce) bottle ketchup

1 (11-ounce) bottle steak sauce (such as A-1)

1 (10-ounce) bottle Worcestershire sauce

1 (12-ounce) bottle chili sauce

Tabasco, to taste

SIDE DISHES

The phrase "side dishes" slights the important role vegetables, salads, and grains play in a meal. Whether it's a tightly focused "occasion" menu or a sprawling collection on the tailgate, side dishes, much like a talented character actor in a film, can elevate a meal from good to great. The beautiful colors and shapes in a fresh salad, the aroma of rice pilaf—these sometimes even surpass the appeal of the entrées. Take a cue from restaurants: sometimes it's the accompaniments that sell the dish. An accomplished host and home cook knows a good side dish can steal the show.

Native Tennessean Kayne Rogers recommends always asking guests if they have any dietary restrictions or food allergies, even if you think you know the answer. Better to avoid the problem ahead of time than spend an hour watching your guests push food around their plates.

Kayne, now of New York City, serves Goober Peas on New Year's Day for good luck. Black-eyed peas and a few sides form a simple menu—she calls the recipe "embarrassingly simple"—to serve family and neighbors a taste of the good fortune in the year to come.

GOOBER PEAS

Heat the vegetable oil in a medium pan over medium heat. Add the onion and bell pepper and cook until softened. Add the sausage and cook, stirring to break up the sausage, until browned and crumbly. Add the black-eyed peas, tomatoes with green chilies, and salt and pepper. Cook until heated through. Serve over rice.

▶ Makes 10 servings

Note: The level of spiciness is easily adjustable by using mild or hot breakfast sausage; plain canned tomatoes can be substituted for the tomatoes with chilies; plain black-eyed peas can be replaced with a variety seasoned with jalapeño pepper for an even spicier dish.

2 tablespoons vegetable oil

1 onion, chopped

1 green bell pepper, chopped

1 pound bulk pork breakfast sausage

2 (16-ounce) cans black-eyed peas, rinsed and drained

1 (10-ounce) can tomatoes with green chilies

Salt and ground black pepper to taste

Hot cooked rice

The marriage of Melissa D. Corbin and her husband, Stuart Lang, of Nashville, Tennessee, started out on a hospitable note: they catered their own wedding. The day before her wedding, Corbin, her family, and friends prepared food for 100 people. They barbecued a hog and made slaw, corn, potato salad, and guacamole. Corbin baked dozens of oatmeal cookies from her Granny's recipe, and a local ice cream shop made them into ice cream sandwiches. Of course, there was a near-disaster: When a huge slow cooker full of beans broke, dozens of servings were lost. "I don't know what I was thinking," says Corbin. "A bride-to-be is supposed to be getting pampered the day before her wedding, and there I was crying over spilled beans." When it was over, though, she was married, and her guests will always remember the wedding and her extraordinary hospitality. The beans include a whole jalapeño pepper that isn't removed before serving. Whoever gets the pepper has a heck of a wedding night.

WEDDING BEANS

2 1/2 cups dried pinto beans

Water to cover

2 1/2 teaspoons salt, divided

Pinch of baking soda

1 clove garlic, knob of ginger, or potato

2 tablespoons olive oil

1/2 teaspoon bacon drippings

Ground black pepper, to taste

Pinch of hot red pepper flakes

1/4 teaspoon dried thyme

1 onion, chopped

1/2 green bell pepper, chopped

1 small whole jalapeño

3 cloves garlic, minced

1 bay leaf

1 teaspoon ground cumin

2 cups chicken broth

3 cups water

1 (14-ounce) can diced tomatoes, undrained

2 links smoked kielbasa sausage, chopped

Combine the beans and water in a large pot. Add 2 teaspoons of the salt and the baking soda. Bring to a boil then turn off the heat. Add the garlic, cover the pot, and refrigerate for several hours. Drain and rinse the beans. Discard the garlic.

Heat the olive oil and bacon drippings in a large pot over medium-high heat. Add the black pepper, pepper flakes, and thyme. Stir in the onion and bell pepper. Cook until tender. Add the whole jalapeño, garlic, bay leaf, cumin, and the remaining ½ teaspoon salt. Cook, stirring, until the garlic becomes aromatic, but not brown.

Add the chicken broth and 3 cups water. Bring to a boil, and then add the beans. Reduce the heat to medium-low and cover. Simmer for about 1 hour, stirring occasionally. Add the tomatoes and simmer, uncovered, until the liquid has reduced by half and the beans have made a velvety soup, about 1 hour longer. Stir in the sausage, cover the pot, and reduce the heat to low until serving time.

▶ Makes 6 to 8 side dish servings

The fortunate guests around Catherine Mayhew's grill in Brentwood, Tennessee, get professional quality Pulled Smoked Pork (page 93) from this member of a competitive barbecue team. Mayhew serves the meat with Corn Cakes (page 85) and Mustard Slaw. The idea for the combination came from a party given by Lodge Manufacturing, maker of classic cast-iron cookware.

MUSTARD SLAW

Combine the carrots, cabbage, mayonnaise, mustard, salt, celery seed, and pepper in a large bowl. Mix well and refrigerate until chilled.

▶ Makes 6 cups, or 8 servings

1 cup shredded carrots

4 cups shredded cabbage

1 1/4 cups mayonnaise

1 tablespoon Dijon-style mustard

1 teaspoon salt

1/2 teaspoon celery seed

1/2 teaspoon ground black pepper

A crunchy slaw from Melissa Denchak of Princeton, New Jersey, gets extra personality from apple, bacon, and pecans. When you're planning an event, be sure to allow plenty of time between the date the invitations are sent and the date of the party. For a formal occasion, that could mean sending the invitations out six weeks before the party. For less formal affairs, a general rule of thumb is to have your invitations in the hands of potential guests two to three weeks before the date. If you're just having happy hour for friends or neighbors, a day or even a few hours might be sufficient notice.

8 slices bacon

1 pound cabbage, finely shredded

2 large Fuji apples, unpeeled, sliced into matchsticks

4 green onions, thinly sliced

1 cup coarsely chopped, toasted pecans

1/2 cup mayonnaise

1/4 cup whole-grain mustard

1 tablespoon cider vinegar

1 tablespoon honey

Kosher salt and ground black pepper to taste

CREAMY CABBAGE-APPLE SLAW WITH PECANS AND BACON

Cook the bacon in a large skillet over medium heat until crisp, 4 to 6 minutes. Drain on paper towels. When cool, coarsely chop.

In a large bowl, combine the cabbage, apples, green onions, and pecans. In a medium bowl, whisk together the mayonnaise, mustard, vinegar, and honey. Pour the dressing over the cabbage mixture and toss until well combined. Garnish with the chopped bacon. Season with salt and pepper.

▶ Makes 8 servings

Memorial Day in the South often means grilling burgers or smoking ribs, but the sides can often be a bit predictable—baked beans and potato salad. Why not swap these old standby sides for something fresher, made with local, seasonal produce? Guests at April McAnnally's Birmingham, Alabama, home appreciate the change of pace that succotash offers. "It's a little more work than potato salad, but so worth it!" she declares. If guests offer to bring something to a cookout, be sure to ask ahead of time whether they'll need a special serving tool. Scrambling around for a melon baller, pizza cutter, or ice cream scoop is not how you want to spend time as guests are arriving.

SUMMER SUCCOTASH

Rinse and drain the peas and lima beans, discarding any leaves and stems. Bring the water to a boil in a large pot over medium-high heat and add the onion quarters and thyme. Boil for 10 minutes. Add the peas and beans and cook until tender, 18 to 20 minutes. Drain and remove the thyme stems and onions. Return peas and beans to pot and set aside.

In a large skillet heat the butter over medium heat. Add the corn and season with the salt and pepper. Cook until tender. Add corn to peas and beans.

Heat the olive oil in the same skillet over medium heat. Add the diced onion and okra, and cook until the onion is translucent, about 10 minutes. Season with salt and pepper to taste. Add the cherry tomatoes and cook for a few minutes longer. Add okra mixture to peas and beans. Bring the succotash to a simmer over low heat and cook 8 to 10 minutes to let the flavors meld. Sprinkle with basil to serve.

▶ Makes 10 to 12 servings

2 cups fresh lady peas

2 cups fresh lima beans or small butter beans

8 cups water

1 large Vidalia or other sweet onion, cut into quarters

2 sprigs fresh thyme

2 tablespoons unsalted butter

6 ears fresh Silver Queen or other white corn, cut from the cob

Kosher salt and ground black pepper, to taste

2 tablespoons olive oil

1/2 small Vidalia or other sweet onion, diced

1/2 pound fresh okra, cut into 1/2 inch slices

2 cups cherry tomatoes, cut into halves

2 tablespoons chopped fresh basil

When in doubt, keep the menu simple, light some candles, create music playlists that are pleasing to every guest (who doesn't like Frank Sinatra?), and keep some good bourbon on hand. "That is the secret to success for any proper Southern-style party, especially if you're a Kentucky girl like me," says Louisville, Kentucky, resident Jessica Pendergrass. This succotash is on the spicy side, so offer plenty of iced tea or adjust the amounts of cayenne and pepper flakes to your taste.

BLACK-EYED PEA AND EDAMAME SUCCOTASH

Soak the black-eyed peas according to the package directions. Drain. Place peas in a large saucepan with the water, onion, and salt, and cook over medium-low heat until the peas are beginning to soften, about 45 minutes.

Combine peas, edamame, corn, tomatoes, chicken broth, sage, cayenne, and pepper flakes in a large pot. Cook over medium-low heat for about 20 minutes. Taste occasionally and add more cayenne, pepper flakes, salt, and black pepper as needed.

Reduce heat to low and simmer for 5 minutes to let the flavors mellow and blend. Do not overcook, as the peas will become soggy.

▶ Makes 12 to 16 servings

1 1/2 cups dried black-eyed peas

3 cups water

1 small yellow onion, diced

1 teaspoon salt

12 ounces shelled edamame, baby lima beans or butter beans, fresh or frozen

2 3/4 cups fresh corn kernels or 16 ounces frozen

1 (28-ounce) can diced tomatoes, undrained (preferably Pomi brand)

2 cups chicken broth

2 tablespoons finely chopped fresh sage

3 tablespoons cayenne pepper

1 tablespoon red pepper flakes

Sea salt and ground black pepper, to taste

A thoughtful host tries, within reason, to accommodate guests' tastes. You may be eager to introduce them to a new cuisine, but unless you are sure they're adventurous enough for Thai salad or stewed kohlrabi, stick with reasonably familiar fare. This lovable stewed corn recipe comes from Ophelia Paine of Nashville, Tennessee, who got it from her great-aunt Ophelia. Try her technique for cutting the corn off the cob: Hold the ear upright over a cutting board and, beginning at the halfway point, use a serrated knife to cut several rows downward onto the board. Rotate the ear of corn and continue until you have cut the kernels off the entire lower half of the corncob. Then flip the ear over and repeat with the remaining half.

6 to 8 ears white corn

1 teaspoon salt

1/2 teaspoon ground black pepper

1/8 teaspoon cayenne pepper

6 tablespoons butter

1/4 cup heavy cream

AUNT OPHELIA'S STEWED CORN

Wash the corn, removing as much of the corn silk as possible. Cut the kernels from the cobs. Put the corn in the top of a double boiler set over a pan of water. Add the salt, pepper, and cayenne, and mix well. Cut the butter into thin slices and dot the top of the corn. Cover the pan and bring the water to a simmer over medium-low heat. Simmer for 45 minutes.

Stir the corn, then add the cream and mix well. Simmer for at least 1 hour longer. Adjust the seasoning, to taste.

▶ Makes 8 servings

Note: Stewed Corn may be made a day in advance and gently reheated.

According to Peggy Sweeney McDonald, a New Orleanian living in Los Angeles, the Sweeney Christmas Eve gathering is the family's big annual celebration. McDonald invites all of her "orphaned" friends who have "nowhere else to go" to share the holidays with her family. The grandchildren perform a short Christmas pageant, and each year a different child has a turn playing Mary. If there's a baby in the crowd, that baby is the star of the tale. The children sing "Silent Night," then one of the boys dresses as Santa "and everyone gets a gift." McDonald's menu always includes honey-baked ham, turkey, a Cajun stewed corn dish called Maque Choux (pronounced "mock shoe"), Spinach Isabel (page 195), and more.

MOMEE'S MAQUE CHOUX

Heat the oil and butter in a large skillet over low heat. Add the onion and bell peppers, and cook until tender, about 10 minutes. Add the frozen corn. It will stick to the bottom of the pan—this is fine. Cook until the corn has thawed. (If using fresh corn, add the corn kernels and milk and simmer 5 minutes.) Add the tomatoes and sugar. Simmer until tomatoes are tender and lose their shape.

Add water a little at a time and cook, covered, until the corn is tender. Season with salt and pepper. If you are using mild tomatoes, add Creole seasoning to taste. Add hot pepper sauce during the last 10 minutes of cooking.

▶ Makes 8 servings

Note: To make ahead, prepare as directed and pour into an 8-inch square baking dish. Refrigerate for 8 hours or more. Remove from the refrigerator and allow the dish to reach room temperature before reheating.

1 tablespoon vegetable oil

4 tablespoons butter

1 large onion, chopped

1 medium green bell pepper, chopped

1 medium red bell pepper, chopped

1 (32-ounce) package frozen corn or 6 to 8 ears fresh corn

1/4 cup whole milk (if using fresh corn)

1 (15-ounce) can spicy or regular tomatoes, undrained

1/4 teaspoon sugar

1/4 cup water

Salt, ground black pepper, and Creole seasoning to taste

Hot pepper sauce, to taste

The complexity of a recipe isn't what makes it welcome at a cookout or potluck dinner—it's the taste and the ease of eating, especially at stand-up functions, that do the trick. Choose dishes that can be eaten with just a fork and that stay safe at room temperature for a couple of hours. All those things earned Broccoli Cornbread a spot as one of the favorites at Tammy Qualls Shaffer's Warrenton, Virginia, home. Add a cup or two of chopped cooked chicken to make it a one-dish supper.

BROCCOLI CORNBREAD

4 large eggs

1 (9-ounce) package frozen chopped broccoli, thawed, drained, patted dry

1/2 cup shredded sharp Cheddar cheese

1/2 cup (1 stick) butter, melted

3/4 cup low-fat cottage cheese

1 medium onion, chopped, or 2/3 cup sliced green onion

1 (6-ounce) package cornbread mix (yellow, white, or buttermilk)

Preheat the oven to 400 degrees. Grease an 8- or 9-inch square pan. Beat the eggs in a large bowl. Add the broccoli and mix well. Add the cheese and butter and mix well. Stir in the cottage cheese and onion. Sprinkle the cornbread mix over the ingredients and mix until no pockets of dry mix remain.

Pour the mixture into the pan. Bake for 35 minutes, or until a wooden pick inserted into the center comes out clean.

▶ Makes 8 servings

Careful with that new oven! Stephen Fries' most memorable dinner party was one that never happened. "The week after moving into a new home in 1987, I had company over. I put a lasagna in the preheated oven and by mistake pushed the lever that locks the oven for self-cleaning. When I realized my mistake, I shut the oven off, but the oven remained locked until it cooled completely. We went out to dinner," says the New Haven, Connecticut, resident. If party prep takes a disastrous turn, order pizza or Chinese, or just heat up soup and make grilled cheese sandwiches.

CORNBREAD AND CHEDDAR PUDDING

2 3/4 cups cubed cornbread

2 tablespoons unsalted butter

1 large sweet onion, thinly sliced

3/4 cup shredded Cheddar cheese

1 teaspoon chopped fresh rosemary

1/2 teaspoon chopped fresh thyme

2 cups heavy cream

1/4 cup canned creamed corn

4 large eggs

1 teaspoon kosher salt

Ground black pepper, to taste

Preheat the oven to 350 degrees. Grease an 8-inch square baking dish and spread the cornbread cubes in it. Melt the butter in a large skillet over medium heat. Add the onion and cook until translucent, about 5 minutes. Reduce the heat to low and continue cooking, stirring often, until the onion caramelizes, about 30 minutes. Spread the onions, cheese, rosemary, and thyme over the cornbread.

In a large bowl, mix the cream, corn, eggs, salt, and pepper. Pour over the cornbread. Let stand for 10 minutes until the cornbread absorbs the liquid. Bake for 40 minutes, or until browned on top and set. Serve hot.

▶ Makes 6 to 8 servings

Whenever you make caramelized onions for a dish, go ahead and make more than you need and store the extras in the refrigerator. Add to grilled cheese, pizza, and other dishes that could benefit from a little sweetness.

To help Susan Josephs stay organized, and to make sure she doesn't forget anything for her meal, she types out a menu for the evening. If guests are bringing a dish to parties at her Boulder, Colorado, home, she also includes their dish and name, and prints out the menus to have at the table. "The menus have become so popular that guests expect them at my table and often take them home," she says.

2 cups water

1 cup white cornmeal

1 1/2 cups fresh or frozen corn kernels

1 medium onion, chopped

5 ounces chorizo or other sausage, chopped

5 large eggs, beaten

1 1/2 cups heavy cream

1/2 teaspoon coarse salt

CORN AND SAUSAGE PUDDING

Preheat the oven to 350 degrees. Grease a 3-quart baking dish. In a large saucepan, bring 2 cups of water to a boil. Whisk in the cornmeal and reduce the heat to low. Stir in corn and simmer until thick, 2 to 3 minutes. Remove from heat and let cool slightly.

Place the onion and chorizo in a medium skillet and stir over medium heat until the onion is tender, about 5 minutes. Add to the cornmeal mixture.

In a medium bowl, mix the eggs and cream. Stir into the cornmeal mixture and add the salt. Pour into the baking dish. Bake for 50 minutes to 1 hour, until set.

▶ Makes 8 to 10 servings

Mara Bovsun regularly fills her little apartment in New York City with guests for Thanksgiving. In search of a better cranberry sauce, she developed this potent fruit-and-nut sauce during a cooking phase when she was "improving" her recipes by adding alcohol.

One nice touch during the holidays is to simmer a pan of apple juice or pineapple juice with cloves and cinnamon sticks on the stove. It smells warm and welcoming and masks cooking smells that pervade the kitchen during intensive holiday cooking.

BOURBON PECAN CRANBERRY SAUCE

1 cup sugar

1/2 cup water

1 cup bourbon, divided

12 ounces fresh cranberries

1 cup coarsely chopped pecans

In a medium saucepan combine the sugar, water, and ½ cup bourbon. Bring to a boil over medium heat. Add the cranberries and return to a boil. Reduce the heat and cook, stirring every few minutes, for about 10 minutes until the cranberries start to pop.

Remove from the heat, let stand to cool for a while, then stir in the remaining ½ cup bourbon. Cover and refrigerate. Mix in the nuts just before serving.

▶ Makes about 3 1/2 cups, or 7 to 8 servings

Cranberry Freeze, from Lori Janaczek of Orlando, Florida, is one of those glorious mid-century Southern recipes that can be served as a salad or dessert. It's a natural at gatherings from Thanksgiving through New Year's. When your holiday crowd includes children, Janaczek recommends having an activity just for them. "Parents are happy and less stressed when their children are being entertained," she says. So break out some gingerbread men (bought or homemade) and give the kids icing, M&M's, raisins, small decorative candies, and sprinkles to decorate their cookies. The little artists will be amused for an hour or two before the meal, or afterward, when adults want to socialize.

1 cup sweetened condensed milk

2 (14-ounce) cans whole cranberry sauce

1 (8-ounce) container frozen whipped topping, thawed

1 (14-ounce) can crushed pineapple, drained

7 ounces miniature marshmallows (about two-thirds of a 10-ounce bag)

1 cup chopped pecans, optional

CRANBERRY FREEZE

In a large bowl combine the sweetened condensed milk, cranberry sauce, whipped topping, pineapple, marshmallows, and pecans, and mix well. Spoon into a large, shallow metal pan. Freeze until set. Thaw for 30 to 45 minutes prior to serving. (Do not let it thaw completely or it will become too watery.)

▶ Makes 12 servings

Note: If you're entertaining friends with kids, consider spooning this mixture into aluminum foil cupcake liners placed in muffin tins for easy serving and clean up.

Nutritional therapist Shane Kelly of Nashville, Tennessee, plans the feel and look of her décor as carefully as she plans the menu. She chooses cloth napkins over paper because "they feel better on the mouth." She likes her centerpieces to be "home-style, not structured" with a loose, organic feel. She might use flowers from her garden or a bunch of nandina branches loaded with berries, tied with a raffia ribbon. Her table also includes candles. Her Eggplant, Tomato, and Vidalia Onion Gratin is a knife-and-fork side dish, and its bold flavors go well with grilled steaks or shrimp over grits.

Coconut oil or butter for greasing the baking dish

1 large Vidalia onion, cut into 1/4-inch slices

1 medium eggplant, cut into 1/4-inch slices

1 large or 2 medium tomatoes, cut into 1/4-inch slices

2 tablespoons extra-virgin olive oil

1/2 teaspoon dried basil

1/2 teaspoon dried oregano

1/2 teaspoon sea salt

Ground black pepper, to taste

3/4 cup grated Parmesan cheese

EGGPLANT, TOMATO, AND VIDALIA ONION GRATIN

Position an oven rack in the upper third of the oven and preheat the oven to 450 degrees. Grease an oval gratin dish or a rectangular baking dish with coconut oil or butter.

Layer the onion, eggplant, and tomato slices in as many rows as the pan will hold. Drizzle with the olive oil. Sprinkle with the basil, oregano, salt, and pepper. Cover with the Parmesan cheese.

Bake, uncovered, for 35 to 40 minutes, until the top is light brown in places.

▶ Makes 6 servings

Making dishes in advance of your dinner party definitely simplifies hosting. This simple green bean recipe from Whit Trumbull of Durham, North Carolina, is ideal for preparing a day or so ahead and works well as part of a buffet spread. Use a slow cooker as a warmer for buffet service. The low setting keeps green beans, dips, stews, and even hot punch at the right temperature so you don't have to keep checking on your dish.

FARM-STYLE GREEN BEANS

4 slices thick bacon, chopped

1 pound green beans, trimmed, cut into 2-inch pieces (about 4 cups)

2 medium onions, diced

3 medium tomatoes, peeled, chopped (about 2 cups)

1/4 cup water

1 teaspoon salt

Dash of ground black pepper

Fry the bacon in a skillet over medium heat until crisp, about 10 minutes . Remove the bacon crumbles from the pan and drain on paper towels. Reserve 3 tablespoons of the bacon drippings.

In a medium saucepan combine the beans, onions, tomatoes, water, salt, and pepper. Bring to a boil over medium-high heat. Reduce the heat to low, cover, and simmer until the beans are tender, 20 to 25 minutes. Stir in the reserved bacon drippings. Season to taste. Serve topped with the crumbled bacon.

▶ Makes 8 servings

Although Martha Hopkins occasionally throws a big party at her Austin, Texas, home, her preference is to entertain just one other couple for dinner. The conversation is more sustained and never cut off by mingling. For the same reason, she says, "It's important to me that I'm not cooking while they're here. I'm an extrovert, but cooking is one thing I like doing by myself." A small dinner is the right occasion for foods like split and grilled whole chicken and Flash-Cooked Okra, which would be difficult to cook for bigger groups. "Prepare for your life to change," she says of her okra recipe.

FLASH-COOKED OKRA

1 pound okra

2 tablespoons lard or olive oil for frying

Salt and ground black pepper, to taste

Rinse the okra in cold water. Trim the stem ends and discard. Slice each pod in half lengthwise.

Heat a cast-iron skillet over medium-high heat. When it's hot, add the lard. Add the okra to the pan in batches, forming a single layer. Sprinkle with the salt and pepper.

Cook the okra without stirring for 3 to 4 minutes. Check a piece or two—they should be nicely browned, almost charred. Turn the okra and let them cook another few minutes until nicely browned all over. Serve immediately.

▶ Makes 4 servings

Note: Choose the smaller pods when you're buying okra. Some varieties taste just fine when they're large, but others become tough and stringy. If you're not sure which variety you're working with, err on the side of smaller pods.

Think about it—if the mashed potatoes are already made, you can spend your last-minute prep time on other dishes, or use the spare minutes to decorate, or just relax a few minutes. Pat Goodyear of Baltimore, Maryland, got this recipe from a friend, and says, "It's a great one to have for entertaining, as having to mash potatoes at the last minute can be a real test of a cook's organizational skills. This method allows for a smooth presentation without all of the last-minute fuss." Amen and pass the potatoes!

3 pounds potatoes, peeled and cut into medium cubes

2 1/2 teaspoons salt, divided

1 1/2 cups sour cream

5 tablespoons butter, divided

1/4 teaspoon ground black pepper

1/4 cup bread crumbs

MAKE-AHEAD MASHED POTATOES

Place the potatoes in a large pot and cover with water. Add 1 teaspoon of the salt. Cook over medium-high heat until tender, 10 to 15 minutes. While the potatoes are boiling, grease a 9 x 13-inch baking dish and set aside.

Drain the potatoes and return to the pot. Add the sour cream and 4 tablespoons of the butter. Mash with a potato masher or electric hand mixer until fluffy and well blended. Spoon into the baking dish, cover, and refrigerate for up to 2 days.

Preheat the oven to 325 degrees. Let the potatoes sit at room temperature for 30 minutes. Bake, covered, for 1 hour.

Melt the remaining 1 tablespoon butter. Combine with the remaining 1 ½ teaspoons of salt, pepper, and bread crumbs. Sprinkle over the potatoes. Return to the oven and bake about 10 minutes, until the crumbs are nicely browned.

▶ Makes 10 to 12 servings

Late winter is a good time for a small dinner or potluck. Cabin fever is rampant, and any invitation to leave the house is likely to be welcome, as are warm, comforting foods. Heather Kokubun of Ponca City, Oklahoma, calls this casserole "one of the most delicious tater tot recipes" she's ever eaten. Serve it as a side dish, or add a pound of browned ground beef to make it an entrée at a casual family gathering.

CHEDDAR TATERS

Preheat the oven to 350 degrees. Grease a 9 x 13-inch baking dish. Combine the soup, milk, sour cream, butter, garlic powder, onion powder, tater tots, and cheese in a medium bowl and mix well. Spread the mixture into the pan. Bake for 25 minutes. Sprinkle the potato chips on top and bake for 5 minutes longer.

▶ Makes 6 to 8 servings

1 (8-ounce) can cream of chicken soup

1 (12-ounce) can evaporated milk

1 cup sour cream

1/2 cup (1 stick) melted butter

1 teaspoon garlic powder

1 teaspoon onion powder

1 (32-ounce) package frozen tater tots

1 1/2 cups shredded Cheddar cheese

1 cup crushed potato chips, optional

Take a cue from Kathryn Tortorici's hosting style and celebrate the small victories of friends and family as well as the big ones. "Celebrating little things in life can be as enormous as celebrating the bigger things we are accustomed to celebrating, such as birthdays, team victories, or promotions," she says. For instance, she serves a special meal when one of her children earns an A in school. So naturally the dinner theme at her family's Birmingham, Alabama, home was "Hey Hey! Who Got an A?" Any small triumph is worthy of a special meal to acknowledge hard work and effort. It doesn't have to be fancy—buy an entrée and make the sides. A pat on the back and a good meal are all it takes to make a loved one feel recognized and encouraged.

4 large baking potatoes, scrubbed

1/4 cup (1/2 stick) butter, plus more for greasing the baking dish

2 green onions, sliced

8 ounces light sour cream

Salt and ground black pepper, to taste

BAKED SOUR CREAM AND GREEN ONION MASHED POTATOES

Place the potatoes in a large pot. Cover with water and bring to a boil over medium-high heat. Cook until tender, 10 to 15 minutes. Drain and peel. Mash the potatoes in a large bowl.

Preheat the oven to 350 degrees. Grease a 2-quart baking dish with butter. Heat ¼ cup of the butter in a small skillet over medium-high heat. Add the onions and cook and stir until tender, about 10 minutes. Add the onions to the potatoes. Add the sour cream, salt, and pepper, and mix well. Spread the mixture in the baking dish. Bake for 30 minutes.

▶ Makes 6 servings

Sweet potato casserole has won plenty of hearts outside the South. Kristen Solomon, of Boulder, Colorado, and her daughter Sophia say their family prepares their dessert-like version most often for Thanksgiving. "We start making it about two weeks before Thanksgiving to 'test it out' again," says Solomon, but it's so delicious they have been known to make it other times, and also to eat it cold, straight from the refrigerator.

When you're organizing a big Thanksgiving crowd, consider asking your guests to bring specific dishes, such as the relish tray, dressing, salad, green beans, broccoli with cheese sauce, creamed onions, and pumpkin pie. Some hosts provide recipes, while others let each cook pick. Either way, you won't end up with two of some dishes and none of others.

NANA KINNEY'S SWEET POTATO CASSEROLE

Preheat the oven to 350 degrees. Grease a shallow 1 ½-quart baking dish.

To make the sweet potatoes place the potatoes in a large mixing bowl. Add the sugar, eggs, milk, and butter, and beat with an electric mixer on medium speed until no lumps remain. Do not overbeat or the mixture will become soupy. Pour into the baking dish.

To make the topping, in a medium bowl combine the brown sugar, flour, coconut (if using), and butter. Mix well with a fork. Sprinkle evenly over the sweet potato mixture. Bake for 25 to 30 minutes. Serve hot or cold.

▶ Makes 8 servings

SWEET POTATOES

3 cups mashed, cooked sweet potatoes

1/2 cup sugar

2 large eggs, beaten

5 tablespoons milk

1/3 cup melted butter

TOPPING

1 cup firmly packed brown sugar

1/3 cup all-purpose flour

1 cup shredded sweetened coconut, optional

1/3 cup melted butter

Jessica Pendergrass of Louisville, Kentucky, says that listening and engaging with guests is what she likes about hosting. "Don't worry about the perfection of the evening. People are happy to be there with you, eating your good food and enjoying the company," she says. And it's true—just about everyone is flattered by an invitation and grateful for company, food, and someone else cleaning up afterward. This recipe was developed for urbansacredgarden.com, a blog where she stores ideas about food, spirituality, and mindful eating.

LEMON MISO SWEET POTATOES

Preheat the oven to 400 degrees. In a large bowl whisk together the miso, rice vinegar, olive oil, soy sauce, and lemon peel and juice. Add the sweet potatoes and leek, and toss to coat.

Spread the mixture on a rimmed baking sheet. Season with the salt and pepper. Roast for about 40 minutes or until the potatoes are soft when pierced with a fork. Serve warm.

▶ Makes 4 to 5 servings

Note: You can find miso in the refrigerated section of the produce department near other Asian foods.

1/4 cup white miso

1/4 cup rice vinegar

3 tablespoons olive oil

3 tablespoons soy sauce or tamari

Finely grated peel and juice of 1 lemon

2 large sweet potatoes or yams, cut into bite-size cubes

1/2 cup coarsely chopped leek (white and light green parts only) or yellow onion

Sea salt and ground black pepper, to taste

Mary Anne Parker and her family open their Harrisburg, Arkansas, homestead to guests for wine tastings, dinners, weddings, and other events. The home is in a reconstructed village on property her family has owned for four generations. Parker's menus feature approachable foods, and she genuinely hopes guests will ask for her recipes. "I always try to serve dishes that people will enjoy and can go home and make," she says. "There is no point in serving a swanky but not replicable menu in the South. The point is for everyone to enjoy, not to feel uptight. The ultimate compliment for the hostess is when guests beg for the recipes so they can serve them at their own parties."

3 or 4 large sweet potatoes, rinsed

1 (8-ounce) package cream cheese, softened

1 cup firmly packed brown sugar

1 teaspoon vanilla extract

1/4 cup (1/2 stick) butter, melted, plus more for greasing the baking pan

1/4 cup walnuts

Marshmallows, optional

TWICE-BAKED SWEET POTATOES

Preheat the oven to 425 degrees. Wrap the sweet potatoes in aluminum foil and place them on a baking sheet. Bake the potatoes for 30 minutes, or until tender. Let cool slightly. Slice the potatoes lengthwise and scoop out the pulp. Discard the skins.

Combine the warm sweet potatoes, cream cheese, brown sugar, vanilla, and butter in a medium bowl and mix well with a spatula. Stir in the walnuts. Grease a shallow 2-quart baking dish. Spoon the mixture into the pan. Bake for 15 to 20 minutes. If using, arrange the marshmallows over the top and bake for 5 minutes longer.

▶ Makes 8 to 10 servings

Stephanie Gore's approach to cooking and serving is to plan a menu around a recipe you have used before, a "star" dish. "It should be something you've made before that's reliable and that you don't have to worry about it turning out well. Then you can experiment with side dishes, or buy a dessert, or ask people to bring other dishes. But you know you have that one dish to anchor the evening," she says. These sweet potatoes are a star at Gore's Nashville, Tennessee, home.

3 pounds medium sweet potatoes

2 cups heavy cream

4 tablespoons butter

2 cloves garlic, minced

1 tablespoon minced fresh Italian parsley

1 tablespoon minced fresh rosemary

1 tablespoon minced fresh sage

1 tablespoon minced fresh thyme

1 1/2 teaspoons fine sea salt

3/4 teaspoon ground black pepper

1 large yellow or sweet onion, cut into thin rounds

1 or 2 diced jalapeño peppers, seeds removed

1 1/4 cups coarsely grated Gruyère cheese

HERBED SCALLOPED SWEET POTATO GRATIN

Fill a large bowl with cold water. Working with one sweet potato at a time, peel, then cut into 1/8-inch rounds and place in the water to prevent browning.

Combine the cream, butter, and garlic in a medium saucepan and bring to a simmer over medium-low heat. Remove the pan from the heat.

Combine the parsley, rosemary, sage, and thyme in a small bowl. Combine the salt and pepper in another small bowl.

Preheat the oven to 400 degrees. Grease a 9 x 13-inch baking dish. Drain the sweet potatoes and pat dry. Arrange half of the potatoes in an even layer in the baking pan. Top with half of the onion. Sprinkle with half of the salt mixture, then half of the herb mixture and half of the jalapeños. Sprinkle with half of the cheese. Repeat with the remaining potatoes, onion, salt mixture, herb mixture, jalapeños, and cheese.

Pour the cream mixture over the vegetables, pressing lightly to submerge the potato mixture as much as possible.

Cover the dish tightly with aluminum foil. Bake for 30 minutes. Remove the foil and bake about 25 minutes longer, until the top is golden and most of the liquid is absorbed. Let stand 10 minutes before serving.

▶ Makes 8 to 10 servings

Note: You can prepare the gratin for baking up to 6 hours ahead.

Once you get an all-purpose recipe, you use it and use it and use it. Spinach Isabel is always on the Christmas Eve buffet at Peggy Sweeney McDonald's family gathering in New Orleans, Louisiana, along with the family's traditional Maque Choux (page 175). Don't feel bound by tradition to serve turkey and ham during the holidays—serve what your crowd enjoys. Rib roast and crown roast of pork are just as celebratory and sure to make a memorable impression. And there's absolutely nothing wrong with lasagna or even red and green Christmas tamales.

SPINACH ISABEL

Cook the spinach according to the package directions. Drain, reserving ½ cup of the cooking liquid.

Melt the butter in a medium saucepan over low heat. Add the flour and stir until blended and smooth. Add the onion and cook until soft but not brown. Add the milk and the reserved spinach cooking liquid, stirring constantly to prevent lumps. Cook, stirring, until smooth and thick. Add the pepper, celery salt, garlic salt, salt, Worcestershire sauce, cayenne pepper, and cheese. Heat, stirring, until the cheese melts. Combine the sauce with the cooked spinach.

Pour the mixture into a 2-quart baking dish. Top with the buttered bread crumbs. Refrigerate for at least 8 hours.

Remove the casserole from the refrigerator and let it come to room temperature. Preheat the oven to 350 degrees. Bake the casserole for 25 to 30 minutes, until warm and bubbly.

▶ Makes 8 servings

Notes: The recipe can be doubled. The whole dish can be made ahead of time and frozen. Spinach Isabel can also be served as a dip with crackers.

2 (10-ounce) packages frozen chopped spinach

4 tablespoons butter

2 tablespoons all-purpose flour

2 tablespoons chopped onion

1/2 cup evaporated milk

1/2 teaspoon ground black pepper

3/4 teaspoon celery salt

3/4 teaspoon garlic salt

Salt, to taste

1 teaspoon Worcestershire sauce

Cayenne pepper or hot pepper sauce, to taste

6 ounces Mexican processed cheese loaf, cut into small pieces

1 cup buttered bread crumbs

Shane Kelly, a Nashville, Tennessee, nutritional therapist, goes to great lengths to create meals that make people feel nourished as well as pampered. "I learned in culinary school to create balance and a variety of salty, sour, bitter, sweet, and spicy. I look at the colors on the plate, the variety of fats. I always serve two vegetables when I'm serving folks, and almost always one of those vegetables will be raw," she says. She avoids sweet drinks ("they can leave people feeling awful") and offers cocktails made from very pure, high-quality liquor, unsweetened juice, lime, and sparkling water. "The biggest compliment I get, whether the next day or right after the meal, is a guest saying, 'I feel really good after eating that meal,'" she says.

ROSEMARY GRILLED SQUASH

2 large yellow squash

1 teaspoon minced fresh rosemary

1 teaspoon salt

1/4 teaspoon ground black pepper

1 to 2 tablespoons extra-virgin olive oil

Cut the squash lengthwise or on the diagonal into thick slices. Combine the squash with the rosemary, salt, pepper, and olive oil in a large bowl. Toss with your hands until the squash is well coated.

Prepare a grill to high heat. Grill the squash directly on the grate or on a grill tray until the pieces have char marks, 2 to 3 minutes. Turn and grill the other side.

Serve the squash warm or at room temperature. You also can use them to top a salad or fold into omelets.

▶ Makes 4 servings

The airy height of a soufflé is a special dish for dinner guests at Deanna Larson's Nashville, Tennessee, home. Everyone has a great story they tell at parties, and those moments make social gatherings memorable. To give your party some extra "flavor," ask guests in advance to prepare a brief story, either their best party story, or one based on a question or theme. A good story session among friends is hard to beat for entertainment.

2 tablespoons unsalted butter

1 cup coarse, soft bread crumbs

2 pounds yellow crookneck squash, sliced

1 medium onion, chopped

1 teaspoon salt

1 cup milk

2 large eggs, lightly beaten

3 tablespoons melted butter

3 tablespoons all-purpose flour

2 cups shredded Cheddar cheese

2 teaspoons fresh thyme

Salt and pepper to taste

SUMMER SQUASH SOUFFLÉ

Preheat the oven to 350 degrees. Grease a 1 ½-quart baking dish. Melt the butter in a small skillet over medium-low heat. When the butter is foamy, stir in the bread crumbs. Cook, stirring, until the crumbs are evenly crisp and golden brown.

Combine the squash, onion, and salt in a large saucepan. Cover with water and bring to a boil. Reduce the heat to low and simmer until the vegetables are tender, 15 to 20 minutes. Drain and mash well. Stir in the milk, eggs, melted butter, flour, cheese, and thyme. Add the salt and pepper, to taste. Spoon into the baking dish and bake for about 30 minutes. Top with the buttered bread crumbs and bake for about 10 minutes longer, until browned.

▶ Makes 4 servings

Patricia Hall, a native of Hendersonville, Tennessee, depends on a recipe that fills multiple roles for feeding guests. Zucchini Parmesan Bake can be a meatless entrée, a side dish, or an appetizer or plated first course. It's safe at room temperature for hours and is good hot or warm. Hall's husband, Andrew, is a serious wine hobbyist, seeking out distinctive bottles for guests and making wonderful pairings with food. He recommends serving an Italian red such as Chianti or Sangiovese with Zucchini Parmesan Bake. The bold red complements and stands up to the strong Parmesan.

ZUCCHINI PARMESAN BAKE

2 medium zucchini

2 medium yellow squash

4 tablespoons olive oil, divided

Salt and pepper, to taste

2 medium tomatoes, cut into 1/4–inch slices

2 cups shredded mozzarella

2 cups grated Parmesan

Slice the zucchini and squash into ¼-inch thick rounds and place into separate bowls. Add 1 tablespoon of olive oil to each bowl. Season with salt and pepper and toss.

Preheat the oven to 375 degrees. Coat the bottom of a 9 x 11-inch glass baking dish with the remaining 2 tablespoons olive oil. Arrange the zucchini, then tomatoes, then yellow squash in layers. Add a layer of the mozzarella. Repeat the layers. Spread the Parmesan on top. Bake for 25 to 35 minutes.

▶ Makes 6 to 8 servings

Note: To serve as an appetizer, omit the tomato and bake a little longer, until the top is browned and crunchy. Serve with a firm, flavorful bread such as focaccia.

This popular seafood salad originated in the 1950s at Bayley's Steak House in south Alabama. Shelly Collins of Durham, North Carolina, was introduced to it at the home of Beth Moore in Wolf Bay, Alabama. "I treasured my time in Beth's kitchen," says Collins. "I was enamored with her ability to transform the food she was preparing into something special. I enjoyed watching her move about the kitchen like she was painting a masterpiece for all of us to enjoy." For 45 years, Moore has served West Indies Salad as a starter for a seafood meal. She often plates it in small crab or seafood motif bowls with a cocktail fork. "In cooking and in life, little touches can make things special. I collect little serving dishes to use at dinner parties," says Collins. "Beth's style of being a hostess of a party certainly inspired me to pay attention to all the little details."

1 medium onion (preferably Vidalia), finely chopped

1 pound fresh jumbo lump crabmeat

Sea salt and ground black pepper, to taste

1/2 cup canola oil

6 tablespoons cider vinegar

1/4 cup ice water

Lettuce leaves and butter crackers for serving, optional

WEST INDIES SALAD

Spread half of the onion over the bottom of a serving bowl. Check the crabmeat and pick out any bits of shell or cartilage. Spread the crabmeat over the onion. Top with the remaining onion and sprinkle with the salt and pepper.

Pour the oil, vinegar, and ice water in that order over the crabmeat. Cover and let marinate in the refrigerator for at least 12 hours. Toss lightly before serving in small individual bowls or on lettuce leaves accompanied by butter crackers.

▶ Makes 4 servings

Personal chef Aly Armistead Greer of Nashville, Tennessee, learned much about entertaining from her grandmother. "My grandmother often entertained formally and had the most beautiful parties that I always wanted to be a part of. All of the fancy dishes and champagne were so glamorous to me and seemed to be out of another time. Although I don't think I'll ever entertain on such a grandiose scale as she did, she had such grace and made every guest feel so special. I always try to be as kind as she was. She took such care in who she invited to her parties. She made sure her dinner guests were seated with people they would enjoy talking to and that every lady had a nice dinner partner," she says.

RAW SUMMER SQUASH SALAD

Use a vegetable peeler to shave the squash and zucchini into ribbons. Put the ribbons in a serving bowl. Add the shallots, Parmesan, mint, lemon juice, olive oil, pepper, salt, and pecans. Toss to combine. Serve immediately.

▶ Makes 6 to 8 servings

2 medium yellow crookneck squash

2 medium zucchini

2 shallots, minced

1/2 cup grated Parmesan

15 fresh mint leaves, julienned

Juice of 2 lemons

2 tablespoons extra-virgin olive oil

Generous pinch of red pepper

Salt, to taste

1/2 cup chopped toasted pecans

Event planner Natalie Dietz Raines of Nashville has the mind of a host and the organizing skills to execute a party. Recipes that can fill multiple roles are a big help. "Sometimes I toss this White Bean Salad with greens and serve it as a salad course. Other times I like it without greens on a buffet or as a side to grilled meats, sandwiches, etc."

Raines recommends starting indoor parties with the thermostat set to an almost chilly temperature, particularly if you're expecting a lot of people. "Indoor parties get hotter than you think they will," she says. Better to start off cool than try to fix the problem once guests are overheated.

1/4 cup extra-virgin olive oil

1/4 cup white or red wine vinegar

1/2 teaspoon garlic powder

2 shallots, minced

2 to 3 tablespoons whole-grain mustard

2 teaspoons Dijon-style mustard

2 (15-ounce) cans white beans, rinsed, drained, or 4 cups cooked white beans

3 carrots, peeled and sliced 1/8 inch thick

1 orange or yellow bell pepper, diced

3 or 4 hearts of palm, diced

Salt and ground black pepper, to taste

5 ounces baby spinach or other baby greens for serving, optional

WHITE BEAN SALAD

In a large serving bowl whisk together the oil, vinegar, garlic powder, shallots, whole-grain mustard, and Dijon-style mustard. Add the beans, carrots, bell pepper, and hearts of palm. Stir to coat the vegetables with the dressing. Season with the salt and pepper. Let stand for at least 30 minutes before serving. Serve over spinach or baby greens, if using.

▶ Makes 6 servings

Susan Josephs of Boulder, Colorado, entertains often, so she finds it helpful to keep track of guests and menus. "I save all the menus on my computer, so I have a record of what I've served to whom and who attended, so I don't repeat the same meal for guests," she says.

KALE PESTO SALAD

1 large bunch kale, stemmed, chopped

Juice of 1 lemon

1 cup packed fresh basil leaves

1/2 cup packed fresh mint leaves

1 cup pine nuts

1 tablespoon extra-virgin olive oil, or more to taste

1/2 to 1 cup grated Parmesan or pecorino cheese

Sea salt, to taste

Stir together the kale and lemon juice in a serving bowl. Refrigerate for 1 hour.

In a blender combine the basil, mint, pine nuts, and olive oil. Blend until the herbs are finely chopped, adding more oil, if needed.

Stir the herb mixture into the kale. The mixture will be thick, so keep stirring until the kale is well coated. Add the cheese and salt, and mix well.

▶ Makes 6 to 8 servings

Note: To serve as an hors d'oeuvre, spoon the kale mixture into endive leaves. Arrange the leaves on a tray or platter.

Donya Mullins of Greensboro, North Carolina, found a clever way to help guests keep up with their wine glasses—etching them with numerals. A dozen wine glasses from a discount department store, an etch kit from a craft store, and one hour later, each glass wore a unique number. Etched glasses or jars make sweet party favors, too, for wedding or reunion parties. Take in some how-to Internet posts and videos on etching to take out some of the trial and error of learning the skill, for better results and fewer mistakes.

COUSCOUS SALAD WITH FRESH PEACHES AND SUGAR SNAPS

1 1/4 cups water

1 cup couscous

2 tablespoons olive oil

2 teaspoons salt, or to taste

1 cup fresh sugar snap peas

2 tablespoons fresh lime juice

1 1/2 tablespoons extra-virgin olive oil

Salt to taste

1 1/2 cups chopped fresh peaches

1/4 cup shelled pistachios

3 tablespoons torn or julienned basil

Bring the water to a boil in a medium saucepan. Stir in the couscous, oil, and salt. Remove the pan from the heat, cover, and let stand for 5 minutes.

Place the peas in a medium saucepan. Cover with water. Bring to a boil over medium-high heat, reduce the heat to low, and simmer until the peas turn bright green. Remove the peas to a bowl of ice water to cool. Drain.

Combine the lime juice, olive oil, and salt in a jar with a tight-fitting lid. Shake to blend. (Or combine in a bowl with a whisk.)

Using a fork fluff the couscous and place in a large bowl. Add the peaches, peas, and pistachios. Drizzle with the dressing. Add the basil and toss to combine. Taste for seasoning and add more salt if needed. This salad is best served at room temperature but can be chilled.

▶ Makes 6 to 8 servings

Perre Coleman Magness of Memphis, Tennessee, likes an "interactive" meal where guests assemble a personal serving. One idea is a pizza party, where she provides dough rounds, sauce, cheese, and toppings. "Roll out the dough, choose the toppings, assemble the pizza, and watch while they bake," she says. "It's fun for kids and grownups alike. Clear off the counter and let everyone work on their creation." Then the host just needs to provide a side dish or salad such as this Purple Hull Pea Salad. Other ideas for DIY party food: sushi rolling, a hot dog bar with all the fixings, and a sundae bar with whipped cream, syrups, sprinkles, nuts, and crushed cookies.

PURPLE HULL PEA SALAD WITH BACON VINAIGRETTE

SALAD

2 pounds fresh purple hull peas

2 cups chicken broth

Water

1 pound bacon

2 fresh pimento (cherry) peppers

4 green onions

BACON VINAIGRETTE

1/4 cup bacon drippings

1/2 cup vegetable oil

1/4 cup cider vinegar

1 tablespoon sorghum or dark honey

1 teaspoon hot pepper sauce, or to taste

Salt and ground black pepper, to taste

To clean the peas, combine them with water to cover in a large bowl. Let the peas settle, then remove any that float. Pick out and discard debris and bad peas. Use a slotted spoon to remove them to a large pan, leaving behind any debris.

Add the chicken broth and enough fresh water to cover by 1 inch. Bring to a boil over medium-high heat, skimming off any scum that rises. Reduce the heat to low and simmer until just tender, about 30 minutes. (For a cold pea salad, you want a little bite to the peas, so don't let them get mushy.) Drain the peas in a colander, rinse well, and drain again. Transfer the peas to a large bowl and refrigerate until chilled.

Fry the bacon in a large skillet over medium-high heat until crisp. Drain on paper towels. Set aside 1/4 cup of the drippings to cool for the dressing, but don't let it solidify. Dice the bacon.

Remove the seeds and ribs from the

pimento peppers. Dice the peppers and add to the peas. Dice the white part and some of the green part of the green onions. Add to the peas and mix well.

For the vinaigrette, combine the bacon drippings, oil, vinegar, sorghum, hot pepper sauce, salt, and black pepper in a jar with a tight-fitting lid. Shake vigorously to blend.

Pour some of the dressing over the peas and stir to coat. You may not want to use all the dressing. Taste the salad and add salt if needed. Refrigerate until ready to serve. Toss the crumbled bacon into the salad right before serving. The salad (without the bacon) will keep for up to 2 days, covered and refrigerated.

▶ **Makes 1 cup dressing. Salad makes 8 to 10 servings.**

Kathryn Mitchell Johnson of Nashville, Tennessee, creates her "company" dishes the way her mother did—by experimenting, which sometimes yields a wonderful discovery, like Grilled Asparagus and Peach Salad. It came about when she was searching for a potluck dish just as the last of the asparagus season met the first of peach season. Bring your best to a potluck dinner, whether your own or someone else's, with dishes that offer a little more—more color, more elaborate prep, more flavors. "I love taking yummy vegetable dishes to potlucks because there never seem to be enough," Johnson says. "This one is so colorful and puts a spotlight on what's in season. It really stands out."

GRILLED ASPARAGUS AND PEACH SALAD

Heat an outdoor grill. Oil the grill racks. Place the asparagus and peach halves on the grill rack and cook until they are tender and have char marks.

In a small saucepan combine the vinegar, brown sugar, salt, and pepper. Bring to a boil over medium-high heat, then reduce the heat to low and simmer until the mixture begins to thicken, 20 to 30 minutes.

Cut the peaches and asparagus into manageable-size pieces and arrange on a platter. Sprinkle with chèvre and basil. Drizzle with the balsamic syrup.

▶ Makes 4 to 6 servings

1 pound asparagus

3 peaches, peeled, pitted, and cut into halves

1/2 cup balsamic vinegar

1 teaspoon brown sugar

Pinch of salt

Ground black pepper, to taste

1 cup chèvre, crumbled, or to taste

Fresh basil leaves, chopped

There are a lot of advantages to including an all-ages activity in a casual gathering of families. It's an ice-breaker for guests who aren't well acquainted, and it focuses the high energy of children. For instance, dessert at Michelle Rosen's gatherings at her Nashville, Tennessee, home is sometimes a session of do-it-yourself s'mores around the family's backyard firepit. "I always keep a stash of crackers, marshmallows, and chocolate bars, and kids and adults love making their own s'mores," she says. S'mores are as much fun to make as to eat—and experimentation is encouraged. "When I've run out of graham crackers, we've used gingersnaps and other cookies, which adds a nice twist."

4 cups peeled, seeded, cubed watermelon

1 small jicama, peeled and cut into 1/2-inch cubes

Finely grated peel and juice of 1 lime

1/3 cup chopped fresh mint

2 tablespoons balsamic vinegar

WATERMELON JICAMA SALAD

Combine the watermelon and jicama in a large bowl. Add the lime peel and juice, mint, and vinegar. Toss to combine. Refrigerate until chilled. Serve cold.

▶ Makes 6 to 8 servings

Note: Chopped or torn basil and cilantro are excellent additions to this cool, summery salad. You can make this recipe ahead, just don't add the herbs until right before you're ready to serve.

A busy schedule requires a little creativity in party planning. Ophelia Paine will always remember a particular dinner party at her home in Nashville, Tennessee, as the night she ordered pizza. "Friday night was the only time we could get together with some friends," she says. "I was working full-time and exhausted. So I ordered pizza from two pizza places and just made a big salad and we compared the pizzas. It wasn't much of a mess, and everyone thought it was a kick." That night confirmed what years of entertaining have taught Paine: "It's more about getting together with friends than what is served. People will remember the conversation more than the meal."

WATERMELON, FETA, AND CUCUMBER SALAD

Combine the watermelon, cucumber, feta, vinegar, and mint in a bowl. Toss to combine. Refrigerate for at least 1 hour, stirring occasionally.

▶ Makes 6 to 8 servings

3 cups cubed watermelon, seeded and drained

1/2 cucumber, partially peeled, chopped

2 tablespoons crumbled feta cheese

2 tablespoons champagne or rice vinegar

10 to 15 fresh mint leaves, julienned

Enid Johnson of Greenacres, Florida, says that for any type of gathering, but especially large ones, she creates the menu two to three weeks in advance. "And once you've set it, stick to it," she says. "Don't change your plans midway or too close to the date because it will only cause you grief of the worst kind." This Southern take on rice pilaf is especially useful if you entertain vegetarians; just substitute vegetable broth for the chicken broth.

ORANGE-PECAN WILD RICE

1 cup wild rice

5 1/2 cups chicken broth

1 cup pecan halves

1 cup golden raisins

Finely grated peel of 1 large orange

1/2 cup fresh orange juice

1/4 cup chopped fresh mint

4 green onions, thinly sliced

1/4 cup extra-virgin olive oil

1 1/2 teaspoons salt

Ground black pepper, to taste

Put the rice in a strainer and rinse under cold water. Transfer the rice to a medium saucepan and add the chicken broth. Bring to a boil over high heat, reduce the heat to low, and simmer, uncovered, for 45 minutes, checking after 30 minutes to make sure the rice doesn't get too soft.

Line a colander with a clean, thin kitchen towel and pour in the rice to drain.

Transfer the rice to a large bowl. Add the pecans, raisins, orange peel, orange juice, mint, green onions, olive oil, salt, and pepper. Toss gently to combine. Adjust the seasonings to taste. Let stand for about 2 hours. Serve at room temperature.

▶ Makes 6 servings

Food with a story, like Red Rice, feeds both the body and the curious mind. Red Rice can be claimed by either Savannah, Georgia, or coastal South Carolina—both are in the Lowcountry, the traditional rice-growing region of the South. The dish's story goes back further, though—Red Rice strongly resembles rice preparations from West Africa. This recipe is from Stephanie Tyson of Winston-Salem, North Carolina, who runs Sweet Potatoes Café with her partner, Vivián Joiner. Their mission is to bring people together over food. Their hosting style is to extend to guests in their restaurant dining room the same warmth and hospitality they would in their home dining room.

RED RICE

Cook the bacon in a Dutch oven over medium heat until crisp, about 10 minutes. Drain the bacon on paper towels and crumble.

Add the oil to the pan. Add the onion, celery, and pepper, and cook over medium heat until tender, 3 to 4 minutes. Add the sausage and cook for 2 minutes longer.

Add the Creole seasoning, nutmeg, tomato sauce, and water. Bring to a boil. Add the rice and cover. Reduce the heat to low, and simmer until the rice is tender and all the liquid has been absorbed, about 25 minutes. Let stand, covered, for 10 minutes. Remove the lid and stir in the bacon and green onions.

▶ Makes 6 to 8 servings

2 slices bacon

2 tablespoons vegetable oil

1/2 cup diced onion

1/4 cup diced celery

1/4 cup diced green bell pepper

1/2 cup diced smoked sausage

1 teaspoon Creole seasoning blend or blackening spice

Pinch of nutmeg

6 ounces tomato sauce

3 cups water

2 cups rice

2 green onions, green part only, sliced

Martha Hopkins doesn't typically throw big parties, but for her 40th birthday, she invited "people from everywhere" and held a Memphis-style barbecue bash at her Austin, Texas, home. "If you throw a party this big, you need help," she says. For the fried chicken, she hired a neighbor who makes excellent fried chicken. For party help, she's had good luck hiring restaurant workers and students from Craigslist. Her helper arrived several hours early to help finish the prep and then set out all the food. The extra hands freed up Hopkins for an hour to attend to other last-minute details.

MANCHEGO THYME MAC AND CHEESE

2 cups shredded sharp white Cheddar cheese

1 cup grated Parmigiano-Reggiano cheese

1 cup grated Manchego cheese

1 pound uncooked macaroni pasta

3 tablespoons minced fresh parsley

1 tablespoon minced fresh thyme

1 tablespoon minced chives

3 1/2 cups whole milk

1 cup heavy cream

1/2 cup (1 stick), plus 1 tablespoon, butter, divided, plus more for greasing the pan

6 tablespoons all-purpose flour

1/4 teaspoon cayenne pepper, or to taste

Pinch of freshly grated nutmeg

2 teaspoons dry mustard

Dash of Tabasco sauce

Dash of Worcestershire sauce

Salt and ground black pepper, to taste

1 cup fresh bread crumbs

Preheat the oven to 350 degrees. Lightly butter a deep 3 ½-quart baking dish.

In small bowl, combine the Cheddar, Parmigiano-Reggiano, and Manchego cheeses.

Bring a large pot of salted water to a boil over high heat and cook the macaroni until barely al dente. (It's okay if the pasta seems undercooked. It will absorb the sauce during baking.) Drain and place in a large bowl. Add

3 ½ cups of the cheese mixture, reserving ½ cup for topping the casserole. Add the parsley, thyme, and chives, and mix well.

Combine the milk and heavy cream in a saucepan. Bring to a simmer over medium-high heat. Keep warm but don't boil.

Meanwhile, melt the ½ cup butter in a large saucepan over medium heat until foamy. Whisk in the flour and cook, stirring, for 1 to

2 minutes. Whisk in the cayenne, nutmeg, and mustard. Cook until fragrant and slightly darker in color, about 1 minute. Whisk in the hot milk mixture all at once. Add the Tabasco, Worcestershire sauce, salt, and pepper, and mix well.

Increase the heat if needed to bring the sauce to a gentle bubble. Cook, stirring, until the sauce thickens enough to coat the back of a spoon, about 3 minutes. Taste and adjust the seasonings as necessary.

Pour the sauce over the macaroni mixture and stir gently to combine. Pour into the buttered baking dish.

Combine the bread crumbs with the remaining 1 tablespoon butter and a generous amount of ground pepper. Add the reserved ½ cup cheese. Sprinkle the mixture over the macaroni. Bake in the middle of the oven for 30 minutes, or until the macaroni is bubbling and the crumbs are golden brown.

▶ Makes 8 servings

Learn to relax so dinner guests can relax. That's the advice of Deanna Larson of Nashville, Tennessee. "That could mean an easier one-pot meal, setting the table buffet-style, or letting guests pour their own drinks, get their own seconds, or help with the cleanup, so they feel more involved and comfortable," she says.

COLLARDS WITH CITRUS AND CRANBERRIES

Tear the collards into small pieces. Pour the water in a large pot and bring to a boil over high heat. Add 1 tablespoon of the salt and the collards. Cook, uncovered, until softened, 8 to 10 minutes. Drain in a colander. Rinse with cold water. Gently press the collards against the colander to squeeze out excess moisture.

Heat the olive oil in a medium pan over medium heat. Add the garlic and cook for 1 minute. Add the collards, cranberries, and the remaining ½ teaspoon of salt. Cook and stir for 3 minutes. Add the orange juice and cook for 15 seconds. Season with additional salt, to taste. Serve immediately.

▶ Makes 4 servings

2 large bunches collard greens, ribs removed, rinsed and drained (or 1 large bag pre-washed collards, larger ribs discarded)

3 quarts water

1 tablespoon, plus 1 teaspoon, sea salt, divided, plus additional salt, to taste

1 tablespoon olive oil

2 cloves garlic, minced

2/3 cup dried cranberries

1/3 cup fresh orange juice

DESSERTS

$g$imme some sugar," enthused generations of affectionate grandmothers, aunts, great aunts, second cousins, and "auntees" across the South. The saying is a metaphor, yet the South's sweet tooth is undeniable. The lure of some favorite Southern desserts is irresistible. A beautiful cake, a dish of homemade ice cream, a bountiful cookie tin, a fragrant pie— they're all a little sweeter when shared.

This boiled custard has always been a family tradition for the family of Wendy Perry of Zebulon, North Carolina. Her late mother, Frances Chamblee Perry, made copious amounts of it for their big family to enjoy at every Christmas gathering, either plain or with some sweetened strawberries she had "put up" the summer before. When Perry's sister Tiana was engaged, the family had a little game for her fiancé: ask him questions and compare his actual answers to what Tiana predicted he'd answer. One question was, "What food do you dislike that Tiana thinks you like?" His answer? "You know that custard stuff your family serves *every* year at Christmas? Well, I don't like it." Still, he'd sampled it every year. Nice manners count for a lot in the South, but there's no accounting for taste. This Boiled Custard is nonetheless a must at Perry Christmas and a nostalgic indulgence for guests who love a taste of tradition.

MAMA PERRY'S BOILED CUSTARD

1/2 gallon whole milk

2 (12-ounce) cans evaporated milk

1 1/2 cups sugar, or more to taste

6 large eggs, beaten or blended until foamy

1 tablespoon vanilla extract

Combine the milk, evaporated milk, and sugar in the top of a double boiler set over simmering water. Cook, stirring constantly, for 20 to 30 minutes until the mixture almost boils. Slowly pour in the eggs, stirring rapidly with the whisk to prevent curdling. Bring the mixture to a gentle boil.

Reduce the heat to medium and cook, stirring often, until the mixture coats the back of a spoon, about 45 minutes. Remove the double boiler from the heat. Add the vanilla and more sugar if necessary. Place the pan in the freezer until the edge of the custard begins to freeze. Transfer to the refrigerator. Stir before serving—the consistency should be thick but pourable.

▶ Makes 14 to 16 servings

For Annette Alexander Calloway of Nashville, Tennessee, music is essential to setting the scene during a dinner party. But she doesn't want to make a soundtrack that's too predictable. She and her husband, Joe, choose CDs beforehand, load up the CD player, and set it to "shuffle." (The process is even easier on an iPod or other portable electronic device.) "I make sure to put in some new music as well as older favorites," she says. "We just make sure there's nothing overpowering. It tends to be slower and mellower, unless we're going to dance. Then it's a whole different selection."

This work of "food art" has been a family tradition for years, a beautiful cake that looks like a present under the Christmas tree, says Calloway.

POLLY'S LANE CAKE

CAKE

3 1/2 cups all-purpose flour

3 1/2 teaspoons baking powder

1/2 teaspoon salt

1 cup (2 sticks) butter, softened

2 cups sugar

2 teaspoons vanilla extract

1 cup milk

8 egg whites

FROSTING

12 egg yolks

1 1/4 cups sugar

3/4 cup (1 1/2 sticks) butter

2 cups pecans

1 1/2 cups raisins, optional

1 1/2 cups sweetened flaked coconut

1 cup red candied cherries

1 cup green candied cherries

1/4 teaspoon salt

1/2 cup rye whiskey or bourbon

To make the cake preheat the oven to 375 degrees. Line three 9-inch round cake pans with parchment paper and butter the paper.

In a large bowl, stir together the flour, baking powder, and salt. Place the butter in a large mixing bowl. Using an electric mixer beat the butter on medium speed until creamy. Add the sugar and beat until fluffy. Beat in the vanilla. Reduce speed to low and add the flour and milk alternately, in two additions, beating just until smooth. In a medium bowl beat the

egg whites until stiff and fold into the batter.

Divide the batter among the three pans. Bake for about 20 minutes, until a tester inserted in the center comes out clean. Let cool in pans for 10 minutes, then invert onto a wire rack and let cool completely.

To make the frosting whisk the egg yolks in a large saucepan. Add the sugar and butter, and cook over medium heat, stirring constantly, until slightly thickened, about 5 minutes. Remove from the heat and add the pecans, raisins, coconut, red and green cherries, salt, and whiskey. Let stand until cold.

Place 1 cake layer on a serving platter or cake stand. Top with some of the frosting, spreading to the edge. Repeat with another cake layer and more frosting. Top with the third cake layer. Spread the remaining frosting on the top and sides of the cake.

▶ Makes 16 to 18 servings

Treat guests to something they won't find anywhere but in your kitchen—that's the approach of Charles Hunter III of Nashville, Tennessee. His dramatic and devastatingly delicious cake announces a special occasion, both on the table and on the fork, for anniversary gatherings, farewell parties, even intimate home weddings. The fresh fruit makes this cake a little top-heavy when cut into wedges, so try Charles's technique: three cuts across the cake, and three cuts perpendicular to those. You'll get 16 rectangular pieces, some with just a little frosting, and some with extra frosting, an innovative solution that yields a piece to suit everyone's preference.

RUSTIC YELLOW CAKE WITH WHISKEY, FRESH FRUIT, AND BROWN SUGAR BUTTERCREAM

SWEETENED FRUIT

1 ripe peach, chopped

1 cup mixed berries

1/2 cup white sugar

Pinch of salt

1 tablespoon fresh lime juice

CAKE

2 1/2 cups all-purpose flour

1 1/2 teaspoons baking powder

1/4 teaspoon baking soda

1/2 teaspoon kosher salt

1 cup (2 sticks) unsalted butter, softened

3/4 cup white sugar

3/4 cup firmly packed light brown sugar

1 tablespoon vanilla extract

3 large eggs, room temperature

1 cup whole milk

BOURBON SIMPLE SYRUP

1 (100-milliliter) bottle honey whiskey (such as Jack Daniel's Tennessee Honey)

1/2 cup white sugar

1 tablespoon water

BROWN SUGAR BUTTERCREAM

3/4 cup (1 1/2 sticks) unsalted butter, softened

1/4 cup heavy cream

3 tablespoons dark brown sugar

1 tablespoon vanilla extract

Dash of kosher salt

1 1/2 cups powdered sugar

Preheat the oven to 350 degrees. Butter two 8- or 9-inch round cake pans and dust with flour, tapping out the excess.

To make the sweetened fruit gently stir together the peach, berries, sugar, salt, and lime juice. Refrigerate 30 to 40 minutes before baking the cakes. Stir occasionally to ensure the sugar is dissolved.

To make the cake, in a medium bowl whisk together the flour, baking powder, baking soda, and salt.

Place the butter in a large mixing bowl. Using an electric mixer, beat on medium speed until creamy. Add the white sugar and brown sugar, and beat until fluffy, 2 to 3 minutes. Add the vanilla, then the eggs one at a time, beating and scraping down the side of the bowl. Reduce the speed to low. Add the flour mixture in three additions and the milk in two additions, beginning and ending with the flour mixture. Mix until combined.

Divide the batter between the pans. Bake until a wooden pick inserted near the center comes out clean. For two 8-inch rounds, bake 25 to 30 minutes. For two 9-inch rounds, bake 22 to 25 minutes. Let the cakes cool in the pans for 15 minutes, then invert onto a wire rack and let cool completely.

To make the bourbon simple syrup, combine the whiskey, sugar, and water in a heavy saucepan over medium heat. Bring the mixture to a low simmer, stirring constantly until the sugar dissolves. Reduce the heat to low and leave the pan on the heat for 1 minute. Remove from the heat and let the mixture cool to room temperature.

To make the brown sugar buttercream, place the butter in a large mixing bowl. Using an electric mixer beat on medium speed until light and fluffy. Slowly add the heavy cream, beating until fully incorporated. Beat in the brown sugar, vanilla, and salt. Add the powdered sugar, a large spoonful at a time, and mix well.

To assemble, trim the tops of the cakes with a serrated knife or cake leveler. Drizzle the bourbon simple syrup over the cake layers, starting from the edges and moving inward.

Frost the tops of the cake layers with brown sugar buttercream.

Drain and reserve the excess liquid from the fruit. Place one cake layer on a cake stand or plate and distribute the fruit over the frosting. Top with the second cake layer. Arrange the fruit over the top layer, heaping it a little in the center. Finish by drizzling a little of the reserved juice over the top of the cake, allowing some to spill over the sides. Serve within a couple of hours. Leftover cake holds well in the refrigerator for a day or two.

▶ Brown sugar buttercream makes about 2 cups. Cake makes 16 to 20 servings.

Note: Cake layers, syrup, and buttercream can be made a day in advance of serving. Prepare the fruit right before assembling.

For holidays, I like to make traditional family recipes like my mother-in-law's oyster dressing or my grandmother's Tennessee Jam Cake. The cake had kind of old-fashioned flavors, and my cousins didn't really enjoy it, so I updated the recipe. Out with the raisins and molasses, in with chocolate, for a cake reminiscent of a chocolate-covered strawberry. I want people to enjoy the food, but I also want to serve dishes that have a family connection, and that they count on. Tradition is important—it's what children remember. Fine-quality ingredients—cake flour, small batch or homemade jam, fresh pecans, gourmet buttermilk, and the best cocoa—give a superior result with a noticeably better flavor and texture.—Nicki Pendleton Wood

TENNESSEE JAM CAKE

Preheat the oven to 325 degrees. Grease a 10-inch tube pan, Bundt pan, or springform pan. Dust lightly with flour.

Place the butter in a large mixing bowl. Using an electric mixer beat on medium speed until creamy. Add the sugar and beat until very well combined. Add the eggs and beat for 2 minutes. Beat in the jam and preserves. In a small bowl dissolve the baking soda in the buttermilk, then mix into the batter.

Combine the flour, cinnamon, cocoa, and salt in a medium bowl. Add to the batter and beat just until combined. Beat or stir in the pecans.

Spoon the mixture into the pan, spreading if needed. Rap the pan on the counter to settle the thick batter into the corners. Bake for 1 ½ hours or until the cake springs back when pressed, a knife inserted near the center comes out clean, or the cake pulls away from the sides of the pan. Invert the cake onto a serving platter and let cool.

To make the frosting combine the buttermilk, sugar, and butter in a 3-quart saucepan. Bring to a boil over medium heat, stirring often. Stir in the baking soda and keep stirring—the mixture will foam up. Cook, stirring, until the mixture reaches soft ball stage (234 to 240 degrees). Let cool slightly to thicken before frosting the cake. If the frosting still seems thin, beat it with an electric mixer for a few minutes to thicken it.

▸ Makes 24 servings

CAKE

1 cup (2 sticks) butter, softened slightly

1 cup sugar

4 large eggs

1 cup blackberry or raspberry jam

1 cup strawberry preserves

1 teaspoon baking soda

1/2 cup full-fat buttermilk

3 cups all-purpose flour

1 teaspoon ground cinnamon

1/2 cup cocoa

1/4 teaspoon salt

1 cup pecan pieces, toasted

BUTTERSCOTCH FROSTING

1/2 cup buttermilk

1 cup sugar

5 tablespoons butter

1/2 teaspoon baking soda

Although Lisa Waddle of Nashville, Tennessee, gleaned much of her cooking wisdom from her maternal grandmother, observing her entertain was more a lesson in what *not* to do. "She was so focused on crowding the table with too many platters and keeping everyone's plate and glass filled, she never had a chance to eat herself," says Waddle. "We used to joke that she didn't need a chair at the table, because she would only sit for a minute or two before popping up to refill the bread basket or reheat a dish she thought wasn't hot enough." Even when everyone had eaten their fill, her grandmother insisted on clearing the table and starting to wash up. "Although I know her selflessness was grounded in love, we all would have been much more relaxed if she just sat and enjoyed the meal with us. Now when I entertain, I plan meals that let me be present at the table and take part in the meal and conversation," she says. That means make-ahead dishes that are served family-style, with an emphasis on quality, not quantity. "It not only makes the meal a gift to others—but also to myself," Waddle says.

CHOCOLATE WHISKEY BUTTERMILK CAKE WITH PRALINE TOPPING

CAKE

1/2 cup (1 stick) unsalted butter

1/4 cup natural unsweetened cocoa powder

1/4 cup water

1 cup all-purpose flour

1 cup white sugar

1/2 teaspoon baking soda

1/4 teaspoon salt

1/4 cup buttermilk

1 large egg

1/2 teaspoon vanilla extract

1/4 cup whiskey

FROSTING

1/4 cup heavy cream

1 (6-ounce) bar bittersweet chocolate, chopped

2 tablespoons unsalted butter, softened

PRALINE

3/4 cup firmly packed dark brown sugar

1/4 cup heavy cream

3 tablespoons unsalted butter

3/4 cup powdered sugar

1 teaspoon whiskey

1 cup chopped toasted pecans

To make the cake, preheat the oven to 350 degrees. Grease and flour an 8-inch cake pan and line the bottom with parchment paper.

In a heavy saucepan melt the butter with the cocoa and water over medium heat. Let cool slightly.

228

In a medium bowl whisk the flour, sugar, baking soda, and salt. In a large bowl, whisk the buttermilk, egg, vanilla, and whiskey. Whisk the cocoa mixture into the buttermilk mixture until smooth. Add half of the flour mixture, whisk until smooth, then stir in the rest of the flour mixture. Pour the batter into the pan and bake for 35 to 40 minutes, until a wooden pick inserted near the center comes out clean. Let cool in the pan 10 minutes, then invert onto a wire rack to cool completely.

To make the frosting heat the cream in a small saucepan over medium heat until just boiling. Remove from the heat and add the chocolate and butter. Let stand until mostly melted, then stir. Let stand at room temperature for about 30 minutes until spreadable. Place the cake on a serving platter and frost the top and sides. Refrigerate for at least 1 hour.

To make the praline, in a heavy saucepan stir the brown sugar, cream, and butter over medium-high heat until the butter melts. Bring to a boil and boil for 1 minute without stirring. Remove the pan from the heat and whisk in the sugar and whiskey. Stir in the pecans and immediately pour over the top of the cake, spreading to the edges. Store at room temperature.

▶ Makes 8 to 10 servings

"King cakes are such a fun tradition," says Jean Button of Fayetteville, Arkansas. "In Louisiana, King Cakes first appear on January 6, known as Twelfth Night or Epiphany, and are available throughout the Mardi Gras season. The King Cake honors the three kings who brought gifts to baby Jesus, who is represented by a small plastic baby. The person who gets the piece with the baby is supposed to bring the next King Cake or give the next King Cake party." Button says the cakes can be hard to find outside Louisiana, so she makes her own. "I typically make about 20 King Cakes each Mardi Gras season. I take them everywhere I go: to work, to meetings, to parties, to friends and family. I give a little prize (usually some special Mardi Gras beads) to the person who gets the baby." Use either the cinnamon or praline filling—both make enough to fill two cakes. Baked King Cakes freeze well.

KING CAKE WITH CINNAMON OR PRALINE FILLING

CAKE

1/2 cup (1 stick) margarine

2/3 cup evaporated milk

1/2 cup sugar

2 teaspoons salt

4 large eggs

1/3 cup cold water

5 1/2 cups all-purpose flour

2 (.25-ounce) envelopes active dry yeast

1 teaspoon grated lemon peel

1 teaspoon grated orange peel

CINNAMON FILLING

1/2 cup firmly packed brown sugar

3/4 cup white sugar

1 tablespoon ground cinnamon

1/2 cup (1 stick) butter, melted

PRALINE FILLING

16 ounces cream cheese, softened

1/2 cup (1 stick) butter, softened

1 teaspoon vanilla extract

3/4 cup brown sugar

TOPPING

1 egg, beaten

1/3 cup purple-tinted sugar

1/3 cup green-tinted sugar

1/3 cup gold-tinted sugar

2 plastic babies

To make the cakes heat the margarine, milk, sugar, and salt in a small saucepan over medium heat or in a microwave-safe bowl until very hot. Let cool slightly. In a small bowl beat the eggs with the water. Add to the milk mixture. Combine the flour, yeast, lemon peel, and orange peel in a large bowl and mix well. Add the liquid mixture and mix well. Knead for 5 minutes. Cover and let rise until doubled in volume.

Punch down the dough and divide into two equal pieces. On a floured surface roll one piece into a 30 x 15-inch rectangle. Cut into 3 long strips.

To make the cinnamon filling combine the brown sugar, white sugar, and cinnamon in a small bowl and mix well. Brush the center of each dough strip with the melted butter. Sprinkle with a little of the sugar mixture.

To make the praline filling combine the cream cheese, butter, vanilla, and brown sugar in a medium bowl and mix well. Spoon a thick line of the mixture down the center of each strip.

To assemble the cakes fold each strip lengthwise toward the center to enclose the filling, pressing the seam to seal. Braid the strips, then form the braid into a circle. Repeat with the remaining dough and filling.

Place the cakes on greased baking sheets. Cover with a damp cloth and let rise until doubled in volume, about 1 hour.

Preheat the oven to 350 degrees. Brush each cake with beaten egg and sprinkle with the colored sugars. Bake for 20 minutes. Remove from the pans immediately so the sugar doesn't harden. Tuck a plastic baby into the cakes while they are still warm.

▸ Makes 2 cakes, about 12 to 14 servings each

An Academy Award-watching party has become the "must-have" invitation for Ray Waddle's film addict friends in Nashville, Tennessee. Everyone is asked to come in black tie, and a variety of appetizers are served. But the highlight is shortly after the halfway point of the telecast, when popcorn is popped and a variety of movie candy in boxes is brought out. Everyone, despite being in formal wear, reverts to child-hood, fighting over who gets the Goobers and Junior Mints. This pound cake, cut into thick slices, which are then cut into quarters, makes a rich alternative for non-candy eaters, and also goes well with coffee (a necessity to get through the long evening).

BROWN SUGAR POUND CAKE

1 cup (2 sticks) butter, softened

1/2 cup shortening

3 cups firmly packed light brown sugar

5 large eggs

3 1/2 cups all-purpose flour

1 cup milk

Preheat the oven to 325 degrees. Grease and flour a tube pan. Place the butter, shortening, and brown sugar in a large mixing bowl. Using an electric mixer on medium speed, beat until well combined. Add the eggs one at a time, beating after each addition. Reduce the speed to low and add the flour and milk alternately in three batches, beating after each addition. Pour the batter into the pan. Bake for 1 ½ hours, or until a wooden pick inserted near the center comes out clean.

Let the cake cool 10 minutes in the pan, then invert onto a wire rack and let cool completely.

▶ Makes 12 servings

A beautiful space with beautiful food—that's how the mind of Teresa Blackburn works in her Nashville, Tennessee, home. Cook, food stylist, and host, Blackburn is always thinking as much about how to present a dish as what to serve. For a themed tablescape for this gorgeous, unusual cake, save grapefruit shells, then fill them with soy candle mix. Line them up and down the center of the table—voilà! Decorative, different, and a sure conversation piece.

RUBY RED GRAPEFRUIT UPSIDE DOWN CAKE

3/4 cup (1 1/2 sticks), plus 4 tablespoons, butter, divided

2/3 cup firmly packed dark brown sugar

1 tablespoon fresh lemon juice

2 large red grapefruits

1/2 cup white whole-wheat flour

1 cup yellow cornmeal

1 1/2 teaspoons baking powder

Generous pinch of sea or kosher salt

1 cup raw sugar

4 large eggs

1/2 cup plain Greek yogurt

1 tablespoon grated grapefruit peel

1 tablespoon vanilla extract

Preheat the oven to 350 degrees. Melt 4 tablespoons of the butter in a 10-inch cast-iron skillet over medium heat. Remove the pan from the heat and stir in the brown sugar and lemon juice.

Slice off the tops and bottoms of the grapefruits. Cut the peel and pith away from the fruit. Cut the grapefruit into ¼-inch rounds. Remove any seeds. Arrange the grapefruit slices over the butter mixture in the skillet.

In a medium bowl whisk the flour, cornmeal, baking powder, and salt. Place the remaining ¾ cup butter and the raw sugar in a large mixing bowl. Using an electric mixer beat on medium speed until well combined, scraping down the side of the bowl as needed. Add the eggs, one at a time, mixing well between each addition. Add the yogurt, peel, and vanilla. Add the flour mixture ½ cup at a time and mix until just blended. Do not overmix. The batter will be thick.

Spoon the batter into the skillet over the grapefruit slices, spreading it to the edge and smoothing the top. Bake for 40 to 45 minutes, until the center is set and a wooden pick inserted near the center comes out clean. Let cool for a few minutes in the pan.

Invert the cake onto a large plate or platter and serve warm or at room temperature.

▶ Makes 8 to 10 servings

So much of what Angie Sarris of John's Creek, Georgia, knows about entertaining she learned from her grandparents. "They were both the most amazing cooks, and wonderful entertainers. She would play the piano and he would sing. They always had many guests stopping by just for a quick visit. I learned from them most of all to enjoy the ones you love, and to welcome drop-ins and drop-bys. And then you will have a home everyone wants to visit. I keep a small supply of homemade gifts, so if I have a guest come by, I send them home with something."

Of this spectacular cake, Sarris says, "Don't knock it, like I did, because it's made with a boxed cake mix." Every bite of this tall, dramatic cake with a light, fluffy filling and a whipped-cream frosting is meltingly delicious. The cake tastes best if kept in the refrigerator for 2 days before serving, an ideal make-ahead holiday dessert.

AUNT DOT'S COCONUT CAKE

CAKE

Butter and all-purpose flour for preparing cake pans

1 (18-ounce) package butter yellow cake mix

3 large eggs

2/3 cup sparkling lemon-lime soft drink

1/2 cup (1 stick) butter, softened

1 (5-ounce) can sweetened coconut milk or coconut cream

FROSTING

1 cup sour cream

1 cup powdered sugar

1 cup white sugar

1 (8-ounce) container frozen whipped topping, thawed

2 cups heavy cream

1 (8–ounce) package unsweetened coconut flakes, shreds or chips

To make the cake, preheat the oven to 325 degrees and butter and flour three 8-inch cake pans. Line with parchment paper. Butter and flour the paper.

Prepare the cake using the package directions, substituting the soft drink for water.

Divide the batter evenly among the pans. Bake according to package directions, 23 to 27 minutes. Let cool in the pans for 10 to 15 minutes. Turn out onto a wire cooling rack and let cool to the touch.

Brush each layer with coconut milk.

To make the frosting, whisk the sour cream, powdered sugar, and white sugar in a medium bowl until well blended. Fold in the whipped topping just until combined (overmixing will make it runny). Spread a thick layer of the frosting over the top of each layer.

Stack the layers on a cake plate. Spread a thin layer of the frosting over the sides to seal in crumbs. Set aside the remaining 1 to 2 cups of the frosting.

Whip the heavy cream in a stand mixer with the whisk attachment for several minutes, until it holds stiff peaks. Fold in the leftover sour cream mixture and frost the top and sides of the cake.

Toast the coconut in a skillet over medium heat for 5 to 7 minutes. Keep a close eye on it and don't let it burn. Once the coconut is a nice brown color remove the pan from the heat and let the coconut cool. Sprinkle the coconut over the top of the cake and gently press it onto the side of the cake. Store the cake in the refrigerator at least two days before serving.

▶ **Makes 16 to 20 servings**

*Angie uses Duncan Hines.

"I always figure out what we're having for dessert first when I plan supper," says Katy Houston of Ridgeland, Mississippi. Houston channeled her lifelong love for baking and desserts into healing help for a college student recovering from a disastrous cycling accident. For 62 weeks, Houston visited her son's best friend each Monday with a homemade dessert, thinking, "If this brings you one ounce of happiness today, I will have done what I tried to do." She collected all the recipes into a book, testing them with her friends, church groups, and anyone else she could recruit. Her Peach Almond Pound Cake turns out to be "great for a picnic or summery type party," she says, because of the seasonal flavor, its generous 16 servings, and its ability to take hot weather. Let Houston's generosity, and her recipe, inspire your own hospitality.

1 cup (2 sticks) butter, softened

3 cups sugar

6 large eggs, room temperature

3 cups all-purpose flour

1/4 teaspoon baking soda

1/2 teaspoon salt

1/2 cup sour cream, room temperature

2 1/4 cups chopped peaches, fresh or frozen and thawed, drained

1 teaspoon vanilla extract

1 teaspoon almond extract

PEACH ALMOND POUND CAKE

Preheat the oven to 350 degrees. Grease and flour a tube pan. Place the butter in a large mixing bowl and beat with a hand or electric mixer on medium speed until fluffy. Add the sugar gradually, then beat for at least 8 minutes or until well blended. Add the eggs one at a time, beating well after each addition.

Stir together the flour, baking soda, and salt in a medium bowl. Combine the sour cream and peaches in a small bowl. Add the flour and sour cream mixtures alternately to the butter mixture, beginning and ending with the flour mixture and beating until just combined. Stir in the vanilla and almond extracts.

Pour the batter into the pan. Bake for 1 ½ to 1 ¾ hours, until the cake is golden brown and a wooden pick inserted near the center comes out clean. Place the pan on a wire rack and let cool for 10 minutes. Invert the cake onto the rack and let cool completely.

▶ Makes 12 to 16 servings

238

"Company" and "cake" were synonymous in the South, even in the tight economic times of the Great Depression and World War II. Warrior Cake was an eggless, milkless, butterless cake popularized during wartime shortages. Pat Goodyear, now of Baltimore, Maryland, says this special cake was served at holiday gatherings during her North Carolina childhood. "My grandmother, Rosa McKrae Winters, made this cake every year. She was a native of North Carolina and was a fine Christian woman who believed in putting her family first," she says. "Money was tight and celebrations few and far between," so Warrior Cake was a welcome delicacy. For a really striking presentation, Goodyear's grandmother added two layers of plain yellow cake between the layers of raisin cake. Warrior Cake is vegan when made with shortening, and a good dessert solution for avoiding allergens like eggs and dairy.

WARRIOR CAKE

CAKE

1 pound raisins

2 cups firmly packed brown sugar

2 teaspoons ground cinnamon

1 teaspoon ground cloves

1 teaspoon nutmeg

1/4 cup shortening or butter

2 cups water

3 1/2 cups all-purpose flour

2 teaspoons baking soda

FILLING

1 fresh coconut, grated, or 12 to 14 ounces shredded unsweetened coconut

2 cups white sugar

2 tablespoons all-purpose flour

1 cup boiling water

Juice of 2 lemons

To make the cake preheat the oven to 350 degrees. Grease and flour two or three 9-inch round cake pans. Combine the raisins, brown sugar, cinnamon, cloves, nutmeg, shortening, and water in a medium saucepan. Bring to a simmer over medium heat and cook for 5 minutes. Let cool, then add flour and baking soda. Divide the mixture between the cake pans. Bake for about 45 minutes, until a wooden pick inserted near the center comes out clean. Let cool in the pans for 10 minutes. Invert onto a wire rack and let cool completely.

To make the filling combine the coconut, sugar, and flour in a saucepan and toss to combine. Add the water and mix well. Heat over medium-low heat, stirring, until the mixture is as thick as jam. Add the lemon juice and mix well.

Place one cake layer on a serving platter. Top with half of the filling. Place the second layer on the filling. Spread the remaining filling over the top of the cake.

▶ Makes 14 to 16 servings

After-party pictures are half the fun of throwing a bash, if Kath Hansen's parties in her Brooklyn, New York, home are the measure. Bottles, cups, hats, musical instruments—clearly a good time was had. The hilarity extends to the food, where she gets creative. She originally created this recipe as a teenager, during what she calls her "crazy teenage kitchen experiments" phase. Other experiments included a Froot Loop pie, a cake shaped and frosted like a vinyl record, and marshmallow-banana dogs. Even though everyone has a cell phone camera, it's still a good idea to set out a few disposable cameras at a big party. Reliving the party is almost as much fun as giving it.

This cake rises a lot in the oven, so be sure your loaf pan will hold 6 cups. The batter should fill the pan no more than two-thirds full. Bake any extra batter in mini loaf pans or muffin tins.

SECRET MOON PIE LOAF CAKE

Butter or nonstick cooking spray

3/4 cup firmly packed brown sugar

1 cup cocoa powder

1 1/2 cups all-purpose flour

3/4 cup sugar

1 teaspoon baking soda

3/4 teaspoon baking powder

1 teaspoon salt

2 large eggs

3/4 cup buttermilk

1/2 cup vegetable oil

1 teaspoon vanilla extract

5 Mini Moon Pies or 2 Single-Decker Moon Pies, cut into quarters

Preheat the oven to 350 degrees. Grease an 8-inch loaf pan. Combine the brown sugar, cocoa, flour, sugar, baking soda, baking powder, and salt in a large mixing bowl and stir until well combined.

In stand mixer whisk the eggs until blended. Add the buttermilk, vegetable oil, and vanilla to the eggs and mix well. Add half of the cocoa mixture to the egg mixture and beat at low speed until just combined. Repeat with the remaining cocoa mixture.

Spoon about one-third of the batter into the prepared pan. Set 3 of the Moon Pies on the batter and press down gently. Spoon half of the remaining batter over the Moon Pies—they should be completely covered. Arrange the remaining 2 Moon Pies over the batter. Cover with the remaining batter.

Set the loaf pan on a baking sheet in the oven. Bake about 1 hour, until a wooden pick inserted in the center comes out with no crumbs clinging to it. (Some of the Moon Pie filling might stick to the tester, and that's fine.) Let cool in the pan for 15 minutes. Invert onto a wire rack and let cool completely before serving.

▶ Makes about 8 servings

241

All the flavors of fresh strawberry shortcake in a tall, beautiful, celebratory cake—that's what professional baker Juanita Traughber of Nashville, Tennessee, envisioned when she developed this cake. She serves it as a birthday cake perched on a tall, clear glass cake stand with a high glass dome for full effect. Just one candle in the center is enough, she says. "I don't want to detract from the beauty of the strawberries." Traughber uses a decorative angled cake server to cut thin slices.

"STRAWBERRY SHORTCAKE" CHIFFON CAKE

CAKE

2 1/4 cups cake flour

1 1/2 cups white sugar, divided

1 tablespoon baking powder

1 teaspoon salt

5 large egg yolks, room temperature

3/4 cup cold water

1/2 cup vegetable oil

1 teaspoon finely grated lemon peel

1 teaspoon vanilla extract

8 large egg whites, room temperature

1/2 teaspoon cream of tartar

FROSTING

2 cups chilled heavy cream

6 tablespoons powdered sugar

1 tablespoon vanilla extract

3 cups sliced strawberries

Preheat the oven to 325 degrees. Lightly grease and flour three 6-inch or two 9-inch round baking pans, or a 12-cup chiffon cake pan.

To make the cake, sift the flour, 1 ¼ cups of the sugar, baking powder, and salt together twice into a large bowl. In a smaller bowl, beat the yolks, water, oil, lemon peel, and vanilla with a hand mixer on high-speed until smooth. Stir into the flour mixture until well blended.

Place the egg whites and cream of tartar in a large mixing bowl. Using an electric mixer beat on high speed until soft peaks form. Add

the remaining ¼ cup white sugar and beat on high speed until stiff peaks form.

Using a large spoon or spatula, gently fold one-fourth of the egg whites into the cake batter until combined. Add the remaining egg whites and stir until well combined. Scrape the batter evenly into the pans. Bake about 30 minutes or until a wooden pick inserted near the center comes out clean. Let cool in the pans for 10 minutes. Invert onto wire racks and let cool for at least 1 hour.

To make the frosting, place the cream,

powdered sugar, and vanilla in a clean mixing bowl and beat on high speed until the mixture forms stiff peaks, about 2 minutes.

Trim the tops of the cakes with a serrated knife or cake leveler. If desired, cut each layer into halves horizontally to make 6 layers. Set the first cake layer on a plate and spread a layer of whipped cream evenly over it. Add a layer of sliced strawberries. Repeat with remaining cake layers.

▶ Makes 10 to 12 servings

Notes: The eggs must be room temperature to beat to a fluffy consistency, so take them out of the refrigerator about 2 hours before beginning this recipe. Overmixing the fluffy egg whites into the cake batter will deflate the batter, which should be light and airy, so handle your whipped eggs with care.

Putting the warm layers on the wire rack into the freezer reduces the cooling time by half.

Alisa Huntsman knows a thing or two about baking for a crowd—she was the pastry chef for years at Loveless Café, the world-famous meat-and-three in Nashville, Tennessee. On the side, she bakes spectacular desserts, such as this cold-weather combination of maple, pecan, and winter squash, and has written two dessert cookbooks.

Check your utensils before your party starts to ensure you have the right gear for each item on your menu. From pie server to ice cream scoop to gravy ladle, the right tool can spare lots of last-minute grief.

MAPLE PECAN PIE WITH BUTTERNUT SQUASH FILLING

1 (9-inch) deep-dish piecrust, store-bought or homemade

PIE

1 1/3 cups mashed baked butternut squash flesh

1/4 cup white sugar

2 tablespoons maple syrup

1/2 teaspoon ground cinnamon

1/4 teaspoon nutmeg

2 large eggs

6 tablespoons heavy cream

TOPPING

1 cup pecan pieces

1/2 cup firmly packed brown sugar

2 tablespoons unsalted butter, melted

1/4 teaspoon ground cinnamon

2 large eggs

1/2 cup maple syrup

Vanilla ice cream or whipped cream, for serving

Preheat the oven to 300 degrees. Place the piecrust into a 9-inch deep-dish pie pan. Line with waxed paper or parchment paper and weigh down with pie weights or dried beans wrapped in aluminum foil. Bake for 20 minutes until firm but not at all browned. Remove the weights and parchment paper.

For the filling, combine the squash, sugar, maple syrup, cinnamon, and nutmeg in the bowl of a food processor and pulse to blend. Process the mixture, scraping the bowl occasionally, until it is completely and evenly pureed. Add the eggs one at a time and pulse to mix. Scrape the bowl, add the cream, and process to mix well. Pour the mixture into the piecrust and smooth the top.

Preheat the oven to 350. Toast the pecans in a skillet over medium heat until fragrant, about 7 minutes. In a small bowl, combine the brown sugar, butter, and cinnamon. Whisk in the eggs, one at a time, then whisk in the maple syrup.

Sprinkle the pecans evenly over the squash filling. Carefully and slowly pour the maple syrup mixture over the pecans, holding the bowl close to the pie so the pecans aren't pushed down into the squash layer. Bake for 40 to 45 minutes, until the pecan topping puffs up and is firm across the top. Let cool before slicing. Serve the pie with vanilla ice cream or whipped cream.

▶ Makes 6 to 8 servings

Notes: For the filling, any sweet, hard winter squash will do, including acorn, turban, or pumpkin of an heirloom variety. Sweet potatoes can also be used in the filling. And if you prefer walnuts, go for it!

Give thanks for an inventive pumpkin pie with a Southern touch. The praline layer on the bottom adds crunch and complexity to a holiday perennial. This favorite of Betsy Watts Koch's family came from a magazine in the early 1960s, and they've been making it ever since for holiday gatherings at their Brentwood, Tennessee, home. To be sure of a bountiful-looking pie, choose the right size pie dish for the amount of filling. There's nothing sadder than a skimpy-looking pie, is there?

PRALINE PUMPKIN PIE

1 (9-inch) deep-dish piecrust, store-bought or homemade

PRALINE LAYER

3 tablespoons butter, softened

1/3 cup firmly packed brown sugar

1/3 cup chopped pecans

CUSTARD

1 cup evaporated milk

1/2 cup water

3 large eggs

1 1/2 cups pumpkin puree

1/2 cup white sugar

1/2 cup firmly packed brown sugar

1 1/2 teaspoons pumpkin pie spice

1 teaspoon salt

1/2 cup chilled heavy cream

Preheat the oven to 450 degrees. Place the piecrust into a 9 ½-inch or 10-inch pie pan. To make the praline layer, combine the butter and brown sugar in a small bowl and beat with a hand mixer until well combined. Stir in the pecans. Press praline layer evenly over the bottom of the piecrust. Bake for 10 minutes. Let cool on a wire rack for 10 minutes. Reduce the oven temperature to 350 degrees.

To make the custard layer, combine the evaporated milk and water in small saucepan over medium-low heat for 4 minutes until bubbles form around the edge. Remove the pan from the heat. Beat the eggs lightly in a large bowl. Stir in the pumpkin, white sugar, brown sugar, pumpkin pie spice, and salt. Add

the milk mixture and stir until well combined. Pour into the cooled piecrust. Bake for 50 minutes or until the center is set but still soft. (Do not overbake—the custard will set as it cools.) Let cool completely on a wire rack.

Place the cream in a small mixing bowl. Using an electric mixer beat on high speed until firm peaks form. To serve, dollop the cream over the pie and spread evenly.

▶ Makes 6 to 8 servings

Note: Any excess filling mixture can be baked in greased custard cups or a small casserole dish alongside the pie for a crustless pumpkin pudding.

247

This Brown Butter Pumpkin Chess Tart, an impressive sounding dessert, is really just a thin, flat pie made with the right pan. The pan is the key, says Mindy Merrell, to easy and pretty finales. "The idea of fitting one more pan in your cupboard might be crazy, but a 10-inch tart pan with a removable bottom is a direct route to a truly impressive dessert for company. We love pie, but find that serving a neat, crisp slice is a real challenge." True, a mangled slice of pie tastes just as good, "but it's so nice when dessert looks really sharp, a result that the two-piece tart pan always delivers." Merrell and R. B. Quinn always serve this beauty at their Nashville, Tennessee, home for holiday meals instead of the usual pumpkin pie. Merrell says, "Some folks just don't love pumpkin pie, but they love this."

BROWN BUTTER PUMPKIN CHESS TART

Preheat the oven to 350 degrees. Roll out the piecrust dough and fit it into the tart pan. Press the dough up the side and over the edge. Cut off any dough that hangs over the edge.

Melt the butter in a skillet over medium heat. Cook, watching closely, until the butter has browned. Let cool. Pour the butter into a medium bowl and add the sugar, cornmeal mix, eggs, sour cream, pumpkin, vanilla, salt, cinnamon, ginger, cloves, and nutmeg. Mix well.

Pour the filling into the crust. Bake for 45 minutes or until set. Let cool on a wire rack. Remove the pan rim and transfer the tart to a serving platter. Slice and serve with whipped cream.

▶ Makes 12 servings

1 (9-inch) piecrust, store-bought or homemade

5 tablespoons butter

1 1/4 cups sugar

2 tablespoons self-rising cornmeal mix or finely ground plain cornmeal

3 large eggs

1/4 cup sour cream or buttermilk

1 cup pumpkin puree

1 teaspoon vanilla extract

1/2 teaspoon salt

1/2 teaspoon ground cinnamon

1/4 teaspoon ground ginger

1/4 teaspoon ground cloves

1/4 teaspoon ground nutmeg

Whipped cream for serving

Retired nonprofit director Pat Lile of Pine Bluff, Arkansas, spent years searching for the World's Best Pecan Pie. This version, made with browned butter, became the namesake of her quest. Lile once made this pie for a dinner party for colleagues. At serving time, instead of the anticipated enthusiastic praise for the World's Best Pecan Pie, she saw only polite smiles and nods. Cleaning up after dinner, she discovered 1 cup of sugar, measured out, sitting on the counter, when it should have been added to the pie filling. Unsweetened pecan pie! The guests, ever the polite Southerners, had just smiled and eaten it. Being a gracious guest is as important as being a good host.

1 9-inch piecrust (must be homemade to be "World's Best")

1/2 cup (1 stick) butter

1 cup light corn syrup

1 cup sugar

4 large eggs, lightly beaten

1/2 teaspoon lemon juice

1 teaspoon vanilla extract

Dash of salt

1 cup pecans, whole or broken into pieces

WORLD'S BEST PECAN PIE

Preheat the oven to 425 degrees. Place the piecrust into a 9-inch pie pan. Place the butter in a heavy saucepan over low heat and cook, watching carefully, until golden. Let cool.

Combine the corn syrup, sugar, eggs, lemon juice, vanilla, and salt in a medium bowl and mix well. Blend in the browned butter. Add the pecans and stir. Pour into the piecrust. Bake for 10 minutes, then reduce the oven temperature to 325 degrees. Bake for 40 minutes longer.

▶ Makes 6 to 8 servings

Mary Dail married into a big family—her father-in-law was one of eight children, and her husband one of 18 grandchildren. The family always held a big Christmas Eve gathering and potluck where her mother-in-law's pecan pies were among others. "I tasted hers and compared it to the other pecan pies there and I thought, 'Gosh, this is the best thing I've ever put in my mouth.' On the long car ride home, she told me how to make it." Dail's pie doesn't include corn syrup, giving it a firmer texture than the "gelled" filling of a Karo pecan pie. The Dail Christmas Eve gathering in Fayetteville, North Carolina, has moved to the Saturday before Christmas, but it's still potluck, to spread the work around the big family. One cousin roasts a hog and grills chickens, others bring sides, and Dail still supplies her distinctive pecan pies.

MARY DAIL'S PECAN PIE

2 (8-inch) piecrusts, store-bought or homemade

1/2 cup (1 stick) butter

1 pound dark brown sugar

4 large eggs, beaten

2 heaping cups pecan halves

Preheat the oven to 350 degrees. Place the piecrusts into two 8-inch pie pans. Melt the butter in a medium saucepan over medium heat. Add the brown sugar and heat, stirring, until it dissolves. Add the eggs, stirring constantly. Cook over medium heat until the mixture is syrupy. Add the pecans. Cook, stirring, until a froth forms on top of the mixture. Pour into piecrusts, dividing evenly.

Bake for 30 to 35 minutes. The pies are done when the center doesn't jiggle when shaken.

▶ Makes 2 pies, 6 to 8 servings each

Note: The pies can be cut into squares and served as a pick-up dessert. Baked pies can be held in the refrigerator for a few days.

The family recipe for Michelle Jerome Rosen's Black Bottom Pie originated in Dallas, Texas, with her grandmother, who handed it down to her mother in Hattiesburg, Mississippi. A cold chocolate dessert may not sound traditionally Southern, but it is—Black Bottom Pie originated in the Deep South, possibly Louisiana, where a cool dessert in warm weather is appreciated. Rosen's parties in Nashville, Tennessee, sometimes move outdoors for a session of s'mores making, which brings up one finer point of hosting: inform guests in advance of conditions at the party or venue. That way, guests can prepare for tight parking, a muddy yard to cross, grumpy pets, or lots of stairs to climb.

FILLING

2 cups milk

2/3 cup sugar

1/3 cup all-purpose flour

1/4 teaspoon salt

2 large eggs

1 tablespoon butter

1 tablespoon rum or 1 teaspoon vanilla extract

CRUST

1 (9-inch) piecrust, store-bought or homemade, prebaked

1 cup semisweet chocolate chips

1 tablespoon water

TOPPING

1 cup chilled heavy cream

2 tablespoons powdered sugar

BLACK BOTTOM PIE

To make the filling heat the milk in a heavy saucepan over medium heat until bubbles form around the edge, 4 to 6 minutes. Combine the sugar, flour, and salt in the top of a double boiler set over simmering water. Gradually stir in the milk. In a large bowl beat the eggs with a fork. Slowly pour the warm milk mixture over the eggs, whisking continuously. Return the mixture to the double boiler and cook until thick, stirring frequently, about 10 minutes. Remove from the heat and stir in the butter and rum. Let cool.

To make the crust place the piecrust into a 9-inch pie pan. Melt the chocolate chips with the water in the top of a clean double boiler. Spread the mixture on the baked piecrust. Fill with the cooled custard.

To make the topping, combine the cream and sugar in a large bowl and beat with a hand mixer on high speed until soft peaks form. Spread over the custard. Refrigerate until serving time.

▶ Makes 8 servings

When Pam Erbes of Denver, Colorado, gives a party she pays attention to the lighting. Instead of bright overhead lights, she opts for lamps and candles for more flattering light and for warmly lit areas that draw guests together for conversation or just offer a pleasant spot to settle in with a slice of pie.

FROZEN LEMONADE PIE

Combine the lemonade concentrate, sweetened condensed milk, whipped topping, and lemon juice in a medium bowl and mix well. Pour into the crust. Freeze for several hours before serving.

▶ Makes 6 to 8 servings

1 (12-ounce) can pink lemonade concentrate, thawed

1 (14-ounce) can sweetened condensed milk

1 (8-ounce) container frozen whipped topping, thawed

1 teaspoon fresh lemon juice

1 (8-inch) graham cracker crust

Joy Harris offers her guests plenty of hospitality, both as they arrive and as they leave her Tampa, Florida, home. "I make personalized goodie bags to take home. They are filled with some of the leftovers in small disposable containers, or baked items in smaller sizes. Sometimes if it's a smaller party, I personalize cookies as place cards and wrap them in plastic so they can take them home."

Lemon juice added to this peanut butter pie helps to blend the sweetness of the condensed milk with the peanut butter to create a smoother flavor. "You don't really taste the lemon juice—it just perks up the flavor, as it does with so many dishes," says Harris.

1 (8-ounce) package cream cheese, softened

1 (14-ounce) can sweetened condensed milk

1 cup peanut butter

1 tablespoon lemon juice

1 tablespoon vanilla extract

1 cup heavy cream, whipped (about 3 cups)

1 (9-inch) graham cracker crust

2 tablespoons chocolate syrup

PEANUT BUTTER PIE

Place the cream cheese in a large bowl and beat with a hand mixer on medium-high speed until fluffy. Add the sweetened condensed milk and peanut butter and beat until well blended. Stir in the lemon juice and vanilla. Fold in the whipped cream. Pour into the graham cracker crust. Drizzle with chocolate syrup. Refrigerate for several hours.

▶ Makes 6 to 8 servings

Grappling with a pie server to cut a big slice of pie in half for just a little taste—it's awkward, but everyone's done it, or seen someone do it. With a rich dessert like Fudge Pie, consider cutting it into at least eight or even ten slices. Mary Dail of Fayetteville, North Carolina, sometimes cuts it into squares, cutting off the rim of the crust first. She serves the squares to her grandchildren with a scoop of ice cream and homemade chocolate syrup. Fudge Pie has been knocking around the South for decades, and for good reason: for a simple-to-prepare dessert, it delivers a powerful chocolaty flavor complemented by a hint of salty crust.

FUDGE PIE

Preheat the oven to 350 degrees. Place the piecrusts into two 8-inch pie pans. Melt the butter in a medium saucepan over medium heat. Add the sugar and remove the pan from the heat. Stir until the sugar dissolves.

Combine the flour and cocoa powder in a small bowl and mix well. In another small bowl beat the eggs until frothy. Add the flour mixture to the butter mixture alternately with the eggs. Pour into the piecrusts. Bake for 30 to 35 minutes. Let cool before slicing.

▶ Makes 12 to 16 servings

2 (8-inch) piecrusts, store-bought or homemade

1 cup (2 sticks) butter

2 cups sugar

1/2 cup all-purpose flour

1/2 cup cocoa powder

4 large eggs

Maria Boccia, an Italian-American transplant to Charlotte, North Carolina, makes sure she's relaxed about her party so guests will be also. "Pick one or two showcase dishes," she advises. "Don't have too many complicated dishes to prepare. If you're anxious, your guests aren't comfortable." She usually has a theme to help shape the menu, such as Italian food or brunch. Beyond that, the kitchen is her playground, and her guests are part of the fun.

PEACH GALETTE

PASTRY

1 cup all-purpose flour

Pinch of salt

1/3 cup shortening (or half butter, half shortening for a richer taste)

2 to 3 tablespoons cold water

FILLING

3 cups peeled, sliced peaches

1/3 to 1/2 cup firmly packed brown sugar

1 teaspoon ground cinnamon

Pinch of freshly grated nutmeg

1 to 2 tablespoons unsalted butter

GLAZE

1 egg yolk

1 tablespoon cold water

Coarse sugar

To make the pastry combine the flour, salt, and shortening in the bowl of a food processor. Pulse until the mixture resembles pebbles. Add the water and pulse until the dough just comes together in a ball. Wrap the dough in plastic wrap and flatten to a disc. Refrigerate for 30 minutes.

Preheat the oven to 400 degrees. Roll the dough on a floured surface to a round approximately ⅛ inch thick. Place it on a sheet pan lined with a silicone mat or parchment paper.

For the filling, combine the peaches, brown sugar, cinnamon, and nutmeg in a small bowl. Arrange (or just pile) the peach mixture in the middle of the pastry. Dot with the butter.

Fold the pastry up and over the filling, pleating as you go around and leaving an opening in the middle so that some of the fruit is visible.

To make the glaze, whisk the egg yolk and water in a small bowl. Brush the mixture over the crust. Sprinkle with the coarse sugar. Bake for 40 minutes, until the pastry is golden and the filling is bubbling. Check occasionally and reduce the temperature to 350 degrees if the pastry seems to be browning too quickly.

▶ Makes 6 to 8 servings

Dr. Carmen April of Nashville, Tennessee, learned from her mother that cleaning as you go makes for the easiest hosting. The house stays clean, and so does the kitchen, which is a good thing, since the party always ends up in the kitchen.

CRUST

1 1/2 cups graham cracker crumbs

3/4 cup white sugar

4 tablespoons melted butter

FILLING

2 (14-ounce) cans sweetened condensed milk

1 cup Key lime or regular lime juice

2 large eggs

TOPPING

1 cup sour cream

1/4 cup powdered sugar

1 Key lime or regular lime, cut into wheels

KEY LIME PIE

Preheat the oven to 375 degrees. To make the crust combine the graham cracker crumbs, sugar, and butter in a small bowl. Mix with your hands. Press the mixture into a 9-inch pie pan. Bake for 20 minutes. Let cool to room temperature. Reduce the oven temperature to 325 degrees.

To make the filling, combine the sweetened condensed milk, lime juice, and eggs in a large mixing bowl. Using an electric mixer beat on medium speed until well blended. Pour the filling into the cooled crust. Bake for 15 minutes. Refrigerate for 2 hours.

To make the topping, combine the sour cream and powdered sugar and mix well. The mixture will be thick. Spread the topping over the pie with a spatula. Arrange the lime wheels over the topping.

▶ Makes 8 servings

Strawberry Pie is a classic Southern dessert. In April McAnnally's version, Pecan Sandies and extra pecans create a crunchy shortbread crust. "My ideas about hospitality and gracious Southern hostessing are simple," says the Birmingham, Alabama, resident. "Prepare and leave nothing to chance. Effortless gatherings require ridiculous (but well worth it) efforts. Always wipe your sink out and never let your prep work show."

STRAWBERRY PIE IN PECAN SHORTBREAD CRUST

CRUST

1 1/2 cups crushed pecan shortbread cookies (such as Pecan Sandies)

5 tablespoons butter, melted

1/2 cup chopped pecans

GLAZE

3 tablespoons cornstarch

1 cup water

1 cup sugar

Pinch of salt

1/4 cup strawberry flavored gelatin

FILLING

4 cups whole strawberries, caps removed

2 cups freshly whipped cream

Preheat the oven to 350 degrees. To make the crust combine the crushed cookies, butter, and pecans in a medium bowl and mix well. Press into a pie pan. Bake for about 10 to 12 minutes. Let cool completely.

To make the glaze, dissolve the cornstarch in 1 to 2 tablespoons of the water in a small saucepan. Add the remaining water, the sugar, and salt and cook over medium-low heat, whisking, until the mixture thickens, about 5 minutes. Add the gelatin and mix well.

To serve, fill the crust with strawberries, reserving one or two for garnish. Top with the glaze. Pile on the whipped cream and garnish with the reserved strawberries. Refrigerate until ready to serve.

▶ Makes 6 to 8 servings

Note: McAnnally leaves the strawberries whole. But if the berries are large, it's a good idea to slice them.

Any host who's assembled a cocktail buffet knows that dessert is always a dilemma. What sweet is small enough and hits the right notes in flavor, festivity, and ease of eating? Nashville, Tennessee, event planner Natalie Dietz Raines has a genius for party food, and came up with a Moon Pie Banana Pudding, plus a fun way to serve it. "I layered it into mini parfait glasses and served them individually on a cocktail buffet. They were a cute bite of dessert to round out the evening." Raines uses chocolate Moon Pies in this dessert, but you can experiment with other flavors.

1 (12-count) package
Mini Moon Pies

1 cup sour cream

3 cups prepared instant
vanilla pudding

5 or 6 bananas

Juice of 2 lemons

1 cup heavy cream,
whipped (about 3
cups) or your favorite
equivalent

MOON PIE BANANA PUDDING SHOTS

Chop the Moon Pies into bite-size pieces. In a medium bowl mix the sour cream with the vanilla pudding and set aside. Slice the bananas and toss with the lemon juice in another medium bowl.

In a trifle bowl or other serving bowl, layer Moon Pies, pudding, bananas, then more pudding. Repeat the layering, ending with pudding on top. Serve immediately or refrigerate for up to a day. Top with the whipped cream just before serving.

To serve in mini parfait glasses, layer the ingredients directly in the glasses.

▶ Makes about 24 (4-ounce) servings

Strawberries and spring go together naturally in the South, and early spring is a good time to invite people over. The weather is reason enough to put together a celebration, and with asparagus, strawberries, and spring flowers in season, the menu and décor create themselves. An early spring get-together is also a good motivator to do all that spring cleaning.

For any spring gathering, a trifle of strawberries in a creamy sweet pudding looks beautiful in a clear bowl, and is simple to serve up, or to let guests serve themselves. This recipe comes from Lori Miller, a Southerner living in Chico, California.

1 (14-ounce) can sweetened condensed milk

1 1/2 cups cold water

1 (3 1/2-ounce) package instant vanilla pudding mix

2 cups heavy cream, whipped

1/2 cup Amaretto liqueur

4 cups sliced fresh strawberries

1 (12-ounce) prepared loaf pound cake, cut into cubes

Toasted slivered almonds and strawberries for garnish

STRAWBERRIES AND CREAM TRIFLE

Place the sweetened condensed milk and water in a large mixing bowl. Add the pudding mix and beat with a whisk or electric mixer on medium speed until well blended. Refrigerate for 5 minutes. Fold in the whipped cream.

Drizzle the Amaretto over the strawberries. Spoon 2 cups of the pudding mixture into a 5-quart trifle or round glass bowl. Top with half of the cake cubes, arranging them in a fan pattern. Top with half the strawberries, making sure to spoon some of the liqueur onto the cake, and half of the remaining pudding mixture. Repeat the layers, ending with pudding mixture on top. Garnish with almonds and strawberries. Refrigerate for 4 hours or until set. Leftover trifle should be refrigerated.

▶ Makes 10 to 12 servings

Marirae Mathis moved from Pennsylvania to Nashville, Tennessee, years ago, bringing along this easy dessert recipe she'd had for a decade. Any berry or soft fruit will do—she's used blackberries, peaches, strawberries, raspberries, and blueberries. Though Berry Pudding is a homey dessert that's simple to make, its warm, comforting flavor holds its own among more elaborate desserts, especially when topped with ice cream or whipped cream. At any occasion featuring lots of desserts, scoop pudding, cobbler, and ice cream into small portions, and cut cakes and pies into thin slices so guests can easily sample a little of everything.

BERRY PUDDING

Preheat the oven to 350 degrees. Grease an 8-inch square baking pan or other 2-quart ovenproof dish.

Combine the flour, baking powder, ½ cup of the sugar, butter, and milk in a bowl and mix well. The mixture will be thick. Spread it in the pan. Spread the fruit over the batter. Sprinkle with the remaining ½ cup sugar. Pour the boiling water over the whole thing but don't stir.

Bake for 50 to 60 minutes. At 50 minutes, the pudding will be gooey; at 60 minutes it will be firmer and drier.

▶ Makes 10 to 12 servings

1 cup all-purpose flour

1 teaspoon baking powder

1 cup sugar, divided

1 tablespoon melted butter

1/2 cup milk

1 cup berries, cherries, or chopped soft fruit, such as peaches, plums, or nectarines

1 cup boiling water

It's happened to every host—dessert's been served and you're exhausted, yet guests are still engaged and socializing. Try offering refills of wine, coffee, or water, or another serving of dessert. If that gesture doesn't bring it home, the phrase, "Well, this has been fun—we need to do it again soon," should get people on their feet and moving toward the door.

Fresh rhubarb has a short season, but a long history, in the South, where it's known as "pie plant" in some areas. This crisp recipe is from Ray Waddle of Nashville, Tennessee.

RHUBARB CRISP

Preheat the oven to 375 degrees. In a large bowl, mix together the rhubarb, sugar, cinnamon, and ¼ cup flour. Pour the mixture into a 9-inch pie plate. In the same bowl, mix together the remaining ¼ cup of flour, brown sugar, old-fashioned oats, and steel-cut oats. Stir in the oil. (The mixture will be clumpy.) Put handfuls of the mixture on top of the rhubarb, squeezing to make it as clumpy as possible. Bake for 50 minutes, until the rhubarb is bubbling.

▶ Makes 8 to 10 servings

6 cups (about 1 3/4 pounds) chopped rhubarb

1/2 cup white sugar

1/2 teaspoon ground cinnamon

1/2 cup all-purpose flour, divided

3/4 cup firmly packed brown sugar

1/2 cup old-fashioned oats

1/2 cup steel-cut oats

6 tablespoons canola oil

From Betsy Burke Parker of Flint Hill, Virginia, comes "a really old-fashioned recipe" developed in her state, "where there are copious amounts of native persimmons each fall." Persimmon Pudding is a pudding in the British sense: a soft, baked mixture. Native persimmons should be put through a food mill or ricer to remove seeds and skins. Big Japanese persimmons available at the supermarket are easier—the pulp scoops out easily with a spoon. "Either works well," says Parker, "but it's sure fun to take some kids and a bucket and go pick persimmons—after frost but before the raccoons get to them!"

"Gracious entertaining starts with a graceful space—it can be a humble cottage or a grand manor—but grace begins with love," says Parker. She decorates the house with cherished emblems: "a deer antler found by the river, a wild turkey feather found in the garden, beautiful local art, warm, soft lighting (candles are best, with dim overhead lights as backup), and glowing silver, the longer the back story the better!"

4 large eggs

2 1/2 cups buttermilk

1 1/2 cups persimmon pulp (see directions in note above)

1 1/2 cups all-purpose flour

1 1/2 cups sugar

1 1/2 teaspoons baking powder

1 1/2 teaspoons baking soda

1/2 teaspoon nutmeg

1/2 teaspoon ground cinnamon or 1/4 teaspoon ground ginger

1/2 teaspoon salt

JEAN ROYAL BRANSCOME'S PERSIMMON PUDDING

Preheat the oven to 400 degrees. Butter a 3-quart baking dish or 2 (8- or 9-inch) round cake pans.

Beat the eggs in a large bowl until they are light yellow. Add the buttermilk and persimmon pulp and mix well. Combine the flour, sugar, baking powder, baking soda, nutmeg, cinnamon, and salt in a medium bowl. Add the flour mixture to the persimmon mixture and stir to blend. Pour into the pan.

Bake for 40 to 50 minutes, until a wooden pick inserted near the center comes out clean. (Overcooked is okay; undercooked is not.) Let the pudding cool for at least 10 minutes before serving. However, this dessert improves after several hours or even a day.

Serve with Buttermilk French Vanilla Ice Cream (page 267), whipped cream, or a sweet sauce of your choice.

▶ Makes 12 to 16 servings

Note: You can add up to ½ cup whole-wheat flour for a denser finished pudding.

"Start with tried-and-true favorites that you know how to cook," advises Betsy Burke Parker of Flint Hill, Virginia. "Practice on your own, try it out on your family, your close friends, your dog, but practice. Make yourself known for a particular dish, or maybe a style—be the person who cooks awesome meatloaf, or the guy who does that incredible chocolate dessert."

Homemade ice cream is always worth the work. Parker makes her Buttermilk French Vanilla Ice Cream with fresh milk from her cows, crème fraîche from the cow's milk, and eggs from her chickens for the deepest, most flavorful result. "Homegrown is always better, especially with recipes that have very few ingredients, like this one," she says. Serve it with Persimmon Pudding (page 266) or with fresh berries.

BUTTERMILK FRENCH VANILLA ICE CREAM

1 cup whole milk

2 cups heavy cream

1 vanilla bean, split, or 1/2 teaspoon vanilla extract

5 egg yolks

1 1/2 cups sugar

1 1/2 cups buttermilk or crème fraîche

Combine the milk and cream in a saucepan over medium heat. When the mixture is hot, add the vanilla bean halves.

In the top of a double boiler set over simmering water, whisk the yolks, then add the sugar gradually. Cook, whisking, until the mixture is foamy and slightly thickened.

Slowly pour the hot milk mixture into the egg mixture. Cook, whisking constantly, until the mixture coats the back of a spoon. Remove the double boiler from the heat and strain (or just remove the vanilla bean halves). Let cool to room temperature.

Add the buttermilk and mix well. Freeze in an ice cream freezer according to the manufacturer's instructions. Scoop into a freezer container and freeze for several hours until firm.

▶ Makes about 6 cups, or 12 servings

Keep the menu seasonal to match guests' appetites, offering lighter, cooler foods in summer and heavier, warmer dishes in cold weather. Watermelon sorbet with a hint of cucumber is as versatile as it is refreshing. Serve it as a heavenly cold dessert. Or use it to make a memorable and celebratory grown-up "float," suggests Perre Coleman Magness of Memphis, Tennessee. Put a small scoop of sorbet into a champagne glass. Top with Prosecco or other sparkling wine, but carefully, as it fizzes up. Magness says this recipe might yield more sorbet base than fits in an ice cream maker. In that case, use the extra to make another small batch, or mix it half-and-half with tea—a treat for the designated drivers.

1 cup sugar

3 cups water

3 sprigs of fresh mint

3 cups deseeded watermelon chunks

1 cup peeled, deseeded cucumber chunks

1/4 cup fresh mint leaves

WATERMELON, CUCUMBER, AND MINT SORBET

Stir the sugar and water together in a saucepan and bring to a boil over medium-high heat. Boil, stirring a few times, until the sugar is dissolved. Remove from the heat and drop in 3 sprigs of mint. Let cool. Remove the mint sprigs.

Place the watermelon and cucumber chunks in a blender. Add the sugar syrup and mint leaves. Blend until smooth. You may need to do this in several batches. Pour through a strainer into a bowl, pressing on the solids. Refrigerate for 2 to 3 hours, until very cold.

Pour the watermelon mixture into the bowl of an ice cream maker and freeze according to the manufacturer's instructions. Scoop into a freezer container and freeze for several hours until firm.

▶ Makes about 2 quarts, or 16 servings

This creamy dessert is from Annette Calloway of Nashville, Tennessee. Her mother created the distinctively Southern ice cream flavor for the family's annual Fourth of July gathering in Alabama.

Mark a big occasion like a reunion with custom napkins (and coasters, if the event calls for them) with your event name and date. Or get creative and print napkins with the event schedule, a family recipe, or a quote from the family history. If you don't have a local party store, plenty of online retailers will print as few as 50 napkins. Try shindigz.com, foryourparty.com, partybasics.com, and weddingfavordiscount.com.

1 1/2 cups sugar

1 (14-ounce) can sweetened condensed milk

1 (12-ounce) can evaporated milk

1 (6-ounce) container frozen whipped topping, thawed

2 teaspoons coconut extract

2 teaspoons vanilla extract

1 cup coconut, toasted

1 cup chopped pecans, toasted

Milk

POLLY ANNE'S TOASTED COCONUT PECAN ICE CREAM

In a large bowl combine the sugar, sweetened condensed milk, evaporated milk, whipped topping, coconut extract, vanilla extract, coconut, and pecans, and mix well. Pour into a 4-quart ice cream freezer container. Add enough milk to reach the fill line of the container. Freeze according to the manufacturer's instructions. Scoop into a freezer container and freeze for several hours until firm.

▶ Makes 16 cups, or 32 servings

For Lindsey Dobruck of Torrance, California, calling a dish "ruined" is subjective. "I've served decapitated Bundt cakes that never fully released from the pan. I turned the broken top layer of my husband's birthday cake into cake pops. But in most of my kitchen mishaps, guests still asked for seconds. As my mom says, 'It's not the Last Supper,' meaning it doesn't have to be perfect. And there's always a next time!" she says.

BOURBON-PECAN ICE CREAM

1 1/2 cups whole milk

1 1/2 cups heavy cream

1/2 cup, plus 2 tablespoons, firmly packed brown sugar, divided

4 egg yolks

1/8 teaspoon salt

1/2 teaspoon vanilla extract

2 tablespoons bourbon

2 tablespoons butter

1 cup pecans

Dash of ground cinnamon

In a large saucepan combine the milk, cream, and ½ cup of the brown sugar. Bring to a gentle boil over medium heat. Remove from the heat.

Meanwhile, in a medium bowl whisk the egg yolks with the salt. Slowly pour in half of the cream mixture, whisking to prevent the eggs from scrambling. Return the saucepan of cream mixture to the heat and whisk in the egg-cream mixture. Stir the mixture constantly, cooking over low heat until a custard consistency forms. The custard is ready when it coats the back of a spoon, or a thermometer reads 160 degrees.

Fill a large bowl with ice water. Set a clean 1- to 2-quart bowl in the ice water. Strain the custard through a fine-mesh sieve into the clean bowl. Stir frequently as the custard cools. Remove the mixture from the ice bath and stir in the vanilla and bourbon. Cover and refrigerate.

Melt the butter in a small saucepan over medium heat. Add the pecans, the remaining 2 tablespoons of brown sugar, and cinnamon. Cook, stirring continuously, until the sugar dissolves and the mixture is thick and brown. When the pecans are completely coated, spread them on an aluminum foil-lined baking sheet to cool. When the sugar coating has hardened, chop the pecans coarsely.

Freeze the custard mixture in an ice cream maker according to the manufacturer's instructions. Mix in the pecans when the ice cream is mostly frozen. Scoop into a freezer container and freeze for several hours until firm.

▶ Makes about 1 1/2 quarts, or 12 servings

Looking for a way to assemble her friends and their daughters over books, Julie Hunt of Nashville, Tennessee, started a mother-daughter book club. If you've ever been at one end of a dining table, wishing you could join a conversation on the other end, you'll appreciate Julie's solution: the group gathered around an oval table for optimum discussing—nothing's better than an oval table to prevent anyone from getting lost in the corner, and let everyone hear everyone else. She serves fruit, salty snacks, raspberry lemonade, and tea cakes. She finds tea cakes to be ideal party food—easy to make, and easier to store and transport than cupcakes.

TEA CAKES

1 1/2 cups white sugar

1 cup heavy cream

1 large egg

1 teaspoon vanilla or almond extract

3 1/2 cups self-rising flour

GLAZE

4 cups powdered sugar

A few drops almond, lemon, or vanilla extract

4 tablespoons water, or as needed

WHIPPING CREAM TEA CAKES

To make the tea cakes preheat the oven to 350 degrees. In a large bowl use an electric mixer to combine the sugar, cream, egg, and vanilla. Add the flour, 1 cup at a time (because the dough can become too stiff), stirring after each addition. Add enough flour to create a dough that's not too sticky to handle.

Roll out on a floured surface to 1-inch thickness. Cut out tea cakes with a biscuit cutter. Set them on a lightly greased baking sheet. (If you rolled the dough too thin, stack two rounds together to achieve the thickness you want.)

Or roll the dough into balls and place on the baking sheet, then flatten slightly with a wooden spoon.

Bake for 10 to 12 minutes. Watch closely, as they typically do not brown on the top, only on the bottom. Remove the cakes from the pans and let cool on wire racks.

To make the glaze combine the powdered sugar with the extract and water in a medium bowl and mix well. The consistency should be thick enough to stay on the cakes but thin enough to spread easily. Spread over the cakes. Let stand until the glaze is firm. (If you want to add sprinkles, do so while the glaze is still wet. If you want pipe a design on top, wait until the glaze dries.)

▶ Makes 24 to 30

The Christmas holiday season is the perfect time for sending guests home with something homemade. Debbie Young of Nashville, Tennessee, makes tea cakes from her grandmother's recipe all year long, but during the holidays, they get extra "dressed up" for company. She dips one half of each cake into white chocolate, lets it set, then dips the other side into dark chocolate. Serve them on a platter, or as part of a cookie plate with tea or coffee. Packed into pretty gift bags or boxes such as Wilton treat boxes, they're a sweet send-off for guests and perfect gifts for teachers. No matter how they're presented, tea cakes have been making guests happy for generations.

BUTTERY TEA CAKES

Preheat the oven to 350 degrees. Combine the butter and sugar in a large mixing bowl. Beat with an electric mixer on medium speed until well blended. Add the eggs one at a time, beating after each addition. Beat in the buttermilk and vanilla. Dissolve the baking soda in the water and add to the mixture. Reduce the speed to low and beat in the flour, 1 cup at a time.

Scoop 1-ounce portions with an ice cream scoop or a heaping tablespoon onto lightly greased baking sheets 2 inches apart. Bake for 8 to 10 minutes, until just beginning to brown at the bottom edge.

▶ Makes about 60

Note: If serving on a platter, refrigerate it until chilled to prevent sticking—these cakes are moist.

3/4 cup (1 1/2 sticks) butter, softened

1 1/2 cups sugar

3 large eggs

3 tablespoons buttermilk

1 teaspoon vanilla extract

1 teaspoon baking soda

1 tablespoon hot water

4 cups all-purpose flour

The Little Debbie oatmeal crème pie is a true daughter of the South. McKee Foods, the Little Debbie bakery, is a Chattanooga, Tennessee, company. Katherine Baronet of Austin, Texas, cobbled together her Oatmeal Crème Pie recipe to get the precise flavors and texture she wanted. "It has accidentally become my signature treat that people always beg for and some have even paid for," she says. "Food has always been a huge comfort for me, so it always makes me feel good to give people a little edible comfort." She included a plate of Oatmeal Crème Pies in a buffet of individual desserts for a friend's engagement party. Also on the table: a vintage tablecloth and photos of the couple among platters and cake stands holding tiramisu and chocolate meringue pies in 4-ounce Mason jars.

OATMEAL CRÈME PIES

COOKIES

1 cup (2 sticks) unsalted butter, softened

3/4 cup firmly packed brown sugar

1/2 cup white sugar

2 large eggs

2 teaspoons vanilla extract

1 1/2 cups all-purpose flour

1 teaspoon salt

1 teaspoon baking soda

3 tablespoons unsweetened cocoa powder

1 tablespoon ground cinnamon

1 1/2 cups old-fashioned oats

FILLING

1/2 cup (1 stick) butter, softened

1 (8-ounce) block cream cheese, softened

1/2 teaspoon vanilla extract

1/2 teaspoon salt

3 cups powdered sugar

To make the cookies place the butter, brown sugar, and white sugar in a large mixing bowl. Using an electric mixer beat on medium speed for 3 to 5 minutes. Add the eggs one at a time and beat until well combined. Beat in the vanilla.

In a medium bowl, whisk together the flour, salt, baking soda, cocoa powder, cinnamon, and oats. Add to the butter mixture in two or three additions and mix well on low speed. Refrigerate the dough for about 5 minutes.

Preheat the oven to 350 degrees. Drop the dough by tablespoonsful 2 inches apart onto greased baking sheets. Bake for 10 to 12 minutes. Take care not to overcook—the cookies should just be turning brown at the edges and appear moist in the center. Using a spatula, transfer the cookies to a wire rack and let cool.

To make the filling combine the butter and cream cheese in a large mixing bowl. Using an electric mixer beat on medium-high speed for about 3 minutes. Add the vanilla and salt and mix well. Sift in the powdered sugar and blend well on low speed.

After the cookies have completely cooled, spread the filling on half of the cookies. Lightly press a cookie on top and then refrigerate for at least 3 hours to firm up.

These oatmeal cream pies last for up to 3 days well covered in the refrigerator.

▶ **Makes 30 sandwich cookies**

Note: Baronet uses a Wilton #12 tip to pipe the filling.

Stash a tin of homemade cookies in the freezer and you're never without a little something for unexpected visitors. This recipe from Paul Verona of New York City makes a big batch of rich, delicate cookies, "more a confection than a cookie," he says, that are excellent with coffee and tea—and company, of course.

PECAN FINGERS

Preheat the oven to 350 degrees. In a large bowl beat the butter with a hand mixer until creamy. Add the sugar, salt, vanilla, and water. Blend until creamy in texture and pale yellow in color. Add the flour and pecans, and mix well. Refrigerate for about 15 minutes.

Scoop level teaspoonsful of dough and roll between your hands into finger-size logs. Place on ungreased baking sheets 1 inch apart and bake for 15 minutes. Start checking for doneness after 8 minutes and turn the sheets around in the oven if necessary to prevent uneven baking. Do not overbake—these cookies are very delicate and if baked too long, they will dry out and crumble.

Let cool for 1 hour. Put the remaining 2 cups of powdered sugar into a bowl. Roll each cookie one at a time in the sugar.

Store in an airtight tin or place in a plastic storage container and refrigerate, or freeze for up to 2 months.

▶ Makes about 120 cookies

2 cups (4 sticks) unsalted butter, softened

1 cup powdered sugar, sifted, plus 2 cups, unsifted, for rolling

1/2 teaspoon salt

2 teaspoons vanilla extract

2 teaspoons water

4 cups all-purpose flour

4 cups finely chopped pecans

For years, Maralie and Richard Exton have opened their Nashville, Tennessee, home to a merry crowd between Christmas and New Year's, when it seems everyone has a hankering for one last holiday gathering. They situate the bar on the screened porch (with outdoor heaters) and the food a couple of rooms away on a buffet in the dining room. The result is plenty of places to eat, bend an elbow with an old friend, sit and talk, and socialize. Their menu combines favorites like barbecue, hot dips, and bourbon balls plus new recipes each year, some destined for the "tried-and-true" list.

1/2 cup (1 stick) butter, softened

8 cups powdered sugar

2/3 cup bourbon

2 cups chopped pecans

4 to 6 ounces unsweetened chocolate

4 to 5 tablespoons paraffin

Pecan halves, optional

BOURBON BALLS

Place the butter in a bowl. Using an electric mixer, beat the butter on medium speed until creamy. Reduce the speed to low and add the sugar and bourbon alternately in four or five additions, mixing until smoothly blended. Add the pecans and mix well. Refrigerate the mixture for at least 8 hours to firm up.

Remove about a quarter of the butter mixture from the refrigerator, keeping the rest chilled. Form 1-inch to 1 ½-inch balls. Set them on baking sheets or plates and refrigerate. Repeat with the remaining mixture.

Melt the chocolate with the paraffin in the top of a double boiler set over boiling water. Use 2 forks to dip the butter balls into the warm chocolate mixture. Roll them until coated. Set them on waxed paper-lined baking sheets. Set a pecan on top and press gently. Refrigerate for at least a day, and up to 4 days in an airtight container.

▶ Makes 48 large or 70 small balls

Here's a festive confection that Pam Erbes of Denver, Colorado, has perfected—divinity made in the microwave. Puffy white and studded with intensely-flavored bits of black walnut, these dainty little tidbits are something special. Choose a dry day for making divinity—humidity can prevent it from thickening and setting properly.

When the sweets and coffee are served, the party's almost over, right? If it's a successful gathering, people may not be ready to go, a tricky situation for a host. Clearing away a few glasses and platters sends a subtle message that the party is winding down. Someone usually offers to help—those who are less inclined to help may take the opportunity to go.

NEVER-FAIL MICROWAVE DIVINITY

Mix the sugar, syrup, water, and salt in a 2-quart round glass casserole. Microwave on high for 20 minutes, stirring every 5 minutes.

Meanwhile, place the egg whites in a large mixing bowl. Using a heavy-duty electric mixer or stand mixer, beat on high speed until very stiff. With the mixer running, gradually pour the hot syrup over the egg whites. Beat on high speed for about 12 minutes until the mixture thickens and starts to lose its gloss. Beat in the vanilla, food coloring, and nuts. Drop by teaspoonful onto waxed paper and let cool completely.

▶ Makes 72 to 84 pieces

4 cups sugar

1 cup light corn syrup

3/4 cup water

Dash of salt

3 egg whites

1 teaspoon vanilla extract

Food coloring, optional

3/4 cup chopped black walnuts

ACKNOWLEDGMENTS

So many people helped transform a cabinet full of ingredients into a fully baked cookbook.

The hyper-competent Lisa Waddle—rarely does a person achieve so much with so little fuss. The super-connected Gwen Crownover Moritz, who introduced me to the marvelous Arkansas cooks who contributed so many excellent recipes and ideas. Connie Crabtree Burritt for her Maryland introductions. Sheri Castle for her network of North Carolina cooks. Sheila Thomas and her deep involvement in cookbook publishing. Nashville Food Bloggers for sharing so generously their beautiful and innovative recipes. To Jennifer Justus, for clarity on the book's introduction.

A big ladle of thanks to my valiant recipe testers: Mindy Merrell, Catherine Mayhew, Mindy Jacoway, Nancy Gent, Beth Cosgrove, Karen Grubbs, Joy Hunter, John Pitts, Brandi Nash Sanders and Coyt Sanders, Jane Hinshaw, Jennifer Orth, and Patsy Caldwell. Truly the finish line was a distant dream without your help.

A heaping helping of gratitude to editors Heather Skelton and Candace Floyd; to the marketing manager Stephanie Tresner; to the staggeringly talented Stephanie Mullins (stephaniemullinsphoto.com); and to food stylist and brilliant recipe developer Teresa Blackburn (teresablackburnfoodstyling.com).

Just as a great pie filling without a great crust isn't pie, so too is my friend of three decades Bryan Curtis the foundation for this whole book and the glue that held it together. Many thanks for the support, the encouragement, and the steady stream of great ideas.

The largest slice of gratitude goes to Tom and Eloise Wood for always supporting and never complaining, even when dinner was cake, deviled eggs, and sweet potatoes . . . again, and especially when the only thing I had time to make was reservations.

BLOGROLL

The blogging world is where home cooking is being reinvented and transformed right now, and I would like to thank these innovative wordsmiths and recipe developers for sharing their kitchen adventures.

Pear, Ginger, and Jack; Slightly Sweet Blueberry Spoon Bread, Teresa Blackburn, foodonfifth.com

Carmen April's Unexpected Mint Julep; Key Lime Pie, Carmen April, dinnerwithnerds.com

Blackberry Shrub; Fried Catfish Fingers with Tartar Slaw; Brown Butter Pumpkin Chess Tart, R.B. Quinn and Mindy Merrell, cheaterchef.com

Texas Ruby Red Grapefruit Pimm's Cup; Lemon Guacamole; Chipotle-Lime Hummus with Sour Cream, Randle Browning, crandlecakes.com

Holiday Spice Punch; Homemade Yeast Rolls in a Bread Machine; Aunt Dot's Coconut Cake, Angie Sarris, angiessouthernkitchen.com

Fresh Squeezed Lemonade with Blackberries and Peaches; West Indies Salad, Shelly Collins, lovingfoodandlife.com

Pimento Cheese Pinwheels; Raw Summer Squash Salad, Aly Armistead Greer, backyardtoballroom.com

Beet Pickled Devilish Eggs; Crab Cake Mac and Cheese, Shamille Wharton, akitchensomewhere.com

Zucchini Fritters for a Crowd; Bacon Cheddar Chive Biscuits; Four-Cheese Sweet Potato Lasagna, Angela Roberts, spinachtiger.com

Hot Black-eyed Pea and Artichoke Dip; Summer Succotash; Strawberry

Pie in Pecan Shortbread Crust, April McAnnally, stovetoptodesktop.com

Shoepeg Corn Dip; Chicken Sliders with Bacon and Avocado-Basil Cream; Shrimp Etouffée, Genet Hogan, raisedonaroux.com

Cheesy Sausage Wontons, Larissa Arnault, killingtimebetweenmeals.com

Wendy's Barbecued Chicken Gizzards; Mama Perry's Boiled Custard, Wendy Perry, wendyshomeeconomics.com

Individual Chicken Pot Pies with Whole Wheat Crust and Kale, Anna Watson Carl, theyellowtable.com

Tater Tot Squash Frittata; Parmesan Basil Mini Biscuits; Grilled Asparagus and Peach Salad, Grant and Kathryn Mitchell Johnson, ladysmokey.com

Mexican Quiche, Dani Meyer, theadventurebite.com

Brown Sugar and Spice Bacon Bliss; Berry Pudding, Marirae Mathis, whocooksforyou.net/blog

Pulled Smoked Pork; Corn Cakes; Mustard Slaw, Catherine Mayhew, thesouthinmymouth.com

Wedding Beans, Melissa D. Corbin, corbininthedell.com

Black-eyed Pea and Edamame Succotash; Lemon Miso Sweet Potatoes; Fried Chicken Nuggets with Honey-Mustard Dipping Sauce, Jessica Pendergrass, urbansacredgarden.com

Rosemary Grilled Squash; Eggplant, Tomato, and Vidalia Onion Gratin, Shane Kelley, chefshanekelly.com

White Bean Salad; Chipotle Chicken "Cobbler;" Moon Pie Banana Pudding Shots, Natalie Dietz Raines, anykitchen.net

Purple Hull Pea Salad with Bacon Vinaigrette; Watermelon, Cucumber, and Mint Sorbet, Perre Coleman Magness, therunawayspoon.com

Couscous Salad with Fresh Peaches and Sugar Snaps, Donya Mullins, asouthern-soul.blogspot.com

Pork Kabobs with Green Chutney, Vivek Surti, viveksepicureanadventures.com

Seafood Creole, Lucy Mercer, acookandherbooks.blogspot.com

Southern Shrimp and Grits; "Strawberry Shortcake" Chiffon Cake, Juanita Traughber, thebruncher.com

Buffalo Blue Cheese Buttermilk Biscuits with Creamy Buffalo Chicken Filling, Ann Wells Parrish, persnicketybiscuit.com

Tennessee Paella, Lisa Cascio Mays, winewithlisa.com

Sandra's Spinach Salad with Hot Chorizo Dressing, Sandra Gutierrez, sandraskitchenstudio.com

Maple Pecan Pie with Butternut Squash Filling, Alisa Huntsman, alisahuntsman.com, downhomedesserts.blogspot.com
Peach Almond Pound Cake, Katy Houston, sweetnessfollows.com
Peanut Butter Pie, Joy Harris, sunshinestatecooking.com
Whipping Cream Tea Cakes, Julie Hunt, cup-a.blogspot.com
Tennessee Jam Cake; Glazed Pork Chops with Wine and Jelly, Nicki Pendleton Wood, theprojectkitchen.com, tupperwareavalanche.com

Thanks to these cookbook authors for permission to use their recipes.

Bloody Mary Bar; Pickled Shrimp; Goat Cheese Queso, Tasia Malakasis. Originally published in *Tasia's Table: Cooking with the Artisan Cheesemaker at Belle Chevre* (New South Books, 2012). Used with permission of the author.

Crunchy Fried Field Peas; BLT Chicken, Sheri Castle, shericastle.com. Originally published in *The New Southern Garden Cookbook* by Sheri Castle (Chapel Hill, NC: University of North Carolina Press). Used with permission of author and publisher.

Strawberry Milk; Heart-Shaped Cheese Bites with Ham; Baked Sour Cream and Green Onion Mashed Potatoes. Originally appeared in *Tables of Content* (Junior League of Birmingham, 2008). Used by permission of the contributor, Kathryn Tortorici.

Momee's Maque Choux; Spinach Isabel, Peggy Sweeney McDonald, meanwhilebackatcafedumonde.com. Recipes originally appeared in *Meanwhile, Back at Café du Monde . . .* (Pelican Publishing, 2012). Used by permission of the author.

Red Rice; Chicken Country Captain. Originally published in *Well, Shut My Mouth: The Sweet Potatoes Restaurant Cookbook* by Stephanie Tyson (Winston-Salem, N.C.: John F. Blair Publisher). Used by permission of the author.

CONTRIBUTOR INDEX

INDEX